The Benjamin Files

Also by the Author

The Poetics of Social Forms
I.   Categories of the Narrative-Historical (forthcoming)
II. Allegory and Ideology
III. The Antinomies of Realism
IV. A Singular Modernity / The Modernist Papers
V.   Postmodernism, or, the Cultural Logic of Late Capitalism
VI. Archaeologies of the Future

Studies
Sartre: The Origins of a Style
Fables of Aggression: Wyndham Lewis, the Modernist as Fascist
Late Marxism: Adorno, Or, The Persistence of the Dialectic
Brecht and Method
The Hegel Variations: On the Phenomenology of the Spirit
Representing Capital: A Reading of Volume One
Chandler: The Detections of Totality
The Benjamin Files

Theory
Marxism and Form: Twentieth-Century Dialectical Theories of Literature
The Prison-House of Language: A Critical Account of Structuralism and
    Russian Formalism
The Political Unconscious: Narrative as a Socially Symbolic Act
Valences of the Dialectic
An American Utopia: Dual Power and the Universal Army

Film
Signatures of the Visible
The Geopolitical Aesthetic: Cinema and Space in the World System

Essays
The Ideologies of Theory
The Seeds of Time
The Cultural Turn: Selected Writings on the Postmodern, 1983–1998
The Ancients and the Postmoderns: On the Historicity of Forms

The Benjamin Files

Fredric Jameson

VERSO

London • New York

First published by Verso 2020
© Fredric Jameson 2020

1 3 5 7 9 10 8 6 4 2

Verso
UK: 6 Meard Street, London W1F 0EG
US: 20 Jay Street, Suite 1010, Brooklyn, NY 11201
versobooks.com

Verso is the imprint of New Left Books

ISBN-13: 978-1-78478-398-3
ISBN-13: 978-1-78478-400-3 (US EBK)
ISBN-13: 978-1-78478-399-0 (UK EBK)

British Library Cataloguing in Publication Data
A catalogue record for this book is available from the British Library

Library of Congress Cataloging-in-Publication Data

Names: Jameson, Fredric, author.
Title: The Benjamin files / Fredric Jameson.
Description: London ; New York : Verso, 2020. | Includes bibliographical
   references and index. | Summary: "A comprehensive new reading of Walter
   Benjamin's major works, as well as a great number of his less well-known
   publications, from one of America's foremost cultural and literary
   critics"— Provided by publisher.
Identifiers: LCCN 2020023370 (print) | LCCN 2020023371 (ebook) | ISBN
   9781784783983 (hardcover) | ISBN 9781784784003 (ebk)
Subjects: LCSH: Benjamin, Walter, 1892–1940.
Classification: LCC B3209.B584 J36 2020 (print) | LCC B3209.B584 (ebook)
   | DDC 193—dc23
LC record available at https://lccn.loc.gov/2020023370
LC ebook record available at https://lccn.loc.gov/2020023371

Typeset in Minion Pro by Hewer Text UK Ltd, Edinburgh
Printed and bound by CPI Group (UK) Ltd, Croydon CR0 4YY

For Susan

. . . to transpose the crisis into the very heart of language . . .

Contents

A Note on References

Unmarked references in the text are twofold: first to the English translation, one of the genuine monuments of US academic publishing, the *Selected Writings* in four volumes (Harvard, 1996–2003, edited by Michael W. Jennings, Howard Eiland and Gary Smith); then to the German originals, the *Gesammelte Schriften* in seven volumes (Frankfurt: Suhrkamp, 1974–89, edited by Rolf Tiedemann and Hermann Schweppenhäuser). Volume V of the German edition has been published as *The Arcades Project*, translated by Howard Eiland and Kevin McLaughlin (Harvard, 1999); references to this edition are marked "A."

The English version of *Origin of the German Trauerspiel* (to be found in Volume I of the German) is translated by John Osborne (*The Origin of German Tragic Drama*, Verso, 2009) the English is referenced as "OT." The *Moscow Diary* (to be found in Volume VI of the German) is translated by Richard Sieburth (Harvard, 1986). References to the letters, marked "B," designate first the English translation by Manfred R. Jacobson and Evelyn M. Jacobson under the title *Correspondence* (Chicago, 2012); and then the German originals in *Briefe* (Frankfurt: Suhrkamp, 1966).

1

Wind in the Sails

1

> For the dialectician, what matters is having the wind of world history in one's sails. For him, thinking means setting the sails. What is important is *how* they are set. Words are for him merely the sails. The way they are set turns them into concepts. (IV, 176; II, 670)

Benjamin is often too readable (or *readerly*) for us to realize that he is incomprehensible, or, in other words, *writerly*. This passage seems to confirm the obvious, namely that everything in Benjamin's work is driven by the passion for history (or at least, for the historical). Beyond that, however, the figure grows devious, multiple implications lead us in contradictory directions, raising unanswerable questions: prevailing wind versus tidal currents, tacking against the wind, rigging, size of the craft itself. Metaphor denarrativizes, with its immediacy of identification; and the wind of history is certainly a conventional figure. But it has become the raw material on which further figures work, producing not a map but a user's manual. As our initial reading begins to disintegrate, sails flapping weakly in a waning breeze, meanings fading away becalmed, we begin to sense that what we have here is no metaphor but rather an allegory: a form that lives by gaps and differences rather than identities, and that develops in time. The twist, the operative figure is, of course, the setting of the sails, by which Benjamin wishes to convey the variety of critical codes or theoretical languages within which we work, depending on the immediate historical situation, which is to say, depending on politics. This is not a philosophical relativism, it is a pragmatism, which does not aim at consistency or the forging of a synthesis of such codes; indeed, it prescribes exactly the opposite: their adaptation to the moment, the crisis, the need. On the other hand, it appeals to cunning, to tactics and to a keen practical awareness of how to use such multiple codes and systems as are available to catch the prevailing wind.

Meanwhile, Benjamin revises his figure as he goes along, without modifying his starting point, leaving apodictic sentences behind him which are haunted by Derridean undecidabilities. The thinker in Benjamin incessantly interferes with the writer and vice versa, producing an unstable fluctuation between words and concepts which the reader must walk like a tightrope. This uncertainty is productive—it makes for a tension between temporality and space which, when maintained to the breaking point, allows us to glimpse the absent center of this work, the famous *Stillstand* in which history and the Now are momentarily indistinguishable. Benjamin has, as we shall see, a number of different languages to characterize this tension, but to settle for any of them even provisionally is to turn that glimpse into a generalized paralysis or, in other words, to reify either his words or his concepts, to produce works in the place of sketches. Baudelaire's notion of the modern as an ephemeral notation in a classical representational language ("the transient, the fleeting, the contingent . . . the one half of art, the other being the eternal and immovable") is as useful a characterization of Benjamin's written thoughts as another.

This skiff is moving, but not only under the momentum of the wind of history; he has no control of the current—it is by way of setting the sail and catching that wind that we can control our own destiny. It is an image that can only multiply our questions, not settle them; and in any case, the shift takes place within the first sentence itself, which problematizes the very notion of history and shifts our attention from the question of whether history has a direction to that of how to register that direction (assuming it exists). Nor is this second problem resolved: only a secondary experimental verification is offered—namely, to see how much historicity your concept is able to register. But inasmuch as history is change as such, this reminder presumably recommends the historical changeability and variability of our own concepts. In thus bringing conceptualization into doubt and sending us back to figuration, the text is not simply designating itself, a gesture without content: it is affirming the variability, the historical ephemerality, of its momentary content and revealing its own temporal structure as a single moment in time; it is an imperative to grasp the volatility of this spatial figure provisionally in a temporal way.

2

It is said that Benjamin was careful to separate his many friends, correspondents, intellectual confidants from each other, opening himself generously and extensively to each one without the partner in question being aware of his other interlocutors or, indeed, of their very existence. There is material here for an intellectual equivalent of the bedroom farce in the many dramas and jealousies that result from unwanted discoveries (Scholem's warnings about the pernicious influence of Brecht, for example). And the astonishing correspondence reveals that for each of these recipients, Benjamin reserved a distinct idiom and set of concerns, themes corresponding to his own working preoccupations to be sure (the letters almost always touch on his own reading and projects), but not necessarily accompanied by those shifts in identity, in personae, which have so often characterized the modernist. Instead, they mark the existence, in his thinking, of a variety of distinct language fields or clusters across which he was able to modulate and which we cannot properly describe either as styles or as unrelated subject matter. Translation was one of his most cherished interests; it is therefore appropriate to claim not only that his writing reveals a process of perpetual translation from one of these language clusters to another, but also and above all that it underscores those discontinuities between them which he was careful to observe and which, as a fundamental principle, he maintained in the content of his thought as well as in its form.

Any conventional acquaintance with Benjamin will at once associate him with three keywords: *flâneur, aura, constellation*. All three are indeed privileged, but their juxtaposition should at first instruct us in the radical gap between their possible meanings and uses. Each one is surrounded by constelled associations of its own: something that might well alert us to the relativity of the term "constellation" itself, a central concept in the notorious "Epistemo-Critical Prologue" to his *Trauerspiel* book. Whatever this third concept means, we must for the moment retain its implication of a radical distance between such constellations and its function to discredit any systematic effort to relate them to each other. Taken in this way, the word "constellation" is a destructive weapon, an instrument to be wielded against system and above all against systematic philosophy: it is meant to break up the homogeneity of philosophical language (and thereby to undermine the very order it seems itself to promote among the stars).

The historical situation will clarify what may seem to go without saying in an age of theory like our own: for Benjamin's time, his youth and the moment of his intellectual formation, have entered the history books as the moment of the hegemony of neo-Kantianism, a moment in which academic philosophy was almost exclusively epistemological and dominated by the sciences and by the ideal of knowledge as the only kind of truth with which philosophy, and thinking in general, should be concerned. Of that period we have ourselves retained only the rebels and the protesters: Nietzsche, Dilthey, Bergson, Croce, the phenomenologists, psychoanalysis, Simmel, and so forth, most of them ultimately failing in their attempts to open up a livable space within this academic and epistemological institutional hegemony.

Benjamin was not a follower of any of these movements or prophets, even though he learned from many of them; he invented his own solution to the problem. But it is clear that his youthful efforts were doomed to grapple over and over again with the problem of Kant: whether to appropriate him by translating his very narrow conception of "experience" into something larger and more existential or metaphysical; or simply, in exasperation, to do away with him altogether ("the greatest adversary of [my own thoughts] is always Kant," he says in an early letter [C, 125; B, 187]). Nor was Hegel ever a solution for him; while the emphasis on language, however large it loomed in the early essays, was an orientation rather than a methodological solution (philology, in any new and comprehensive sense, still awaiting its reinvigoration in this period). History, with the one great exception of Riegl, only offered idealistic and evolutionary continuities (the target later identified as "progress"), rather than the breaks that were the preconditions for the kinds of periodization that later absorbed his energies (the Baroque, the Second Empire, the "situations" of contemporary French and Soviet writers).

"Constellation" will only be one name for the discontinuous yet peri-odizing focus Benjamin is seeking, and it will lose its reason for being if we turn it into a philosophical concept of some kind, into a universal. What accompanies the translation process we have proposed for describ-ing Benjamin's thought requires a different kind of language than that of philosophical abstraction: we will call it "figuration" and illustrate its results by way of another name and another version altogether of what the constellation was meant to convey.

This is the panorama, an institution of mass entertainment still exist-ing in Benjamin's youth and evoked in several places in his work, but which originated in Baudelaire's time; the panorama will, in fact, like so many of Benjamin's exhibits, serve multiple purposes. It will furnish the contents of autobiographical sketch (in *Berlin Childhood*), while serving as the very form of the work called *One-Way Street*, itself not only a panorama of Weimar inflation but of urban life as such. In its classical form, static tableaux of historical moments form a discontinuous sequence: "because the viewing screen, with places to sit before it, was circular, each picture would pass through all the stations" (III, 346; V, 388; VII, 388). This discontinuity will therefore (in a third use, after form and content) serve as a foreshadowing of the great theme of media technology: its spectacle thus "prepared the way not only for photogra-phy but for film" (III, 35; V, 48).

And characteristically, in another essay, Benjamin takes the time to treat us to a miniature biography of the panorama's inventor, who also invented an early form of photography called the daguerreotype. Benjamin wants here, in his portrait of Daguerre, to train us in a sensi-tivity to the great innovators and inventors, in order for us to learn to classify the artists and writers among their number and thereby to understand their achievements in a new way, as technical advances. But the reader is not omitted; the entry on panoramas will also read them as the sign of a new kind of perception, that of the city-dweller, and of an attention to multiple details and attractions, which will, however, be grasped one by one, as we circulate from one image to the next. (That in this they also announce the arcades, and also the use of iron in construc-tion, is yet another bonus of this figure.)

Figuration is thus a complex form of language, in which a certain discontinuity is captured and named, and which is nonetheless available for multiple and, as it were, lateral uses and exploitations. In the same way, the constellation can become the occasion for a reflection on astrology (and graphology) or, on the contrary, an association with the matter of stars in Baudelaire's poems. But the same search for an adequate figure for the conceptualization in question will turn up an adjacent phenomenon:

> It cannot be overlooked that the assembly line, which plays such a fundamental role in the process of production, is in a sense represented by the film-strip in the process of consumption. (III, 94; I, 1040)

Here we not only have base and superstructure bundled together but also the possibility of a new characterization of that "aesthetic of discontinuity" in Eisenstein's "montage of attractions," with its family likeness to other modernist practices such as the Poundian ideogram. If so, however, it would be better to associate Benjamin with a heretical modernism like that of Brecht, rather than with the standard academic variety. There is, indeed, much in common between Benjaminian writerly practice and (leaving aside the famous V-effect) Brechtian epic theater, with its analytic relationship to its contents: breaking every act or event down into its constituent parts, naming them, as you might supply a motto to a picture (or an intertitle to a silent film) by lowering a banner over the scene which, as in eighteenth-century novels, announces the subject matter of the chapter to come: "In which Mr. Peachum . . .," etc.

Yet despite the temptation—"an aesthetic of discontinuity," for example—it may be best not to attribute some official aesthetic to Benjamin, about whom it seems safer and more productive to list his aversions—progress, psychology, art history, aestheticism, aesthetics itself—than to endow him with any positive formulas. He does have a certain canon, but it is characterized by marginality and eccentricity, by a stubborn anti-canonicity, rather than any list of shared formal values.

It is this preponderance of the negative—even *Erfahrung*, or experience, that moment of truth most highly prized in the Benjaminian scheme of things, is ultimately defined against the *Erlebnis*, or punctual shock; even aura is defined against that reproducibility that renders it obsolete—that inclines me toward a less affirmative account of what makes the Benjaminian (if not the Brechtian) episode possible: that is

interruption as such, the break, the gap, separation (a central category
for the young Marx as well). Tearing a quotation out of its native place,
the original text is, as we shall see, a thoroughly characteristic process (a
Benjaminian *gestus*); destruction is here an unexpectedly congenial
modus operandi.

But we must not allow it to tempt us into Friedrich Schlegel's language
of the fragment, either, even though Benjamin himself is sometimes so
tempted (and in any case, Schlegel's term was meant to suggest that literary works are themselves simply fragments of an absent whole, a figure
Benjamin will reinvent for Language, as we shall see). On the contrary,
episodes that may at first look like fragments in Benjamin are as fully
formed as stanzas or verse-paragraphs. What gives them their fragmentary look is the inevitable gap between them, which will anachronisti-
cally remind us of the oneiric flashes or the obligatory gaps within the
surrealist image, a practice that also greatly fascinated Benjamin for a
time.

Nor, in a more nihilistic spirit, should the hegemony of the interruption suggest the infinite divisibility of the peeling of the onion, the
Beckett-like practice of a division into the smallest atomic units which
eventually leads to nothingness (I have, in any case, elsewhere argued
that Beckett's apparent voids are always haunted by the dreariest bourgeois domestic memories). This bad infinity of the subdivisional process
is explicitly arrested by a suggestive Benjaminian note:

> The task is to make a stopover in every one of these many little
> thoughts. To spend the night in a thought. (II, 122; VI, 200)

In fact, it is not as a dwelling in the fragment, even in transit and over-
night, that Benjamin finds the definitive formulation of this process; it is
rather with a term drawn from the other end of the philosophical spectrum, namely the "monad," that he prefers to characterize it. We will see
later on that we must be equally suspicious of the language of the
"image," and in particular of the famous "dialectical image"; still, it is as
the image which is a whole world in itself that Benjamin sees (and
collects) his monads.

And this is why he does not have to solve philosophy's most urgent
problem since Plato, namely that of universals and abstractions: for
him these are problems of figuration and of writing, of monadic

representation, rather than problems of thinking and conceptualization. For the latter—Plato's Ideas, Lévi-Strauss's *pensée sauvage*—he has a different solution, an idiosyncratic and rather untraditional German one—namely Goethe's notion of the Ur-form, the smallest intelligible forms of our "blooming, buzzing confusion," what he likes to call their "origin" (and this also is the moment to distinguish Benjamin's use of this word, also derived from Karl Kraus, from what gets denounced philosophically in poststructuralism). "Origin" in Benjamin is not a temporal word, but rather something closer to the phenomenological "essence." All of which, in Benjamin, will lead to Goethe's formula "tender empiricism," delicate empiricism (the term which, in the Greek, equally gives rise to two other concepts of the greatest significance to Benjamin and Brecht alike: experience and experiment).

> *Es gibt* (says Goethe) *eine zarte Empirie, die sich mit dem Gegenstand innigst identisch macht, und dadurch zur eigentlichen Theorie wird.*[1]

> There exists a delicate or tender empiricism which makes itself utterly identical with the object, thereby becoming true theory.

(It may be worth noting in passing that it is in his idiosyncratic reflections on color that Benjamin rehearses his doctrine of the universal most strikingly: pure color is therefore that "idea" in which colored objects somehow "participate.")[2]

Still, even this stubbornly antiphilosophical position must claim some philosophical basis, which I will locate in the dialectic of the boundary and the limit: the distinction, in other words, between an ending beyond which nothing exists and a borderline between two entities. This dialectic was a vital instrument for Hegel in his transcendence of Kant (and of the latter's "limit," the unknowable thing-in-itself); it will equally afford Benjamin a productive ambiguity in mediating between the isolation of his episodes as so many discontinuous monads, and their interrelationship as elements within a larger monadic field. The constellation is a monad, so much is certain; but how we explore it

---

1 Sprüche in Prosa, 167; *Maximen und Reflexionen*, 509.
2 Howard Caygill, in *Walter Benjamin: The Colour of Experience*, London: Routledge, 2016 offers an intricate and thorough discussion of this thematic interest.

[handwritten margin notes: "Constellations let us explore & map it out → but they don't relate? / how we use constellations depends on what we have, where we find ourselves."]

and map it out, as a set of more infinitesimal monads in their own right—that is a decision to be made on the basis of the historical raw material and also on our historical (which is to say political) "current situation."

It must also follow, from this aesthetic or dialectic of the interruption, that Benjamin never wrote a traditional book (and never could or wanted to). Or if that seems rash (or harsh), then let's say he wrote only one, called *One-Way Street*, which ratifies the very phenomenon of gaps we have begun to examine. Even the thesis on German *Trauerspiel* falls, on closer inspection, into distinct and unrelated chapters; while those chapters themselves, like the great program-essays, prove on yet closer inspection themselves to disintegrate into distinct and unrelated moments and topics (and are indeed sometimes organized that way). The failure to cohere of the *Arcades Project*, then, is no mere historical accident; it corresponds to the deeper movement of Benjamin's genius, and constitutes, if you like, the new form that the impossibility of the book such brings forth in its place. It thereby takes its place in that illustrious sequence of works—Pascal's *Pensées*, Gramsci's *Prison Notebooks*, Lacan's seminars—which it would be abusive to call unfinished, let alone collections of fragments, but also misleading to characterize as journals or notebooks, and which can serve as cousins to what Frye or Bakhtin called Menippean satires in their worthy and stimulating, yet unsatisfying, attempts to recreate a system of genres (a kind of constellation in its own right, as Claudio Guillén pointed out), a system which can alone guide formal analysis, provided the latter finds a way to transcend it (just as Benjamin himself managed to transcend the self-conscious reflections on the essay form by Lukács and Adorno).

3

Still, there remains one distinct conceptual language whose identity Benjamin seems to have been willing to respect and to preserve, for the very reason that it is not altogether philosophical; and that is theology as such. Nothing has wreaked more havoc among the Benjaminian commentators than this interest, and that is why it is essential to insist from the outset that theology, in his sense, has nothing to do with God, and that it is to be considered a language or a code and not a system of

beliefs. Theology exists because a void has been left in the areas traditionally assigned to philosophy—(a void) which can no longer be
adequately organized by the meager instruments assigned to ethics by
neo-Kantianism and Enlightenment thought in general. That void or
lack becomes apparent with the appearance of genuine historical thinking in the late eighteenth century (with that unique and as yet untheo-
rized, unphilosophical event called the French revolution); "history"
here also meaning the gap between individual and collective dynamics
or the unsuitability of academic concepts devised in each of these historically new areas for use in the other.

Ethics, a set of concepts designed for individual behavior, are only
fitfully (and figuratively) suitable for the historically new collective
dynamics that govern large-scale national and revolutionary movements. The centerpiece of individualistic ethics—the binary opposition
of good and evil—is at best ideological when it comes to collectivities.

The theological code, meanwhile, although traditionally deployed for
both individual and collective categories, cannot be said to mediate
between them, let alone to suppress their incommensurabilities, between
which it at best modulates as between two musical keys. Translation,
therefore, however mysterious a process in its own right, would seem to
offer the most adequate characterization, and the most Benjaminian, for
its function. The theological is to remain a distinct language-field in its
own right, with which—as in all true translation—other languages are
put in contact in order to measure the extent of their possibilities of
meaning.

Yet we do not remember often enough that there is a branch of ethical
thought—I would rather call it an ethical genre, a way of writing the
ethical, or representing it—which, call it *Lebensweisheit*, wisdom literature, or the paradoxes of the so-called *moralistes*—has a completely
different orientation than the academic one. I should like to say that in
it the relationship between the personal and the collective is reversed;
and while so much political thought involves the illicit transfer of individualistic categories to the collective, this other kind of discourse sees
the personal-ethical as the political, and focuses the new categories of a
late feudal or raison-d'état politics on the complexities of human relations, particularly in the court situations of absolute monarchy. Here it
remains Machiavelli, who is the true originator of these new categories
(however openly his readers are willing or not to acknowledge him),

and it is the French moralistes and, above all, Balthazar Gracián who undertake to codify a new set of political categories for the novelties of individual yet social relationships, all of them in one way or another derived from the implicit assimilation to the art of war, strategy and tactics alike. Characteristically, Benjamin's gift of a copy of Gracián to Brecht at Svendborg seals this affinity and alerts us to the attention in both to this rarely formulated level of intercourse, which eludes the visibility of history and yet remains undetected on the level of individual subjectivity.

Benjamin's sense of the timeliness of older theological categories is therefore symptomatic and prophetic all at once. He finds the most useful ones in Jewish theology, as it was in his period re-elaborated by Hermann Cohen and Franz Rosenzweig; and this for a paradoxical reason, namely because the Jewish tradition—regressively, if you like—still invokes a collective history and has not yet had to take into consideration the individualisms confronted by both Christianity and Islam (their dilemmas will come into their own historically with the problems of predestination and providential determinism, as we shall see later).

Theology in general constitutes a compromise between secular logic and figuration: the forms it thereby produces, and not only in the Christian Middle Ages, are unique verbal conceptualities whose structures are determined by the impossible effort of incorporating narrative into purely secular abstractions whose logic has been bought at the price of cleansing them of myth or storytelling temporality. If religion, as Max Weber thought, is a specialization whose task is consolation, then it must necessarily deal in human time and traffic in narratives; the transcendental content or sacred nature of such narratives is a secondary matter. To acknowledge this narrative basis of theology is, to be sure, always somehow to step outside it, but there are two ways in which this can be done: on the one hand, a reductive Enlightenment, with its denunciation of theology as superstition (something which Benjamin will repeatedly invoke with the word "myth") and, on the other, a more mystical "third way" which rises above both religion and rationalism, beyond the subject/object split, to offer some heightened and depersonalized yet narrative mode of thought, as in Origen, Plotinus, and Spinoza or, in modern times, Hegel's speculation, Nietzsche's beyond good and evil, and historical materialism. Benjamin's curious word *Geistesgegenwart*—often translated as "presence of mind"—occasionally

seems to mean an attentiveness beyond mere awakened secular perception: presumably its findings—undeveloped in his work—are what "the
historical materialist" knows, and perhaps even what is available in
"profane illumination" or Hölderlinian *heilige Nüchterheit*.[3]

At any rate, recourse to theological language—which is not a matter
of stages of personal or intellectual development and which persists
from the beginning of Benjamin's career to its end—is to be understood
in the context of this representational dilemma which is at one and the
same time an intellectual one and against the background of which his
politics must also ultimately be grasped.

The basic categories of the theological language-field are, then: reconciliation (*Versöhnung*), redemption, the Messiah, allegory and myth. As
for that other all-important category, which is language, even though
one of Benjamin's basic statements on it will take the form of a commentary on Genesis, it is not strictly a theological matter and seems best
dealt with in another context. Insofar as the first of these categories,
reconciliation—so important in Rosenzweig—implies a consent to the
world, we may assume that Benjamin's critique of it is no different from
Adorno's, although less strident in a situation in which the outcome—
reconciliation here means reconciliation with fascism—is obvious
enough and, equally obviously, unacceptable.

Redemption (*Erlösung*) is, however, another matter altogether and
must be understood in a collective rather than an individual way. It
governs Benjamin's thinking, if not of history as a whole, then at least
of the past and the dead: it functions for him as a debt and an obligation and is assimilated for him to communist and revolutionary ideals.
We will be obliged to confront it in some detail in a final chapter, on
History.

There, too, the notion of the Messiah will necessarily find its place,
along with the peculiarly dialectical structure of what Benjamin meant
by "hope." Inasmuch as both Christianity and Islam are founded on the
conviction that revelation has already taken place in one way or another,
only the Jewish concept of the Messiah (which has its own history) is
available to do something rather different to temporality and in

---

3 The problem of "attention," however, is central in the intellectual life of this
period, as Jonathan Crary demonstrates in *Suspensions of Perception*, Cambridge: MIT
Press, 2001—it becomes something like a synonym for consciousness.

particular to its future dimension, to its way of conceptualizing futurity. Insofar as this concept or vision is irredeemably condemned to the narrative representation of an individual figure, its conceptual impossibility is already marked and, for Benjamin, discounted in advance; but by virtue of that very impossibility, it gives him a different way of thinking of Utopia and revolution than what is available in more secular modes (including Marxism). We will return to this issue as well.

As for myth, it designates a kind of pre-theological realm before the past itself; it can be taken, as Adorno and Horkheimer do in their Benjamin-inspired *Dialectic of Enlightenment*, as another word for the irrational. Like theology, "myth" is a term that straddles the boundary between narrative and philosophy, an unsatisfactory concept which cannot be used either way except in a negative form, as what is nonphilosophical but also nonhistorical. It will be as problematic in its "usefulness" as the whole notion of dream and phantasmagoria—central to Benjamin's thinking and writing in the early stages of the *Arcades Project* in the late 1920s and powerfully criticized by Adorno. The rational exploration of this area, as it were, is to be found in his protocols on the uses of hashish (in which he followed his alter ego, Baudelaire). But the issue was never resolved, I believe, and this is why his proximity to Klages and Jung remains so sensitive (Horkheimer suggested he clarify his thoughts by way of an analysis of their "irrationalisms," a critique which he was never to write).

But the issue is all the more crucial since, at least in Jung's so-called "collective unconscious," it raises another quasi-theological dilemma for Benjamin's thought in general, namely that of the category of multiplicity. For here we meet, in its most abstract or Hegelian form, the category which necessarily governs Benjamin's omnipresent thinking about the masses, a presence that runs from the Baudelairean crowds (and their *flâneur*-observer) to the redemption of the dead. This is the unthinkable level of the collective and the very source of Benjamin's strongly revolutionary and Leninist convictions. But for philosophy it cannot be thought in its own right (something even clearer for us today in globalization, where, as Sloterdijk has put it so well, who can come to terms with the presence of billions of other people?); nor are its theological forms anything more than an imperative to think and not the thought itself. The sequence of historical terms for this mass of other people— from clan and people to race and nation, and back to sociological notions of group and *ethnie*, testifies to the urgency of this missing term and its concept.

4

Finally, it seems important, in a work so profoundly dedicated to history, to note a conception of "access" in Benjamin's work: access, which he sometimes calls "legibility" (*Lesbarkeit*, and "only at a certain time" at that [A N3,1, 462; V, 577]) is the point at which the position of the analyst in the present is evoked and which officially becomes the philosophical problem of historicity (something otherwise memorably reformulated in R. G. Collingwood, in Gadamer, and implicitly in Gramsci's conception of Marxism as an "absolute historicism"). It should be remembered, in this context, that Benjamin's formula of "the now of recognizability" (often shortened to *Jetztzeit* or "now-time") is designated as a variable attribute of the past, the moment when a specific past becomes accessible as a part of our present.

The problem seems less pressing in a time in which the writer is so completely absorbed in a single period—the Second Empire—and in the place—Paris—with which that historical period is indissolubly wedded that the question of access needs less attention. But before that, this simple term (*Eingang* in the original) serves as a warning and an alert for historical distance, for the otherness of periods to which it is we ourselves who no longer have "access." Of Hölderlin's world, for example, he says: "It is difficult to gain any kind of access to this fully unified, unique world" (I, 24; II, 111). He thereby evokes, at the moment of the great Hölderlin revival or, indeed, its virtual discovery (with the first editions of the collected works, and in particular of the later ones, stricken by madness), the force of this revelation. It is also a term he will use about tragedy, whose essentials he gleans from Hofmannsthal and from Florens Christian Rang, and that for a twofold reason: first, once again to heighten the force of the discovery of the radical otherness of that "speechlessness" which the original forms of tragedy were able to stage (but which is now lost to us); and, second, in order to bring home the radical difference of the modern *Trauerspiel*, whose true form and spirit he claims to have discovered—to which itself he has managed to gain "access"!—from an ancient tragic drama to which it is so often assimilated (with the subsequent loss of the historic originality of both).

The notion of the requirement of "access," then, secures the radical difference of the past, in all its moments, at the same time that it preserves the freshness of its rediscovery, under conditions which make it alone possible and demand explanation in their own right. (So it is, for example, that he will evoke Expressionism as the climate in which both *Trauerspiel* and Riegl's rediscovery of late Roman art were able to be recovered [II, 668; III, 336].) This shock of revelation of the past—elsewhere he will famously call it a "tiger's leap"—is a crucial feature of Benjamin's experience of history. "Empathy," a word redolent of experimental psychology and only invented in 1903 (and subsequently popularized by Worringer) seems a misleading guide to "access": it will be radically rearticulated in Benjamin's appropriation of it as the "dialectical image." Still, it must remain a crucial feature of our own access to Benjamin himself. Can we expect to relive his work without the situation of the 1920s and '30s flashing up before our eyes? Without some "empathy" for the mortal struggle between communism and fascism which defines this period and casts its light over everything he wrote?

2

The Spatial Sentence

1

There are interesting reasons for thinking that *One-Way Street* (I, 444–487; IV, 85–148) was Benjamin's only real book, a box of chocolates that should bear the warning: addictive substances! Too rich to be devoured all at once, the items are like the aged photos you lift one after another out of an old carton, wondering who their subjects were. Each one can consume more time than you imagine, plunging you into the state induced by riddles and puzzles. These are impressions all right, *choses vues*, but spiked with dialectical twists. It would be a mistake to take them for the purely visual, but also to confuse them with simple thoughts, interesting observations. The latter are as treacherous as the detail; a separation here, the mind–body elements hooked together in a rare molecule. Complete paragraphs, these, the danger being now the gap between them, which no thematic ingenuity can bridge, absolute and non-generic, a blank abyss that corresponds to nothing experiential, the blink, the moment of rest, the withdrawal—it is not the leap of the dream logic or the temporal distraction of the journal entry, lapses of attention, changes of place. The oddities of the paragraph give way to the mysteries of their succession.

This dangerous stimulant can be identified by the way in which, quite against your will and knowledge, your very relationship to reading and writing has been modified by the pages you have been absorbing. It wants you to perceive, no doubt; but then to fashion those perceptions into a kind of paradoxical metaphorics without the profit of an abstraction or any kind of thought into which you might translate the operation. This is Simmel's lesson, whose almost unreadable density always turned on an empirical content ("tender empiricism") impossible to generalize after all that effort, a lesson which our present writer has, dispelling the fog, revealed to be the most resistant and crystalline of Baudelairean precisions. The city is still here and central, but an almost caricatural German philosophical incomprehensibility has given way to its opposite, an overly attentive examination of every storefront at which we linger, will we ever get to the end?

So this is, as the title half suggests, the actual stroll of the as-yet-unthematized *flâneur* through the self of an urban agglomeration whose streets and byways Asja has "cut through like an engineer." These words (from the dedication) suggest some unusual conception of his own work as a writer—a leaving out, which is also an urban renewal: this particular one-way street is new, carved out of a traditional urban landscape, or bulldozed through it; and it is moving in a single direction, perhaps toward that future at the back of the *Angelus Novus* facing the wind from the past.

And indeed, the first entries suggest the random observation of the exteriors through which we are passing (gas station, numbered houses, apartment buildings, an embassy, a construction site) but also evoking the hidden interiors behind some of these and in particular their rooms (breakfast room, vestibules, furniture, underground works, even Goethe's study in Weimar). Nothing, however, betrays what lies before us, what might serve as our goal or even our terminus: does this street end up in the countryside? Does it cross the whole city? Does it ignominiously dead-end in some larger thoroughfare?

In fact, the concluding section, "To the Planetarium," seems to point beyond the city limits to something as yet unidentified. What precedes it grows ever more populated, with more and more buildings, with festival, carnival, and beerhall spaces, from which, paradoxically, our perceptions are ever more isolated. "Again and again, in Shakespeare, in Calderon, battles fill the last act, and kings, princes, attendants, and followers 'enter, fleeing'" (I, 484; IV, 143).

So the separated stops on this journey never do fit any proper generic category: it is surely not a set of fragments; it is not Goethe's "aperçu" which designated the crystallization of an inner or Ur-form within the single sudden perception; not an aphorism, either, however closely Nietzsche and Adorno both peer over Benjamin's shoulder and ask us to assimilate the completion of their great one-sentence leaps to this equally complete entry or paragraph; not really a *fait divers*, inasmuch as the latter generally draws out the paradox of an event or action. It is a conceptual complex without an abstract concept: Benjamin's occasional use of the Platonizing word "idea" seems to have involved a movement in this direction, even though in *Origins* it designated a whole historical movement or style, such as the Baroque, which then effectively renames it and consigns it back into intellectual history. Impressions, *choses vues*, diary entries, sketches, notes in passing, all register what Baudelaire called the "modernity" of the thing—its ephemerality, but far more faintly do they capture that eternal "other half" on which the poet also insisted (in "*Le Peintre de la vie moderne*") and which takes us back to the ahistorical dimension of Goethe's Ur-forms.

Benjamin's procedure is best grasped, I sometimes feel, as the preparation for the definitive sentence ("writers are people who love sentences," someone once said): the nonconceptual yet figural formulation which rounds the words off and makes them complete. Or maybe our definition ought to run the other way and begin with the series: the entry is what can be included, discontinuously, within the series or the collection, what by its precision and arresting fulguration raises the question of its relationship to the items that precede it.

Those assemblages—not a bad Deleuzian expression for *One-Way Street*, either—are also assuredly a kind of form in Benjamin's mind and work: in *Berlin Childhood*, they have been subjectivized into Proust-like evocations and thus misleadingly point us on toward autobiography as their absent climax. Meanwhile, in the big program-essays, the discontinuous montage is concealed by continuous paragraphing: it is only when we begin to take these apart in their turn that we begin to glimpse their fundamental discontinuity, their episodic form and essence. *Central Park* then offers its collected aphorisms as the anticipation of that later, well-nigh accidental generic form which stands as a kind of ruin (in the language of *Origins*), the so-called convolute, namely the surviving older files containing clippings and notes on single subjects which, piled up, were to constitute the raw materials of the future *Arcades*. An imaginary thematic unity then lends its theoretical cast to the form, a sham and illusion not really dispelled even by holding firmly to the unnamed genre or "*einfache Form*" (Jolles) we have full-blown before us in *One-Way Street*.

Each paragraph is complete in itself and is in fact sealed in with a title. One is tempted to evoke such units in a dual way, such as text and picture, picture and caption, words and music, particularly inasmuch as the alleged titles are in fact wry commentaries on the little entries, such as "Come Back! All is Forgiven!" or "Caution: Steps" or, more ominously, "Lost-and-Found Office" or "Stand for Not More than Three Cabs." This last, indeed, does contain three separate paragraphs, but they are depressing: the vendors' hawking of the local papers while he is waiting for a bus; though out of doors and in the middle of the city, it makes him feel as though he were in a cell. An unrefreshing dream of a shabby dwelling awakens him to the unpleasant condition of having briefly and in a state of exhaustion fallen asleep with his clothes on. A final, more direct association of the strains of music in tenement buildings leads to a more forthright declaration of taedium vitae: "It is music of the furnished rooms, where on Sundays someone sits amid thoughts that are soon garnished with these notes, like a bowl of overripe fruit with withered leaves"—rotten and dried out all at once. Taxis have not left from any of these three stations, the empty spaces waiting for them in the street do not bode well for the traveler in any of his three conditions. Something unpleasant happens to waiting here. It becomes an object of contemplation, it grows symbolically, asks for endless exegesis since nothing definitive can be said or thought about it. It becomes a kind of parable, like the Hasidic tales of which Benjamin was so fond, except without the rabbi to point us to the didactic conclusion. And yet we're in the city, the newspapers have lots of headlines every day, taxis are prowling back and forth everywhere, we will need a hotel room at night even if we're sleepless.

So now the external gaps between the entries are echoed inside each one in the form of different but analogical inner distances, gaps, discontinuities—not only the still relatively physical one of text and caption, but of what reigns within the figures and the thoughts themselves, the syntax, the analogies that are veritable syllogisms.

At this point, if a bit of overinterpretation is permitted: it may be wondered whether any significance is to be attached to our uncertainty (and Benjamin's?) as to whether the navigation of this street—this freshly perforated street—is to be understood as a stroll or a drive. We begin, after all, with a vehicle; even before Marinetti, it is vehicle and velocity which are the very operators and signifiers of artistic modernity. Yet the pace of the inspection of storefronts and signage inclines one to posit a slower, more leisurely movement; in any case, who ever imagined a *flâneur* behind the wheel? If there is anything symptomatic here, it must have to do with Benjamin's relationship to technology and in particular to the machinery of movement (very much including the camera itself—think of Dziga Vertov and his triumphant tours of urban Bolshevism!). One is tempted to suggest a unique conception of modernity as a heightened speed which allows for a more intense concentration on smaller and smaller segments of the environment it perambulates (indeed, this is more or less the description of cinema that emerges from Benjamin's famous essay "The Work of Art in the Age of Its Technological Reproducibility").

Still, sometimes we are officially strolling, and multiple perspectives confront what we may call the spatial sentence, a rhetorical move that shifts the content itself rather than its syntax or destination:

> Only he who walks the road on foot learns of the power it commands, and of how, from the very scenery that for the flyer is only the unfurled plain, it calls forth distances, belvederes, clearings, prospects at each of its turns like a commander deploying soldiers at a front. (I, 448; IV, 90)

It is a commonplace to observe that the modernists discovered temporality, not only as a reality that demanded a new method of representation, but as material to be incorporated into the representation itself. Le Corbusier constructed his villas with temporality, in the form of the trajectory; even music, already a seemingly temporal art, deployed pulses and duration in new and inescapable ways. Benjamin's sentence, however, as we have quoted it, is neither an exercise in point of view, nor is it a theorization on the order of Virilio's magisterial studies, even though, as Deleuze might put it, the sentence "thinks," but by way of representation rather than by concept.

Surely, however, its juxtaposition of several modes of perception, the foot-bound, the aerial, the forgotten vehicle of the opening, is phenomenological? Surely it incites us to an awareness of the distinction between various forms of temporal experience? But I would prefer to argue that the distinction and the radical difference lies in the turning itself, the break, which alone secures comparison and a sense of the uniquely distinctive modes that lie on either side. "The unfurled plain" ("*die aufgerolle Ebene*") is a perceptual abstraction which slyly inserts the temporality of the flight, the surface rolling out before us, in place of the aerial panorama in all its map-like concreteness and reduction: it only sets the stage for a return to the earth-bound perspective of the pedestrian (who is not yet, not at all, a *flâneur*; he's going somewhere!). Abstract are also the contents of the country landscape on foot ("distances, belvederes, clearings, prospects"), which merely serve to demonstrate that there is no such thing as space in the abstract at which we might gaze. Space is, as Benjamin says of architecture, distraction; as in Lewis Carroll, we can only see it laterally, out of the corner of our eye; when we turn to confront it with a head-on frontal gaze, it vanishes.

Still, where is time in all this? Was it merely syntactical—in the correction that replaces the "landscape . . . for the flyer" with what is called forth with each turning of the road on foot? (That construction, however, secretly contains the two other elements of the spatial sentence we have mentioned above—the peremptory correction and the positioning of the recipient: "only he who.") No, temporality comes with an unexpected, I daresay a completely gratuitous, simile: "like a commander deploying soldiers at a front" ["*herauskommandiert, wie ein Ruf des Befehlshabers Soldaten aus einer Front*"]. It is the road itself that so commands. We obey its orders as readers and shift our inner mimetic perspective accordingly. But I also want to evoke a parade-ground, with rows of soldiers standing at attention. At a single shouted command, these lines wheel about with geometric precision: the flank turns in a grand movement; these bodies, arrayed, move together to the very harmonies of the cosmos.[1]

So the movement of a small thing, my own insignificant person on a stroll or drive, taking in the sights, assumes the broader dimensions of the multitude, indeed of the universe itself. This makes for a well-nigh physical displacement within the reading mind itself, a regulated spasm in which the mimetic categories are unexpectedly substituted for one

---

1   See William H. McNeill, *Keeping Together in Time*, Cambridge: Harvard University Press, 1995.

another like the prestidigitation of a shell game or the unmistakable tremors of an underground detonation. This writer has visibly tampered with our mental infrastructure; his sentence has reached inside the mind with an imperceptible violence that ought to be illegal and denounced as such.

The difference between these perceptual dimensions is called upon metaphorically to function like an identity: turning a corner is "like a commander deploying soldiers at a front." The military aircraft has suddenly infected the metaphorical field of the *flâneur*, his slow arrival at a new batch of storefronts becomes the unison collective of troops wheeling in a new direction: but is it a review? Or a tactical maneuver? Such are the ancillary uncertainties with which this unexpected play of figuration leaves us. In these uneasy shifts from tenor to vehicle, from foreground to background, minimal to maximal, subject to object, there is a gradual slippage from the metaphorical to the allegorical. The object in the lost-and-found office is the fresh first sight of an unfamiliar landscape; habit gets lost the way you forget your wallet somewhere. The blue sky, however, so dazzling and refreshing, turns out to be a painted stage prop, restored to you with a certain contempt, that you should have bothered to look for so worthless an item in the first place (*Marnie*? The simulacrum? Here, to be sure, speaks the official spokesman of *aura*).

It is rare, however, for these random observations to come together in that simultaneity of possible worlds that the popular language of the period identified with Einsteinian relativity. Benjamin admired Giedion's book on glass architecture long before the immense manifesto which made him famous (*Space, Time and Architecture*, 1941), so the latter's rather facile Einsteinian account of architectural modernism in terms of relativity and perspectival multiplicity finds its definitive formulation, instead, in the phenomenology of the sailor's world (I, 485; IV, 144), the stroll in the port that reminds one of the sources of the storyteller (travelers' tales, sailors' even taller tales, the adventures spun out for the gullible and sedentary villagers). The shift, the shock, lies in the realization that however extensive the seaman's travels on the vasty deep, he never really knows much of the real city itself: his life on land is limited to bars and whores, and then he sets sail again on emptiness, undergoing the agonies of Conrad's *Typhoon* with nothing to show for it afterward but the memory of fear and crisis, without the slightest idea of real human

life, of routine, of the city and the everyday. His is not a flight from any
of that because he has never known it in the first place; and the port is
truly an incommensurable world, with hodological paths unknown to
the city-dwellers, whose habits are themselves unsuspected by the sailors in their unimaginable haunts. Every city is no doubt a superposition
of incommensurable villages, sometimes overlapping, sometimes wholly
unimaginable for each other, and whose very existences may be incomprehensible to their neighbors. But rarely is this juxtaposition so
dramatic as between the natives of the ports and those of the great
downtowns, with their distant suburbs.

The exhibits thus begin in time to disintegrate into a heterogeneous
collection of jottings: erotic, sociological, *choses vues*, childhood memories, moral reflections (à la Nietzsche or Gide), traveler's notes, flea-
market collections, the zeitgeist, the literary, the phenomenology of
bars, detective stories, fortune tellers, techniques and maxims, like any
interesting personal journal or diary, to be leafed through idly and
sometimes marked with a pencil. But just a minute! This is a writer for
whom the collection itself is a theme and an obsession: stamp collecting,
books, any boxful of carefully selected oddments—these are the objects
of his heightened attention, as a foot fetishist might take more than an
idle interest in the closets of his neighbors and friends. So there is some
higher vantage point we seem to have missed here; a lookout point not
included in the program, a more comprehensive secret plan or strategy,
a set of sets, a new genre? One perhaps slyly designated in passing by a
remark on children's hoards, leading one on to children's hiding places
and the reorganization of space they achieve in the most familiar of interiors, a thought that cannot but reverberate back on what is happening
to the street we are currently reading and which is opening up into a
nest of backrooms and hidden toys and dolls. Lacan thought the collection was a sign from *das Ding* (the first dawning infantile sense of the
as-yet-unconceptualized Other): his example was a uniquely constructed
endless series of interpenetrating wooden match boxes from all imaginable places on Earth.[2] Maybe these jottings interpenetrate (he says
"copulate") each other in some such mysterious way, their linkages
remaining undiscovered by us and in our frustration sometimes simply
pointing back to Benjamin himself, his own private "themes" and

---

2   Jacques Lacan, *Seminar, Livre VII*, Paris: Seuil, 1986, 136.

obsessions (including collecting), his own personal unconscious "signifying chain." And if he has become part of ours, then of course we're never uninterested; but alas, our investment in other people's wish-fulfillments is at best limited, as Freud pointed out.

We have forgotten, however, in all this—in the jumble of personal impressions and public observations, the record of an active mind almost exhausting in its diligent attentions—we have forgotten one thing, maybe the most relevant of all (and the most annoying). "Polyclinic: the author lays the idea on the marble table of the cafe." He lays out his instruments, operates, sews the patient up, "inserts a foreign term as a silver rib." The text is finished, he pays the waiter, "his assistant" (intern, colleague, nurse, etc.), in cash. He has written the article commissioned by his editor as you might order your espresso, read the paper, smoke a cigarillo and perhaps enjoy the view or examine the flora and fauna of the neighboring tables (open-air cafés, being for the Berliner, a decidedly Southern experience). At least half this book is taken up with *writing*! Are you disappointed or excited? The old '60s manias—*écriture*, text, tattoos, the letter, the mark, the trace, the recording apparatus, the stylus, reading, the book—all are here avant la lettre, a seedbank ready to spring into flower in the hot Parisian summers of the postwar Western intelligentsia. But maybe this particular purloined letter has arrived at its destination too late? Perhaps literature itself, around which so much of Benjamin revolves, is itself outmoded in the era of the media, new and old, and in the age not just of reproducibility, of which Gutenberg and the book remained the privileged example, but of computability and big data, the PowerPoint and the algorithm, artificial intelligence, translation machines and posthuman high-frequency trading. You can still talk about reading all of this, but, as with the Kindle, Benjamin's physical book has all but vanished, and his thoughts about it make us just about as uncomfortable as the daring references to radio throughout this period.

Benjamin's attention to writing, however, was certainly a thrust toward materialism unusual even in the most advanced philology of the time: Spitzer and Auerbach were not much interested in the physical book (despite Dante's celestial "volume" binding together "*ciò che per l'universo si squaderna*"), but Benjamin actually collected them—so his thoughts on books are fully as objective and sensory as his thoughts on pavements or on whores: indeed, did not one of the more striking ones read: "books and whores can be taken to bed" (I, 460; IV, 109)? (It should be said in passing that it is not the frequency of his references to brothels throughout his oeuvre that "may not be suitable for all audiences," but rather the frequency with which they function as casual metaphors: both sexual institutions and literature are among the signs of the aging of this work, which any good defense lawyer would urge us to replace in its historical situation and context.)

So, cutting through the city will also turn the thoughts of the engineer to his own instruments, his tools and maps, the challenges faced by his urban project, techniques as well, traditional and experimental, and the forms of the labor—excavations, demolitions, bridges, negotiating the cables, sewers, underground waterways that lie in his path. Each of these— and mapping each of these—will take a different form, different dimensions, as the very first entry warns us: "leaflets, brochures, articles, and placards." And the caption ("Filling Station") reminds us of something else, namely that the gas with which we fill our car has a very different function when compared with the more viscous liquids with which we oil other parts of the engine. The term "literature" covered a broad and varied array of writings in the eighteenth century—"letters" (belles lettres)— after which the category shifted toward the different kinds of experts involved in its production. How universal, then, was the vocation and practice of the "man of letters" Benjamin aspired to be in the Weimar period? This vocation no longer exists, and we must read his work through its absence, along with the related disappearance of reading publics, journals, newspapers and the array of print media that used to constitute the "public sphere," the realm of exchange and opinion. "Opinions," indeed, (*Überlegungen*) "are to the vast apparatus of social existence what oil is to machines," or so Benjamin completes his materialist analogy.

The newspaper, meanwhile—Hegel's "morning prayer of modern man," Mallarmé's Thousand-and-One-Nights prototype for his Book of the World—the newspaper would seem to be at least one of the models for that Eisensteinian "montage of attractions" which is the cornucopia of *One-Way Street*. As a theme, it is necessarily part of itself, a set which includes itself as its own subset: notes about typography, book reports, an encomium for self-publishing, Karl Kraus, typewriters versus calligraphy, even multiple theses and adages about writing, criticism, the cultural public, the document as discourse . . . "Post no bills!"—this injunction is itself a kind of schizogenetic placard against itself, just as the analysis of opinion forces Benjamin's own personal opinions into the medium of perception and toward the *fait divers*. And perhaps even into the advertisement, like the Soviet avant-garde visual art of the period (El Lissitzky): "today, the most real, mercantile gaze into the heart of things is the advertisement." This is that nominalist trend of the Zeitgeist against which Adorno philosophically warned.

But this "spirit of the age" poses its own problems for the generalization, for the central diagnosis this picture book so desperately calls. When it comes, then, in Benjamin's "guided tour through German inflation," we find only scanty notes on collective psychology, the paradoxes of national behavior and the state of the Germans in what ought to be a heroic crisis time. There is a way in which Benjamin's own method condemns him to this rather disappointing anticlimax.

For the deeper subject of this history—"subject" in the sense of protagonist and even demiurge—is not that collective national psychology called The Germans, it is the child. It is not the macrocosm of a whole population but rather the pre-individual, pre-collective, pre-national being so active in its exploration of space, its search of pantries, its collections, its decipherment, its constructions, that is the secret subject of so much of Benjamin's writing and perception: a kind of estrangement-effect by way of regression, an innocence recaptured in his other great montage, the *Berlin Childhood*. Benjamin thought he had found his first genuine political praxis in the early German youth movements, but they proved to have already overshot the mark; and if for one whole strand of Benjaminian exegesis, the writer's soul was torn between the German language and the Jewish identity traditions, then the child was already the solution avant la lettre, still ignorant of its participation in either one, let alone of their tension with each other. This is not to say anything so simpleminded as that Benjamin loved children, a doubtful proposition at best for this loner; nor did he aspire to any Wordsworthian childlike state, an ideal at the extreme other end of the linguistic and perceptual complexities in which he reveled. Childish, perhaps, were those bombastic seventeenth-century German dramas he undertook to study, but scarcely his readings of them.

Yet the fantasy image of the child somehow offered a methodological way out of the great form-problem of the age, if not a solution to it: how to operate with hyperintellectual intensity in a situation in which ideas have become commodities and sheer opinion? How to create the new out of universally debased ideological materials? How to think after the end of philosophy and the reification of the academic disciplines, or to perceive after the wholesale transformation of reality into images and commonplaces? His contemporaries Pound and Eisenstein came up with similar conclusions: the ideogram, the montage, are means toward an art that thinks without opinion, that combines the multiple levels of the Real without filtering it through a "temperament." The stacks of notes that were to have become the *Arcades* promised just such another monument, no longer a one-way street but a whole city in its own right. Adorno, who chose the path of using thought against itself, expressed his doubts about the possibility of the enterprise, which only left sentences behind it. Yet those sentences are precious enough, and they give a good sense of what Barthes meant when he tried to distinguish between the *lisible* (the readerly) and the *scriptible* (the writerly), for their latent scriptible power and concision still works—it makes you want to write.

The opening asked us to fill the gas tank in advance; the closing leaves us outside the planetarium to come, as it were—the recovery of the relationship of Dasein, of the individual human body, to the cosmos. Has it been broken by the all-encompassing city form to which *One-Way Street* and life and history all condemn us equally? Or are we on the knife's edge of Heideggerian metaphysics, of some relationship to the universe which, having lost it, we cannot even any longer imagine? Benjamin was fond of that strange little treatise in which Blanqui, from his lifelong prison cell, imagined not only the universe itself beyond the visible stars but their repetitive eternity, history repeating over and over again in unimaginably vast cycles—that history into which he himself vainly tried to intervene and will then do so again and again for all eternity. That is, no doubt, to repeat over and over again our failure to reach the planetarium, and yet, as well, to approach its presence, so close, nearby, over the next bend in the road, over the next hill. True ontology is the effort to reach an as-yet-nonexistent ontology, the one we can still only imagine.

2

One-Way Street therefore sends us in a number of different directions. Space and the city, obviously enough; they will be dealt with in a later chapter (VI). But there is also the destination of this journey, seemingly stalled or broken off just outside the city limits at the planetarium itself. Presumably more is at stake here than the mere casting of horoscopes, in which Benjamin took some personal interest (an area we will explore in the next chapter). For Benjamin's theory of language, implicit in his seemingly mystical early conception of "language as such," as well as in his own critical dealings with sentences and texts, is not so convention- ally academic as that of his contemporaries in the *Stilstudien* movement (Leo Spitzer, Erich Auerbach and, later on, Werner Krauss), even though he liked the term "philology." The limits on linguistics in general remain the limits of the sentence, no matter what kinds of larger frameworks (discourse, text grammar, performativity) are proposed; and we have already seen that in what we may call his "spatial sentences," the syntac- tical limits of the sentence itself are subject to underground tremors and perturbations even if they are not altogether breached. I anticipate on a later discussion by suggesting that Benjamin sees his sentence (and that of others) in an altogether different and potentially nonverbal context. When he compares Baudelaire's verses, for example, to the insurrections and coups d'état envisioned by Blanqui, what is at work is not a meta- phor. Rather different from the elegant violence he admired in Baudelaire's own phrasing—knife strokes so clean you do not even feel them until you notice the blood beginning to seep through the water— Benjamin's comparison with Blanqui, which combines the two distant domains of the stylistic and the political in an arbitrary and willful gesture, can be felt to be an act in its own right, an intervention in the serene autonomy of the verses for which the current language of performativity or the speech act seems too academic and well-behaved. Brecht's conception of the *gestus* is preferable, which subsumes the words under a more physical and situational unity; and as a critical act (or *gestus* in its own right), it demotes linguistics to a subordinate posi- tion under what Kenneth Burke would have called dramatistics. Conventional interpretation is thereby interrupted, we might say, even though all the great interpretations of so-called "style studies" have always acknowledged a secret allegiance to the logic of the *gestus* (I think again of Spitzer, or of Sartre's literary essays, in which the style of a Faulkner or a Dos Passos, of Camus's *Stranger*, are grasped as so many metaphysical acts).

But I also want to underscore the not-so-secret violence of Benjamin's critical practice; he did so himself, in his call for the "destruction" of the text in its analysis, a terminology he found in the German Romantics: "criticism [for Friedrich Schlegel] irrevocably and earnestly dissolves the form in order to transform the single work into the absolute work of art ... 'We must elevate ourselves above our own love and be able in thought to annihilate what we adore, otherwise we lack ... the sense for the infinite.' In these statements, Schlegel expressed himself clearly about the destructive element in criticism, its decomposition of the art form" (I, 163–4; I, 85). In Benjamin, this principle will take the form of a rhetorical violence in which a given passage is "wrenched out" (IV, 173; I , 670: *herausreissen*) of the writer's text. But above and beyond that transcendental level, which was for the Romantics art as such (and for Benjamin, occasionally, language), this "annihilation" is also a production:

> Good criticism is composed of at most two elements: the critical gloss and the quotation. Very good criticism can be made from both glosses and quotations ... a criticism consisting entirely of quotations should be developed. (II, 290; VI, 162)

Thus, to wrench a passage out from a given text is not merely to disrupt the text; it has the consequence of producing that new thing, the quotation, which has a generic life of its own. As we shall see shortly, not only is it secretly grounded in the logic of similitude, it has its own deeper *Gleichnis* and, as it were, its Ur-form in history itself. There is thus a movement of expansion in which the tearing out of the quotation slowly becomes the discovery of the New, which in Baudelaire is "wrenched with heroic effort from the 'ever self-same'" (IV, 175; 1, 672: "*dem 'Immerwiedergleichen' abgewonnen*"). It is a process which then becomes world-historical when that well-known figure, "the historical materialist," undertakes "to blast a specific era out of the homogeneous course of history; thus, he blasts a specific life out of the era, a specific work out of the lifework" (IV, 396; I, 703).

It might well be said that this violent will to expansion (intensification, *Steigerung, amplificatio*) in reality amounts to little more than a fantasy promotion, Kenneth Burke's "symbolic *act*" shriveling back into a "merely *symbolic* act," Baudelaire's versification likened in derision to Blanqui's (equally impotent) insurrections. The figural violence is that of the literary critic trying desperately to endow his cultural column with the historical and political significance of revolt and praxis. This interpretation, of course, depends very much on the historical value one attaches to culture and on the way in which superstructures are seen as an active part of the mode of production (and it has been argued that the modern and, even more, the postmodern—and with it, so-called Western Marxism—represents a shift of the social center of gravity from production to consumption).

More significant, however, seems to me the form of the figural expansion itself, in which the positive and the negative alternate in an uncertain dialectic. On the face of it, destruction (this was also Heidegger's word for his revision of the history of philosophy, later rewritten as "deconstruction") would seem, as a synonym for and expression of violence, to be a negative term. Yet in another moment, for Benjamin, destruction produces and indeed constitutes a new kind of production, which would in general not be equal to its own meaning without the destruction of its own raw materials. So it is that the critical "destruction" of the aesthetic work is not necessarily so negative a phenomenon as the revival of a regressive aestheticism will be found to be. Figuration in Benjamin consists in a neutral establishment of the materials of the figure, as it were, the initial data of an undetermined situation in which a constellation of images is set in place, then to be inflected with either positive or negative outcomes depending on our political requirements. "Aura" can be Utopian or dystopian as one likes, and can stand in the service of a progressive or a reactionary politics: itself a judgment to be made politically, as Benjamin insists over and over again (even in his earliest youth-movement writings, in which it is a question of "wrenching" the concept of experience from its Kantian epistemological limits and endowing it with a more energizing generational force).

But the syntactical act, if it is permitted to call it that, is not in Benjamin limited to the literally explosive ("the historical materialist blasts the epoch out of its reified 'historical continuity'" [III, 262; II, 468]: "*sprengt*"); it also underscores a temporality which detects significant movement and ephemerality within the reified time of a historical "grand narrative." So, "the dialectical image is an image that flashes up. The image of what has been—in this case, the image of Baudelaire—must be caught in this way, flashing up in the now of its recognizability" (IV 183; I, 682; also A, N3, 1; VII, 578 and K2, 3; VII, 495). *Aufblitzen*—a peculiarly Benjaminian verb, which has its own inner kind of violence—can best be appreciated by way of its multiple equivalents: flash up, flare up, sparkle, coruscate, glint, gleam, glimmer, streak, twinkle, and so on—where for the overt violence of the act of wrenching has been substituted its temporality, and the violent physical act has been replaced by its fleeting appearance. Thus, the ephemerality of the entity, its luminosity, is emphasized by yet another privileged expression, *vorbei-huschen*—to flit past, to fly past, to slip, to flash, to scurry, to whisk, to dart, and so on, where speed is then substituted for visual appearance. "The nexus of meaning of words or sentences," he tells us in a significant passage, "is the bearer through which, like a flash, similarity appears . . . its production by man—like its perception by him—is . . . tied to its flashing up. It flits past [*Es huscht vorbei*]" (II, 722; II, 213).

But this "similarity," which is itself a "flashing" that "flits past," demands a more extensive explanation. It is in fact the mark and symptom of one of the most fundamental categories of Benjamin's thinking, namely the similitude (or *Gleichnis*), which is not to be confused with metaphor or tropology but is a well-nigh metaphysical principle which governs his view of history as well as his practice of perception (his tender empiricism) and which will be approached in the next chapter. Suffice it for the moment to observe that these are by no means the only tics of style that will be isolated and examined in the present work, but also that they all have a secondary, perhaps unwanted, consequence which now demands attention in its own right.

As we have seen, these recurrent and seemingly metaphoric expressions not only underscore the multiple faces of the figural situation itself, they also presuppose that initial figural violence of the "wrenching out," the autonomization of the part becoming a new whole. Yet this was itself possible only on the basis of what can be termed the dialectic of the point and the line, the moment in which the violence of a break initiated a production and transformed a limit into a boundary, producing a whole new episodic space in the gap left it behind.

There are also moments in which Benjamin's linguistic habits serve other, more dubious purposes. I would in that sense characterize the neutral yet strangely scientific-technical terms whereby he links base and superstructure and claims the authority of a link and a meaningful connection by way of words that do not exactly bear interpretation: such are "carries the index of," "an extract of," "precipitates," and the like, about which we may venture endless conjectures that remain eternally unverifiable, if elegant in their papering over of an awkward moment. More meaningful are the radical opposites of all these figural movements, namely Benjamin's lifelong insistence on speechlessness and expression-lessness, which will begin with Greek statuary (Baudelairean beauty) and persist as the very fulfillment of language in its own opposite, the silence and emptiness of the radical break itself. This truth of the radical interruption will indeed, reinforced by the authority of Rang and Rosenzweig, form the basis for his theory of tragedy, as we shall see shortly. Finally there is the speaker of these turns of speech, who is also their observer, their analyst and their operator: this is the "he who," the "whoever," later openly identified as "the historical materialist," who will play a significant if enigmatic role in Benjamin's cast of characters.

Figure 2.1

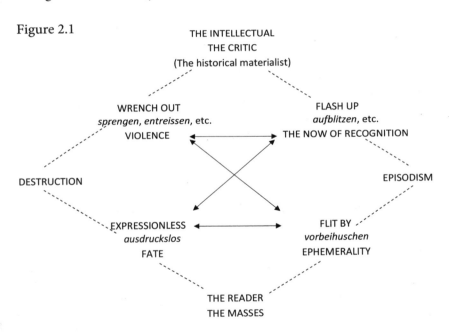

3

It will not have escaped the reader that sentences—whether those of his object of study and philological attention or those of Benjamin himself—thus "wrenched" from their context or work become a new text in their own right, perhaps one can even call them a new genre. That genre is the quotation, and it may be more than appropriate to quote the passage in which, in *One-Way Street*, Benjamin describes them:

> Quotations in my work are like the wayside robbers who leap out,
> armed, and relieve the idle stroller of his conviction. (I, 481; IV, 138)

The stroller is an old friend, Baudelaire's and Benjamin's *flâneur*; while
"conviction"—the oil with which our vehicle was to have been lubricated
at the outset—is another word for the one Benjamin uses so sparingly,
namely ideology. So these are robbers whose motivations are pedagogical: they want to <u>leave us at a loss</u>, without prejudices or preconceptions,
in just that state that Brecht's *Verfremdungseffekt* was also supposed to
induce, namely the state in which new thinking begins.

But perhaps the formal implications of the quotation will not be clear
unless you have worked through the convolute on Baudelaire himself.
Benjamin does occasionally note down his own impressions of the poet;
but despite three essays on his poetry, I hesitate to call them literary criticism. What seems above all to have interested him are the interpretations
of Baudelaire by other writers of the period, ranging from denunciations
of Baudelaire's immorality to the subtlest stylistic observations of a
Lafargue or a Bourget. Now it is certainly the case that few writers have
been open to so many varied reactions and readings as this poet, about
whom one is tempted to say that it is this variety itself, and the impene-
trability it suggests, that is the very sign and mark of his greatness. But I
also think that Benjamin reveled in the multiple voices and opinions, the
sheer polyphony, of the public sphere as it formed around what literally
became a public scandal, and what was across all the languages of the
world recognized as a stylistic crystallization of something more than
mere novelty, as the beginning of a whole new era. But it is Benjamin's
passion for the multiplicity of these voices that above all interests me, yet
another symptom of his not unpolitical fascination with the multiple,
with the masses as such (despite the fact that these are almost exclusively
bourgeois critics). It is worth observing that here also the poet preceded
him, who, in his *Fusées*, reflects: "*Le plaisir d'être dans les foules est une
expression mystérieuse de la jouissance de la multiplication du nombre.
Tout est nombre. Le nombre est dans l'individu. L'ivresse est un nombre.*"[3] I
translate: "The pleasure we take in crowds is a mysterious expression of
our jouissance in the multiplication of number. *Everything* is number.

---

3   Baudelaire, *Oeuvres complètes, Bibliothèque de la Pléiade*, Paris, 1975, 649. Benjamin
will himself quote this passage in *Arcades* J34a3, 290.

Number is in the individual. Intoxication is a number." Indeed, it is this very polyphony of the quotations that sometimes makes one grateful he never "completed" the *Arcades* in any discursive form and left us with that collection of clippings which becomes our own hobby.

There remains, however, a generic effect whereby suddenly another book speaks through the text, and the aesthetic of interruption rather than the plausibility of its content does something to the reader's internal equilibrium. Perhaps it also from time to time has the effect of discrediting the text's primary voice, namely that of Benjamin. In either case, we seem to be confronted here with an unusual pedagogy which has to do with the shifting of perceptual levels within the mind, a kind of pedagogical surgery that can be characterized as a cultural revolution within the reading process. But now we also inevitably remember a persistent dream of this writer, the notorious and no doubt somewhat impish project of writing a book wholly made up of quotations, a project that maddened Adorno:

> Method of this project: literary montage. I needn't say anything. Merely show. I shall purloin no valuables, appropriate no ingenious formulations. But the rags, the refuse—these I will not inventory but allow, in the only way possible, to come into their own, by making use of them. (A, 460, N1a8; V, 574)

Probably he did not have so ambitious a project in mind in 1924, when he wrote Scholem, "I have at my disposal about six hundred quotations, and, in addition, they are so well organized that you can get an overview at a glance" (March 5). The testimony, however—it has to do not with the future *Arcades*, but with Benjamin's research on his *Trauerspiel* thesis—makes us realize that, in fact, long before the Baudelaire project, he had already written such a work. For as we shall see, the *Trauerspiel* book is itself scarcely more than a tissue of quotations, lined up in parade formation, to be marched solemnly across the field, an army of discontinuities. But this particular army, like Blanqui's, is disguised as a discourse.

Still, Benjamin himself was perfectly willing to extract just such combinations from his own notes, as evinced in his "essay" "Central Park," which is constituted by a series of his own observations, in episodic or fragmentary form, selected from the J or Baudelaire convolute, without any strong overall direction (wind in his sails?) or, less metaphorically, without any central thesis or connecting tissue (without *mediations*, in Adorno's indictment). This practice might then be seen in two ways: it is a kind of pastiche of the pure form of juxta-posed quotations alluded to above, with his own notes standing in for the clippings from other works; or else it is the primary form or arche-type of the discontinuous string of theoretical observations—à la Nietzsche or La Rouchefoucauld—of which the "quotation book" was itself merely an imitation or a realization, but now in the form of a collage of impersonal materials.

Here, then, an aesthetic begins to appear, the traces of a formal prin-ciple (or *Kunstwollen*) which is profoundly characteristic of the modern-ist period and can find parallel realizations in Pound's *Cantos*, on the one hand, and Eisenstein's "montage of attractions," on the other: both of them discontinuous and seemingly a patchwork of unrelated images which, for one reason or another, eschew the direction of the personal voice, of the subjectivity of sheer opinion, of subjective intention and interpretation, thereby illustrating the drive, in modernism, to escape psychology and the conscious direction of the ego in the search for a more objective aesthetic. At the same time, all three bodies of work are obsessively pedagogical (we might add to them Godard's *Histoire(s) du cinéma*) and betray a heightened commitment to dogmatic theses and lessons all while they are able to take credit for an enlargement of the role of the readers, whom they seem to ask to make their own judgments (as also in Brecht's epic theater). The paradox, indeed, the contradiction of this unique aesthetic impulse has perhaps its political analogue in Maoism: bombard the headquarters! Make your own judgments (inso-far as they coincide with mine)! It is the strong personal conviction that wishes to disengage itself from the personal (or from the "author," in all its poststructural senses) and that acknowledges some new freedom of interpretation of the readership at the same time that it longs to annex that readership to its own ends, which it prudently omits to specify. This is perhaps the place to evoke a fundamental stylistic principle Benjamin often reiterated: "If I write better German than most writers of my generation, it is thanks largely to twenty years' observance of one little rule: never use the word 'I' except in letters" (II, 603; VI, 475). As for the larger forms into which these sentences, whether quotations or not—and often enough quotations from himself!—are embedded like a

mosaic (a figure Benjamin himself uses tellingly in his essay on translation), those seem limited to the essay, a topic on which Lukács had
himself famously written and to which Adorno will return after the war
(in an argument used against Lukács himself, as it turns out).

But this is to reckon without the virtuosity with which Benjamin
handled this form, if indeed what we have already seen to be an assemblage of separate sentences can even be called that. Our view of that
"form" has, however, been biased by the editions in which the writings
were issued (let alone the ideological struggles around them). In
Germany, the decisive reappearance of Benjamin took place in 1955,
with the publication of the two volumes of essays selected by Scholem
and Adorno; in America, with Harry Zohn's translation of *Illuminations*
in 1969 (in a collection chosen and edited by Hannah Arendt).
Meanwhile, the beginning of the publication of the *Gesammelte Schriften*
in 1974 put the debate on another footing altogether, while the monumental American four-volume *Selected Writings*, whose publication
began in 1996, might have been expected to do the same for American
critical efforts as well.

Still, the Benjamin of an English-language reader remains that of
Illuminations; but the German reader was no less limited, for whom the
great two-volume collection of 1955, assembled by Scholem and Adorno
(as it were the West-German or revisionist canon), traced the outer
limits. To be sure, it also included *The Origins of German Trauerspiel*,
which remained legendary over here until its 1998 translation. Other
selections included only what I have called "essays," which I will now
rebaptize as program-essays, by which I am trying to designate the
opposite of the "occasional" piece or the structure as a collation, as well
as to underscore the effort, in each one, to make a complete theoretical
statement of some kind. These begin in 1929 with the essay on Surrealism
and end with the essays specifically drafted for the Frankfurt School
journal, the *Zeitschrift für Sozialforschung*. (I omit the so-called early
writings—mostly fragments—from this discussion, even though they
include the formal predecessor of the longer form in the study of
Goethe's *Wahlverwandtschaften* [192, 2], to which Benjamin always
attached special significance.)

It is also instructive to compare the two collections, the American
translations and the German originals—which is to say, it is instructive
to see what *Illuminations* itself left out: the early ("theological")

materials, to be sure; many literary essays and reviews, excepting those on Kafka and on translation; *One-Way Street*; "The Destructive Character" (on the historico-political role of Kraus and Brecht); and the three significant previews of the *Arcades Project* ("Paris, Capital of the Nineteenth Century," "The Paris of the Second Empire in Baudelaire," and "Central Park"). We may also note that the essay on "Eduard Fuchs: Collector and Historian"—often described as Benjamin's most orthodox expression of a Marxist method—was omitted by both collections; nor did either show any awareness of the second version of "The Work of Art in the Age of Its Technological Reproducibility" while both grudgingly include the Brechtian "What is Epic Theater?" at the same time that they renounce what became Benjamin's most influential literary-theoretical text of the 1960s, namely "The Author as Producer," which both Adorno and Arendt seemingly deplored. But perhaps the latter work, for its brevity, is not really to be considered a "program-essay" any more than "The Critique of Violence" (omitted by Arendt) and "The Task of the Translator"—both influential texts for Benjamin's 1960s afterlife. Nor does either include what became the foundational text for Benjamin's more mystical readers, namely the early "On Language as Such and on the Language of Man" (1916, but unpublished in his lifetime). So, as little Marxism as possible, and a certain distance from the theological as well as what would become the 1960s political traditions of Benjamin.

Still, despite a sampling by Adorno-Scholem, even the German public could not have been aware of the tidal wave of short articles and reviews that would strike the public sphere with the 1972 publication of Volume III of the *Gesammelte Schriften*, an immense 600-page meteorite, which, fallen inexplicably among the more respectable "literary" essays, suddenly, with its rich cornucopia of hundreds of one- or two-page book reviews of all kinds, made it clear that the industrious Benjamin was a very different kind of writer than the one canonized by so many diverse literary ideologies and academic tendencies.

If we accept the proposition that the book review (although itself almost always determined by arbitrary and contingent external commissions) is a genre or form related to the diary entry (for example, that of André Gide, canonical for the twentieth century and the object of a good deal of admiration on Benjamin's part), and if we then make so bold as to add to our list that now-extinct form, the letter, in which

Benjamin was able to deploy so many of his varied intellectual interests and personal mannerisms, we begin to gain a very different picture of this figure, one about whom it may be possible, having already asserted that he never wrote a book, to affirm that he never even wrote an essay as such.

At any rate, a case can be made not merely for including the "quotable sentence" in the repertory of Benjaminian genres or "small forms"— where it joins the maxim or the epigram, Goethe's "aperçus"—but of extending the catalogue further, of submitting the essay form itself to Benjaminian "destruction" and identifying not only the spatial sentence, the quotation, the art-paragraph, the tonal sequence and "montage of attractions," but also the failed genres, the tractatus, the incomplete medieval treatise, which survive only here and there as "theses," the political speeches and manifestoes, the journals or diaries.

Nor must we omit his children's entertainments and plays and his radio broadcasts, which would seem to fall under the somewhat different heading of narratives. He told stories, certainly—entertaining his public of mixed ages with selected and memorable catastrophes, such as "The Lisbon Earthquake" or "The Railway Disaster at the Firth of Tay"— but he was not a storyteller in the sense in which his great essay of that name evokes the vocation of that now-extinct institution. Rather, he strikes me as what one would call a raconteur, particularly in the form in which, from Maupassant to Conrad and Somerset Maugham, that traveler's pastime became a literary practice (and, according to the Sartre of a particularly venomous denunciation in *Nausea*, a vehicle for imposing an authoritarian and generational respect for "experience" on a captive audience).

In Benjamin's case, however, one is inclined to sense a delight in sharing such exotic experiences, which goes so far as to include a good deal of pleasurable and Brechtian instruction, such as the history and economics of shipping (II, 646–8; VI, 447–8). More often, though, the entry serves as a pretext for exercising the narrator's virtuosity.

Thus, for example, he will start out a newspaper sketch on various exotic Italian foods with a few obligatory thoughts on taste, on eating, on new gastronomical sensations. Almost at once, however, the anecdote appears, in the guise of a travel entry: "How did I learn all this?" (II, 350) (Nothing really personal about this first-person: it is the persona of the professional travel guide.) Yet the experience rises against a background of emptiness; what makes it visible as an "experience" is the solitude and the emptiness of traveling, of the isolation in a foreign place, of boredom ("boredom is the dream bird that hatches the egg of experience" [III, 149; II, 446]), or of isolation ("how sad it makes you not to be able to share it"—as with the complex business of a breakfast alone in a French cafe [II, 360; IV, 376]).

But then the wonderful anecdote, orgiastic in its enthusiasm, pockets stuffed full of figs, which get transferred to his mouth—"the ultimate mountainpeak of taste ... the utter transformation of enjoyment into habit, of habit into vice. A hatred of those figs ... I was desperate to finish with them, to liberate myself, to rid myself of all this overripe, bursting fruit. I ate to destroy it" (II, 359; IV, 375). Shades of Herr Jakob Schmidt, the *Mahagonny* character who, now that money can buy anything and everything, allegorically devotes himself to eating another whole calf, to have peace with his desire (he dies of it). What in Brecht is dramatic and materialistic, I almost want to say ontological, is here in Benjamin psychological somehow, until we remember his translation of it into that peremptory truth ("no one who has never eaten a food to excess has ever really experienced it") of which the anecdote becomes the verification.

But supposing the book reviews really just share the same form, isolated experiences against the void of an empty boredom, perceptions transmogrified into events—which, since the reader/listener partners in them, get transformed into anecdotes—we must nonetheless appreciate the boldness with which Benjamin converts the humble essay form into a well-nigh symphonic display of tones and levels, a virtuoso performance that ranges from the child's finger exercise all the way to the sublime. Indeed, a brief 1928 account of the Berlin Food Fair for the *Frankfurter Zeitung* ("Epilogue to the Berlin Food Exhibition" [II, 135–9; IV, 527–32]) would at first glance seem to have all the appeal of a notice of farmers' markets in a small-town newspaper. In fact, or perhaps for that very reason, it turns out to be one of Benjamin's most dazzling essays, not only for the grotesque proportions of this exhibit, seemingly rivaling Henry Ford's mechanical museum in Deerborn, but also for the unobtrusive yet unerring way in which Benjamin pursues a path from reception through politics to apocalypse in the vignettes he constructs with such gusto and with a writerly pleasure in its own energies quite at odds with his ostensible subject.

After an initial throwaway observation about the relationship between exhibits, popularization, and the art of advertising, he stages an account of the Brobdingnagian proportions of the initial offerings ("sacrificial loaves of bread as tall as a man on the altar of statistics"—a note to which he will return); characteristically locating the delight in such monstrous immensities in the reactions of one of his favorite spectators, namely children ("what these things mean for science escapes me entirely. But their meaning for children is obvious").

The quotient of instruction in the child's fun fair then becomes revealed for what it is in the appearance of a second type of spectator, namely the masses ("who do not wish to be 'instructed'"). Now the giant landscapes of the child's spectacle take on a somewhat different, perhaps more premeditated and thereby sinister, intent: for the masses "can absorb knowledge only if it is accompanied by the slight shock that nails down inwardly what has been experienced. Their education is a series of catastrophes that befall them at fairs, in darkened tents, where anatomical discoveries enter their very bones." Here lessons are being surreptitiously administered, and the trajectories of the edible are conveyed, along with "little lights going on and off, illustrating crop cultivation in different seasons or the process of metabolism in the human body." A dose of history is imbibed as well, where "Egyptians, Greeks, Romans, Germanic tribes . . . dine in illuminated niches but consume nothing, like spirits meeting for a midnight feast." The Christians, meanwhile, teach the pros and cons of infant nourishment, including the bad nurses, who "put the bottle in their own mouths, hold the drinking child head-down, chatter all the while to another one of the damned, and produce a picture that is enough to warm the heart of any devil." (Perhaps this last exhibit was calculated to keep the riotous child observer of the opening in check and under caution.)

At any rate, we ultimately emerge into statistics, and from beautiful landscapes reduced to the spaces of food production and delivery, we "come into our own from our least-known side, the fourth or fifth dimension that we did not even know existed—namely as providers of yardsticks." All this then proceeds logically through "food in wartime" to the ghastly synthetic foodstuffs—"all of them registered trademarks in which the unaccommodated truth of the day found refuge, as if in ultimate linguistic exile." The now of this degradation seems destined for the contemplation of some Benjaminian *Grübler*, picking among the rubble of the outmoded for allegorical bits and pieces, for the telltale "remnants of the first 'guaranteed gas-proof' foodstuffs."

This trajectory bodes no good, and predictably the essay duly arrives without a whimper at the end of the world: this "food exhibition [which] would be no bad model of the place where the world gets boarded up and nailed shut." Apocalypse then quietly consists of a numerical linguistics in which "we see twelve sacks containing 650 kilos of concentrated feedstuff, 900 kilos of straw, 2,700 kilos of hay in two cartloads, and 11,000 kilos of turnips in five heavy cartloads." What would he have thought of the automated chicken runs and chemical pig farms of the present day, whose misery and toxins far outweigh the destiny of sheer enumeration and statistical planning?

Yet he regrets the climactic absence of the final form of gastronomical science, "that stretch of beach littered with human bones" where Robinson Crusoe discovered the secret of cannibalism. The omission does not diminish the value of this henceforth immortalized exhibit as a fever-chart of human pedagogy or, if you prefer, of the techniques of cultural revolution; for what we discover in Benjamin's cast of characters here—the exhilarated children, the slow-witted masses, the historical specters and the only-too-vivid nurses, the "absence of the touring medical expert" as well, the cannibals who live on in Europe's as well as in Robinson's memory—is Benjamin's careful observance and measurement of the ways in which instruction comes to society, to a social order always in need of "social reproduction," whether of a revolutionary or a conservative type. His characters are then always the objects of pedagogy: this is the deeper secret of his political and aesthetic kinship with Brecht and also that of his attention to the archetypical subjects of such pedagogy, namely the children themselves, whose very relationship with their toys betrays not enjoyment or consumption, but rather the delight in production as such. He himself, the *flâneur* and, as it were, the academic monitor of such collective and social pedagogies, remains an observer—but, at the same time, scarcely a neutral one, the time traveler from some messianic future who can alone express his delight and amusement in the grotesque forms these classrooms of social reproduction take in capitalism's random marketplace today.

3

Cosmos

. . . the stars, which Baudelaire banished from his world . . . (IV, 173; I, 670)

1

It would be hard to overestimate the significance of this observation, not only for Benjamin's reading of the poet, but for his assessment of the modern world as such. To be sure, Baudelaire imagined lofty dwelling places, "*auprès du ciel*":

> *Ich will um meinen Strophenbau zu läutern*
> *Dicht unter Himmel ruhn gleich Sternendeutern.* (IV, 23)

> I want a bedroom near the sky, an astrologer's cave
> Where I can fashion eclogues that are chaste and grave.[1]

Ashbery's unsolicited introduction of a "cave" has the merit of stressing a less obvious motivation—namely, to get as far away as possible from

---

1   Benjamin's translations are to be found in Volume IV of the *Gesammelte Schriften*, here page 23; he does not seem to have tried his hand at "Spleen IV," whose first line is cited later on. Ashbery's version of "Paysage" is to be found in *Baudelaire in English*, eds. C. Clark and R. Sykes, New York: Penguin, 1997, 111, as is Roy Fuller's of "Spleen IV," 102. Quotes from Baudelaire's own work refer to the two-volume Pléiade series *Oeuvres Complètes*, Paris: Gallimard, 1975.

society. The garret may be closer to the stars than the street, but it remains as inaccessible as the sky in bad weather:

> And when winter casts its monotonous pall,
> Of snow, I'll draw the blinds and curtains tight
> And build my magic palaces in the night.

In fact, what replaces the stars as some outer limit of Baudelaire's world is in fact the ceiling that conceals them: the "lowered ceiling" of weather is here scarcely metaphorical. It makes the streets themselves, the whole of the formerly outside world of the city, into an interior and a space of enclosure:

> *Quand le ciel bas et lourd pèse comme un couvercle . . .*

> When, a great manhole lid, the heavy sky
> Falls and fits neatly on the horizon's ring . . .

This permanently asphyxiating spatial temporality, which differentiates Baudelaire sharply from the impenetrable fog of his London contemporary, Dickens, is what for Benjamin makes the urban into a city and an object of his lifelong representational ambition ("the city became a book in my hands," he says about Marseilles in the early morning [I, 477; IV, 133]). Benjamin's early translations of Baudelaire were indeed limited to that section of *Les Fleurs du mal* called "Tableaux parisiens" (the selection no doubt also motivated by its absence from the magnificent German renderings of Stefan George, whose translation of "Spleen et idéal" as "Trübsinn und Vergeistigung" he particularly admired). He often joked that the young Adorno was his only disciple, but his own thoughts were certainly crystallized by the disciple's now-classic chapter "Intérieur," in which the subject's origins in the object world are dramatically unmasked by existentialism's ecological kinship with the bourgeois room as a closed form: "Inwardness presents itself as the restriction of human existence to a private sphere free from the power of reification. Yet as a private sphere it itself belongs . . . to the social structure."[2]

Rooms are, indeed, always of heightened significance for Benjamin, as

---

2   T. W. Adorno, *Kierkegaard, Construction of the Aesthetic*, Minneapolis: University of Minnesota Press, 1989, 47.

though the angel had driven Adam and Eve from the garden straight into a boarding house. Proust's hotel bedrooms were certainly archetypal, but somehow Benjamin's own Berlin childhood made those of the German capital into the privileged spatial expression of a classical European bourgeoisie. Yet, in another sense, the room as form can be considered a very old spatial genre, only recently menaced by Le Corbusier's "free plan": we will see, when we get to Benjamin's essays on cities, that rooms are always a clue for him and an object of the greatest scrutiny. But perhaps it is not anticlimactic to observe that the combination of these figures—the city considered as a room, the room transformed into a city in its own right—can only be fulfilled in the phenomenon of the arcade itself, whose popularity was due to the shelter it afforded from the heavens, as well as the well-lit security that distinguished it from streets before gas lighting: here the "lid," the "ceiling," becomes a benefit and, as Aragon demonstrates in the scurrilous irony of *Le Paysan de Paris*, stimulates the flourishing of a whole varied cityscape in miniature.

As for the stars that interiors render inaccessible, their reappearance in Blanqui's final manuscript, *L'Éternité par les astres*—whose revolutionary version of the eternal return, with its undecidability of hope and fate, haunted Benjamin's last years—they there have a wholly different meaning, which is reflected back on Baudelaire himself: they are the self-same, the ever repeating identical, which now "represents a picture puzzle of the commodity. They are the ever-same in great masses" (IV, 164; I, 660). But we are here at some remove from the stars promised by "To the Planetarium."

The latter then reenact the dialectic of the limit and the boundary already rehearsed above. Their absence becomes the limit of the modern, beyond which it cannot go; yet which, on more insistent meditation, proves only to be the boundary beyond which something else, another cosmos, can be imagined.

2

> *Alles Vergängliche ist nur ein Gleichnis.*
> Mortal ephemerality is but similitude.
>
> Goethe, *Faust II*

Still, Benjamin is intent on reminding us, on the very doorstep of the building in which their simulacra are offered in display, that "it is a dangerous error of modern men . . . to consign [the experience of the cosmos] to the individual as the poetic rapture of starry nights" (I, 486; IV, 146–7).

The experience of the stars, if we still had access to it, would not be a visual one, contrary to what the experience of their absence might suggest, but rather a bodily relationship. Benjamin associates the visual with the measurable:

> Nothing distinguishes the ancient from the modern man so much as the former's absorption in a cosmic experience scarcely known to later periods . . . The exclusive emphasis [by Kepler, Copernicus, and Tycho Brahe] on an optical connection to the universe, to which astronomy very quickly led, contained a portent of what was to come. The ancients' intercourse with the cosmos had been different: the ecstatic trance [Rausch]. (I, 486; IV, 146)

It is an intoxication (derived no doubt from Nietzsche's usage) that has less to do with Baudelaire than with Hölderlin, where it is the "*heilige Nüchternheit*" that is somehow in itself a visionary drunkenness, in which (an early form of the definition of "aura") it alone holds "knowledge of what is nearest to us and what is remotest from us" simultaneously.

There follows a fateful sentence, which redefines the place of the body in all this: "This means . . . that man can be in ecstatic contact with the cosmos only communally." Visuality and its sciences are properties of the individual body, and thereby symptoms of modernity. The body is certainly central to Benjamin's materialism, but not, as we shall see, in its currently fashionable poststructuralist a postmodern sense. In any case, Benjamin's cosmos is a lost prehistory, to which we can invent a relationship only through a few traces, such as the poetic fragments of Hölderlin: "It is difficult to gain any kind of access [*Zugang*] to this fully unified, unique world" (I, 24; II, 111).

No, what sets the body in relationship to this ancient cosmos, in which the stars and their constellations still exist, is the doctrine of similitude (*Gleichnis*); and here we touch on the productive angle from which to approach Benjamin's allegedly mystical notions of language and his occasional allusions to Christian as well as Jewish theological motifs. I am trying, in these pages, to avoid as much as possible any comparative or anachronistic references to our current poststructuralist doxa; yet here we stumble unexpectedly across a wholly unforeseeable confirmation in Michel Foucault's lyric celebration, quite as unforeseen a moment in his own hermeneutically suspicious work, of what he takes—fortified by Borges and the obscure Latin medical treatises of the Bibliothèque nationale—to be the medieval/Renaissance episteme of illimitable similitude: "a linking of resemblance with space, this 'convenience' that brings like things together and makes adjacent things similar, the world . . . linked together like a chain. At each point of contact there begins and ends a link that resembles the one before it and the one after it: and from circle to circle these similitudes continue, holding the extremes apart (God and matter), yet bringing them together in such a way that the will of the Almighty may penetrate into the most unawakened corners."[3] (And, linking this particular Foucault to a Benjamin whose very existence he can have known nothing of, we may also set in place the "correspondences" of Baudelaire.)

For Foucault's account of resemblance has a deeper kinship with what Benjamin, in his most concentrated "fragment" on the subject, calls his "doctrine of the similar" (II, 694–8; II, 204–10):

> Our gift for seeing similarity is nothing but a weak rudiment of the once powerful compulsion to become similar and also to behave mimetically. And the lost faculty of becoming similar extended far beyond the perceptual world in which we are still capable of seeing similarities. What the state of the stars—millennia ago, at the moment of their birth—affected in human existence was woven there on the basis of similarity.

Despite a variable terminology, it will be conceptually desirable to separate what we will translate as "similitude"—*Gleichnis*—from the more garden-variety "similarity" or *Ähnlichkeit*, for reasons already implied in this text: similarity being the modern or "fallen" form of similitude, as we shall see in a moment.

---

3 Foucault, *The Order of Things: An Archaeology of the Human Sciences*, New York: Vintage, 1994, 19. The relevance of Foucault's account is strengthened by the kinship between Paracelsus's "signatures" and Benjamin's "similitudes" (see Ian Hacking, *The Emergence of Probability*, Cambridge: Cambridge University Press, 2006, 42).

We may well want to add this charged term, "similitude," to what we think of as Benjamin's theological categories, although it weighs them down in the direction of language itself. One of the temptations of a thematics of language is, however, subjectivization and also a Kantian inclination to count the linguistic as one more mechanism whereby we project our own categorial system onto the outside world in order to organize it. Even though Benjamin will follow the biblical attribution of the power of naming to Adam, his notion of the linguistic organization of the world seems to me a more objective one, in which word and thing are ontologically conjoined and objects speak to us before we ever get around to describing them.

Two features of this cosmic situation express an objective rather than a subjective or psychological conception of similitude. The first is that emphasis on the communal or collective experience of this cosmos, which designates modern individuality as a barrier to its recovery. The second is the role played by similitude in Benjamin's unique vision of history—something we will need to disentangle from the conventional misunderstanding of the so-called "dialectical image" in a later chapter.

For the moment, a different misunderstanding must be addressed: one propagated and compounded by the now-famous thinker whom Benjamin sometimes, in ironic modesty, called his disciple (the others—Bloch, Sternberger—he tended to denounce with a kind of anxious exasperation as plagiarists). Adorno, indeed, borrowed Benjamin's theme of mimesis and transformed it into the rather inexplicable cornerstone of an anthropology he only partly, with Horkheimer, explicated in *Dialectic of Enlightenment*, where it pursues a tenacious existence as "the mimetic impulse" or, in other words, a theory of human nature avant la lettre. Whatever we may think of this doubtful philosophical presupposition, and however critically we may wish to judge the use of this term in Benjamin, it will be desirable to disentangle them and keep them distinct.

For in Benjamin mimesis is not the fashioning of a likeness nor the imitation of a posture; it is neither aesthetic nor the expression of an instinct of play. It is, rather, the source of language itself, as a "non-sensuous similitude"; and this paradoxical and perhaps even deliberately self-contradictory definition will be called upon to designate the relationship of words to things. This is to say that for Benjamin, the notion of mimesis has nothing of the visual about it, something which removes his usage from any of the standard ones and above all from Ähnlichkeit or similarity. What relates this idiosyncratic view of language to the status of the body in some primal cosmos is no doubt the related conviction that "experience"—another crucial Benjaminian concept, at which we have not yet arrived—is essentially something "*einverleibt*"—that is, absorbed by the body (*Leib*) itself.

As for the traces of a Foucauldian metaphoric episteme, however, they solicit Benjamin's attention in all the nooks and crannies in which secret correspondences between seemingly unrelated dimensions of the world are to be found: in astrology, for example, or in graphology, of which we may be startled to learn Benjamin was himself a trained practitioner, and in which a taste for the hieroglyph is married to the habits of the body itself. The philosopher Ludwig Klages, who will shortly appear, alongside Carl Jung, as an archetypal spokesman for the irrational in the Weimar era, was a foundational theoretician of this "discipline," whose frequentation by Benjamin was for more Enlightenment intellectuals a rather doubtful matter. (Horkheimer will later on in the Nazi period urge him to write an analysis of Klages and Jung as much to distance himself from them, no doubt, as to clarify his own position on such suspiciously "mythic" relationships with the cosmos.)

To read Benjamin's views in a mythic-nostalgic sense is no doubt strengthened by the narrative form in which he conveys them, as well as the sense of decline and fall, of modern deterioration, conveyed by passages such as this one:

> The sphere of life that formerly seemed to be governed by the law of similarity was much larger. This sphere was the microcosm and the macrocosm . . . It can still be claimed of our contemporaries that the cases in which they consciously perceive similarities in everyday life make up a tiny proportion of those numberless cases unconsciously determined by similarity. (II, 694–5; II, 205)

We will not be able to gauge the extent of the role similitude (*Gleichnis*) plays in Benjamin's social and historical thought until we confront the rather doubtful and enigmatic notion of the "dialectical image" in which *Gleichnis* is dramatically (and allegorically) fulfilled. Meanwhile, and as for the sense of origin that lingers over this evocation of a lost and seemingly paradisal world, we would do well to remember that for him,

"origin" is explicitly identified with "essence." Origin is meant phenom-
enologically (whatever his other objections to this philosophy, itself
already distorted by Heidegger into an equally unacceptable ontology),
rather than chronologically; and no doubt something of Benjamin's
linguistic "doctrine" is derived from the Romantics, particularly from
Schlegel's critique of the visual:

> Schlegel's manner of thought, unlike that of many mystics, is distin-
> guished by its indifference to the eidetic; he appeals neither to intel-
> lectual intuitions nor to ecstatic stakes. Rather . . . he searches for a
> noneidetic intuition of the system, and he finds this in language.
> Terminology is the sphere in which his thought moves beyond discur-
> sivity and demonstrability. For the term, the concept, contained for
> him the seed of the system; it was, at bottom, nothing other than a
> preformed system itself. Schlegel's thinking is *absolutely conceptual*—
> that is, it is linguistic thinking. (I, 139–40; I, 47)

"Terminology" here stands for the primacy of words and names, and
naming will be at the heart of Benjamin's early ruminations on language,
as in the characteristic remark he finds in Schlegel, "it is an advantage
for an idea to have several names" (I, 140; I, 48).[4] From Schlegel also
derives the Mallarméan idea that all concrete, early or "national"
languages are derived from an Ur-speech of which they are so many
emanations or approximations:

> *Les langues, imparfaites en cela que plusieurs, manque la suprême:
> pensée étant écrire sans accessoires, ni chuchotement mais tacite encore
> l'immortelle parole, la diversité, sur terre, des idiomes empêche personne
> de proférer les mots qui, sinon se trouveraient, par une frappe unique,
> elle-même matériellement la vérité.* (I, 259; IV, 17)

Languages being imperfect owing to their very multiplicity, the
supreme one is lacking: if thinking is writing without accessories, no
whispering but the word still tacit, that very diversity of idioms on

---

4   This is either the reverse or the enlargement of a saying of Hermann Cohen, the
great professor of Benjamin's youth, that it is desirable for a single word to have many
meanings.

earth prevents anyone from proffering words which otherwise, owing to their unique stamp or coinage, would materially turn out to be the truth.

I am inclined to think that "*tacite encore*" offers a muffled confirmation of Benjamin's obsession with the speechless or expressionless; at any rate, this notion of an Ur-language is central to Benjamin's theory of translation.[5]

Far from being a twofold process, indeed, translation summons a third spectral entity up between them and that is Language itself, in which both contingent and historical languages participate as in a Platonic Idea. If there is any Platonism at all in Benjamin's thought (as readers of the infamous "Epistemo-Critical Prologue" have often been led to imagine), then it can be found here, in this version of abstraction as participation (methexis). But Benjamin's "Ideas" are not the reified abstractions of the idealist tradition; closer to phenomenological essences, they seize the concrete fitfully, as so many unrelated phenomena in that dispersed and "fallen" world we call modernity (or capitalism).

Meanwhile, this primal language, whose dynamics we will examine in a moment, also stands at the center of Benjamin's idiosyncratic notion of mimesis, whose original form—whatever its later associations with copying and the like—we have seen to be "non-sensuous similarity," namely the likeness of two entities with wholly different modes of being, such as that between word and thing. In the Ur-language things speak, they are their own names, it is the name which is the mimesis of the thing. All of which, couched in an essentially biblical discourse, would seem to mark Benjamin's thinking here as "theological" in our (and his) sense of the word; thus, the notion of a "fall," a fall of man from the Ur-language into the contingent and concrete currently spoken one, demonstrates the narrative advantages of Benjamin's "theological" code. What rescues these linguistic speculations from metaphysics or idealism is their form, which consists in a commentary on the Book of Genesis (a commentary which, like so many other youthful projects,

---

5 For a demonstration that this is not a metaphysical fantasy but can inspire concrete linguistic practice, see Clive Scott's extraordinary *Translating Baudelaire*, Exeter: Exeter Press, 2000, especially chapter 2.

remained unfinished, let alone unpublished). The text, "On Language as Such and on the Language of Man" (1916), is neither mythic nor religious; it is a parable of the language of modernity, a "fallen" language given over to "communication" and instrumentality.

This is a discourse we must now translate into that of alienation. What is lost at the moment of the Fall is, first of all, the dialectic of the name and the nameless, which gives way to the "human word, in which name no longer lives intact." This human word will now transform language into a vehicle of communication: it will convert the former "word" into a mere sign and now foreground the content of those sentences we speak in our local tongues rather than their medium. Benjamin goes so far as to associate that now wordly and human content with Kierkegaard's expression, *Geschwätz* (or "prattle"), from which Heidegger's analogous *Gerede* equally derives (the gossip of the "man," of *Massenmensch*, the masses, modernity, and the media).

> For the essential composition of language [he means fallen language, human language, today], the Fall has a threefold significance . . . In stepping outside the purer language of name, man makes language a means . . . and therefore also, in one part at any rate, a *mere* sign; and this later results in the plurality of languages. The second meaning is that from the Fall, in exchange for the immediacy of name that was damaged by it, a new immediacy arises: the magic of judgment, which no longer rests blissfully in itself. The third meaning that can perhaps be tentatively ventured is that the origin of abstraction, too, as a faculty of the spirit of language, is to be sought in the Fall. (I, 71–2; II, 153–4)

These crucial qualifications allow us to translate this seemingly theological account into the more secular and distinct codes, on the one hand, of Lévi-Strauss's *pensée sauvage* and, on the other, of the dialectic. Both can be grasped as a response to the historical crisis of the universal in our time (something to which Adorno's conception of nominalism is also profoundly related); and in that sense, they obviously have all kinds of social and political consequences, as well as a heightened relevance for the contemporary or postmodern period.

Taking the second consequence first, I will argue that judgment means here the ethical binary, the distinction between good and evil. This distinction, insofar as it means anything in the state from which

language has fallen, was implicit in things rather than in external "judgments": to be freed from the essential moralizations of judgment is to
gain access to Spinoza's third way of knowledge or to the dialectic (and,
in contemporary terms, to the properly historical, which excludes ethics
and moralizing and only grasps necessity). The moralizing judgment of
things as good or evil is thus a degradation imposed on us by a fallen
language; and to see things in this way is to grasp the philosophical
significance of the Nietzschean injunction "beyond good and evil"
(which, it ought not be necessary to add, is something quite different
than a call for unbridled wickedness and immorality; it is a call for
historicity).

Now we can conjoin the third and first of Benjamin's enumerations:
for it is the repudiation of the abstract and the universal which leads us
back to *pensée sauvage*, a thinking without abstractions in which, like a
mathematical set which is a set of itself, a particular must also do double
duty as its own genus—an oak leaf, for example, meaning at one and the
same time its own species and leaves in general. Consequently the very
landscape in which an individual language is embedded speaks in its
own right, as in Lévi-Strauss's reading of the Tsimshian "Epic of Asdiwal."

(Still, the evocation of a legendary event like "the Fall" would seem to
make at least some perfunctory acknowledgement of the presence of
traditional theology unavoidable. I will attempt to elude even this
concession, however, by anticipating a later discussion of Benjamin's
idiosyncratic notion of history, to be characterized as a practice of "periodization without transitions." It is a position which posits a critical
presupposition, to be found everywhere in the early twentieth century
(and owed, no doubt, primarily to Bergson), of a kind of temporal
double standard, in which we live a superficial and measurable, "linear"
time in our official daily lives, while from time to time glimpsing the
deeper "synchronic" temporality that governs life as such. The first of
these, denounced by Benjamin as "homogeneous" time, is that of narrative sequence and causality, the second that of his "periods without transitions," his "dialectical images." The Fall would certainly seem to belong
to that category of sequential events which defines the first or "homogeneous" kind of temporality and, as an event, would seem available to
characterize the transition from some earlier unfallen cosmos of correspondences and similitudes to our own current world of slow deterioration. One cannot conceptually overcome this contradiction, or at least

Benjamin did not. But I believe it is best to take the "concept" of the Fall as the marker between the two discontinuous and incommensurable systems of homogeneous time, as two periods without transitions, rather than as an event which belongs to either order. The structural contradiction lies, in other words, in the simultaneous status of the Fall as an event and as, at the same time, a marker of the separation of the field of events in general from a radically different kind of temporality.)

3

But there is another side to that vision of the cosmos as an unfallen world of resemblances and similitudes, a darker side which it would be better to identify as the archaic, the world of myth. This is a word which in Benjamin (and in the Frankfurt School who followed him in this) has none of its original Greek sense of a narrative or story, but always signals a world of guilt and fate from which Greece itself (and Greek tragedy, in Benjamin's idiosyncratic version of it) was to lift and free us.

That prehistory should thereby come in two distinct forms or with the simultaneity of these two positive and negative faces—cosmos and myth—is a problem he never addressed, but which he might have confronted in the unwritten essay on Jung and Klages already mentioned. Fortunately, the great and neglected program essay on Bachofen, the inventor of "Motherright" and the theory of primal matriarchy, is there to spell out its general direction. For Marxism has its own tradition of such mixed feelings, which are to be found in Frederick Lewis Morgan, the grandfather of anthropology (according to Lévi-Strauss) as well as the father of Marxist anthropology as such. Morgan evoked a heroic prehistory in the Iroquois confederation—a military democracy, as Engels put it—only to discern, behind this Utopian age, a more baleful nightmare of social chaos: "a stupendous promiscuity," Morgan called it, mindful as any good Victorian of the absence of the incest taboo; leftists ever since, mesmerized by the ethical binary, have found themselves inclined either to Utopianize the world of the hunters-and-gatherers or to denounce the oppressiveness of tribal societies organized on the basis of age and gender. Perhaps, with Benjamin, we might call these classifications "judgments" in the bad sense and chalk them up to the overlap of various incommensurable historical narratives. He now grasps Bachofen as the missing link, and takes pains to demonstrate the way in which, alongside its appeal to fascism's mythic thought, the latter's conception of matriarchy (*Mutterrecht*) dramatized a communism which "appealed hardly less to Marxist thinkers" (III, 12; II, 220).

Bachofen thereby becomes the more truly Marxian theorist of that archaic that holds sway before the Viconian thunderclap of the law. Here the harmonious cosmology of Foucault's episteme is united with the unformed lawlessness of the archaic by way of the idea of the "chthonic," the still primordial bodily proximity to earth, to evoke "a creation whose vanishing calls for no lament," an "*unbeweinte Schöpfung*" which leaves material traces behind it in the form of the tombstone, the boundary stone, the walls "which formed the unity of the res sacrae" (Bachofen, quoted on III, 14; II, 221). The passionate archeological and anthropological debates about matriarchy are there to demonstrate the resonance this seemingly purely historical theory arouses in our individual and, as it were, existential being; just as the dual descendency of the fascist precursor Klages and the anarchist Elisée Reclus testify to the changes in valence operated by historical punctuation and, in particular, by the initial choice of discontinuity or continuity in any commerce with these primal materials.

But there can be no mistaking Benjamin's far more decisive judgment on the archaic in the Weimar period; its detection will entail the elaboration of a second concept, this one a psychoanalytic one, namely the phenomenon of regression. But it is the detection which is risky business: as with graphology, any keen interest in the traces of the mythic in a streamlined, modern culture might well be considered to be an endorsement of it, in which the resistance to the modern and to capitalism is as difficult to evaluate as the difference between communism and fascism.

For the mythic in culture, there is at least an interesting solution, borne to us from the past itself: it is the fairy tale, the peasant wish fulfillment, as the redemptive alternative to the somber myths of fate entertained by a death-oriented feudal aristocracy. Benjamin's interest (coincidentally contemporaneous with the development of the Propp school of narrative analysis in the Soviet Union) can be discerned in its family likeness with "The Storyteller" and with a whole undeveloped canon of nonrealistic works, ranging from Hebel's *Hausfreund* anecdotes (what

Lukács might have called minor epic forms, and the object of a suspiciously parallel interest of Heidegger) all the way to the bizarre science
fiction of Scheerbart's *Lésabendio* (itself to be sure interrelated with the
modern architecture this author also promoted). Theoretical work on
fairy tales certainly revived in our own time, but more in the interest of
narrative analysis (of which Propp, unknown to Benjamin, became a
fashion and an archetype) than for a class analysis of this essentially
peasant form of Utopianism. One glimpses here, indeed, the possibilities of a new kind of genre analysis, based on class antagonism—epic
versus fairy tale—which remains undeveloped, not least because around
the world, in postmodernity, peasantries have themselves finally disappeared, along with their feudal masters. Still, it is a pity that Benjamin
never managed to disengage himself enough from the *Arcades Project* to
initiate this field.

(This is not to suggest that his work deals any more fully with the epic
as an extinct genre. It is always worth reminding the non-German-
speaking reader that this matter is scarcely simplified by the German
term *episch*, which simply means narrative: thus, Brecht's epic theater is
not one of heroic battles and legendary deeds, but simply "narrative"
theater as opposed to some older "dramatic" kind.)

What is far more significant for the assessment of Benjamin's work is
the notion of the regressive as a historical substitute for the more
Enlightenment-inspired epistemological concept of "the irrational": it is
a substitution we can observe ever more clearly by distinguishing
Benjamin's thinking here from its late and rather different elaboration
by the Frankfurt thinkers in their *Dialectic of Enlightenment*. Both
Benjamin and the Horkheimer-Adorno team are, to be sure, still caught
up in the ideology promoted by bourgeois Enlightenment and formulated in a sharp opposition between reason and the irrational (or the
superstitious). I have argued elsewhere that the anthropological and
Habermasian enlargement of reason and communication in our time,
colonizing all the former hiding places of Otherness—in which not only
religious or premodern belief, but also madness, obsession, criminality,
drugged states, "deviancy" and the thought of excluded minorities are
housed—has rendered the critical use of the term "the irrational," plausible enough in the Hitler period, no longer very serviceable polemically
and indeed exclusionary in political contexts. It is this notion of the
archaic as such, which has worn the least well in Benjamin's intellectual

arsenal, save as a "vision of history," and which therefore needs to be deployed with some caution.

The judgment whereby the regressive is detected and denounced is, however, the principal form of Benjaminian ideological analysis (he does not use the word "ideology" much otherwise). It serves, for example, to define an otherwise positive opposite number or positive term, that of "the advanced," which plays so central a role in his aesthetic—we will later on read "The Author as Producer" as an alternative call for what we still call modernism. Indeed, the historicity of canonical modernism—"Make it new!"—finds itself powerfully displaced in the direction of media studies by this notion, in which, as we shall see, both the relations and the forces of production need to be taken into account.

At any rate, the ideological Geiger counter with which some presence of the regressive and the reactionary is to be detected, while it stands in the service of attempts to recuperate this "irrationality" for the left, is also subject to suspicion by that same left for the complicity it necessarily shows for its archaeologies and the interest it necessarily has to entertain (graphology! astrology!) for its objects of study.

Nowhere is this ambiguity, an ambiguity which reigns on both sides—in the subject as well as in his object—more visible and potentially damaging than in the interest in the archaism of the dream, which Surrealism will shortly promote into the raw material of one of the most "advanced" modes of artistic production of the day. Benjamin seems to have fitfully consigned the protocols of his dreams to paper, followed in this by the far more disciplined and systematic practice of Adorno and corresponding to Benjamin's equally dutiful record of his drug visions. For the latter, at least, he did not have to wait for the Surrealists (Breton was, in any case, I believe, rather strict in his exclusion of artificial stimulants, something he made up for in a far greater tolerance than Benjamin himself for the occult); the example of Baudelaire, and his own example in de Quincey, were also models to follow.

But where this interest goes off the rails, it seems to me, is in the elaboration of the experience, of the oneiric into a generalized cultural category he will call phantasmagoria. This was, I think, a false step, what Deleuze would have called a "bad concept," and we will examine it further in chapter VII, where I believe we can find a more satisfactory substitute in Benjamin's own elaboration of the diagnosis of "aestheticism."

Meanwhile, as for dreams, Benjamin's incisive critique of aesthetics—
Schein or beautiful appearance—proved to be a more productive place
to assign such phenomena their proper position. Regression, however, is
everywhere, while the analysis of phantasmagoria is best reserved for
the stage, and the Baroque stage at that. (I will here add another personal
opinion, namely that the evolution of contemporary film has richly
demonstrated the obsolescence of dream sequences—along with flash-
backs—in the postmodern age, where, despite my objections, phantasmagoria might well be said to have made a comeback as a theoretical
concept: Surrealism loses its power when the dream itself is commodified, but so, perhaps, does the idea of "commodification" itself.)

Figure 3.1

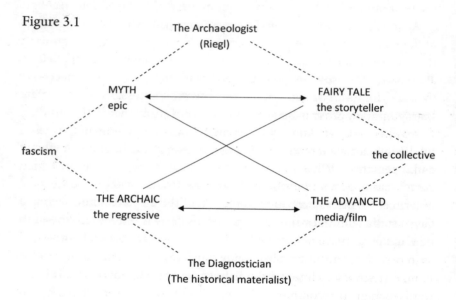

4

Nature Weeps

1

But if *One-Way Street* is Benjamin's only book, then what is *The Origin of German Trauerspiel*? And is not this celebration of the German Baroque in full Weimar a blatant regression to pre-Enlightenment theatrical ornament and superstition? What the "book" is, of course, is "the two hundred filing cards" rearranged, without much comment ("I need not say anything"), according to the categories in force for dissertations in the then-rigid German academic humanities. (This seems to have been the case even in a new and progressive university like Frankfurt, whose modernity was such as to permit the institutionalization of what will come to be known as the Frankfurt School; its future director, however, was methodologically backward enough to recommend the repudiation of this very thesis by his future collaborator.) I want to show that the rich and original Benjaminian thematics developed in the thesis are seriously weakened and underdeveloped by their obligatory academic organization.

Before deciding what Benjamin has to tell us in this thesis, however, it will be useful to see what he does not tell us. I claim that the deeper subject of the investigation, the one hampered by the requirements of its academic function, is the distinction between tragedy and *Trauerspiel* and in particular the nature of tragedy as such. It is a topic he discussed with Florens Christian Rang, a Christian theologian and interlocutor whose unexpected death in 1924 cut short any number of Benjamin's projects; a topic for which he also drew on its rich elaboration by Franz Rosenzweig, in the latter's Judaic-heretical *Star of Redemption* (1919). Both of these sources, then, are theological in the stricter disciplinary sense of the word, and their theories of tragedy clearly emerge from and reflect the shattering experience of World War I.

So framed, then, Benjamin's (unwritten) book joins a long tradition of theories that from the seventeenth century onward attempt to rationalize the impossibility of modern tragedy and to grasp its absence as a key to the understanding of modernity. In addition, we may detect a distant kinship here with Nietzsche's relationship to antiquity, who, as a classicist, promoted Wagnerian opera for a time as a substitute for so extinct a form as tragedy itself. Benjamin's relationship to the classical is an undeveloped, only faintly audible ground bass in his work, reviving briefly with his attention to Baudelaire's putative classicism ("It is very important that the modern, with Baudelaire, appear not only as the signature of an epoch but as an energy by which this epoch immediately transforms and appropriates antiquity" [A 236, J5, 1; V, 313]): the classical, the eternal, being for Baudelaire "the one half of art," the other half being the modern and the ephemeral. Still, it would seem that the author of *Les Fleurs du mal* finds his kinship with Rome rather than with ancient Greece ("it would be important to determine Poe's relation to Latinity" [A240, J7, 7; V, 313]), a classical tradition in which Christianity can also claim its place, and thereby richly providing for blasphemy and satanism as well.

Greece on the other hand, and in particular Greek tragedy, offers a cultural constellation in which the all-important motif of fate can be circumscribed, a theme which concerned Benjamin his whole life long and which he was reluctant to extrapolate into the modern category of character (and thereby of physiognomy). For here history intervenes decisively: "contemporary ideas do not permit immediate access to the idea of fate" (I, 201; II, 171), and Benjamin associates our attempts to think it with that category of "foretelling the future . . . under which the foretelling of fate is unceremoniously subsumed" (I, 201; II, 171).

Thoughts on guilt and innocence, on happiness, are explored as possible modes of "access" to the classical idea of fate, but the following sentence is decisive: "In tragedy pagan man becomes aware that he is better than his god, but the realization robs him of speech, remains unspoken . . . The paradox of the birth of genius in moral speechlessness, moral infantility, is the sublimity of tragedy . . . probably the basis of all sublimity, in which genius, rather than God, appears" (I, 203–4; II, 175). Benjamin does not return to this, Hamann's language of "genius"—a kind of Enlightenment version of regression—nor does he ever seem to have been much interested in the sublime and its capacity to promote art into a kind of Hegelian absolute (indeed, we must reckon with a persistent anti-aesthetic strain in Benjamin, and one seriously antithetical to Adorno's inveterate defense of the famous "autonomy of the work of art").

Speechlessness is, however, the crucial motif here; and its classical version may be thought to be quite different in spirit from any of its modern privative forms.[1] Still, one wants to read onto the record one of the most sublime of all modern silences, one of the most stunning speech acts of a speaker who was surely a great master of the modern sentence, namely Karl Kraus. This silence has to do with the coming of World War I:

> In these great times, which I have known since they were this small; and which shall become small again if they are given time for it; and which we, because such a regressive transformation is not possible in the world of organisms, prefer to greet as obese, and the truly hard times they are, weighing heavily on all of us; in these times in which the unimaginable occurs and where what is coming cannot be imagined (since if it could, it wouldn't happen in the first place); in these so earnest times which have laughed themselves to death at the idea they could ever be taken seriously, and which, surprised by their own tragedy, now long for distraction and having been caught doing so are trying to find words for it all; in these loud times, booming with a nightmarish symphony of deeds causing news and with the nightmarish symphony of news responsible for deeds; in these times, expect no words from me . . . Whoever has something to say, let him step forward and be silent![2]

---

1   See, on all of this, Carrie L. Asman, "Theater and Agon/Agon and Theater," *MLN* 107: 3, 1992, 606–24. Her very rich discussions of Benjamin and Rang, which range from sacrifice to carnival and raise a tangle of Bakhtinian—and Girardian—speculations, including cross-references to Hofmannsthal, as well as to Brecht and Kafka, do not include any mention of the equally important input of Rosenzweig.

2   Karl Kraus, *In these Great Times*, trans. Harry Zohn, Chicago: University of Chicago Press, 1990, 70–1.

It is the maximalist expression of the later and appropriately minimalist reaction to Nazism (*"zu Hitler fällt mir nichts ein"*—"about Hitler I can think of nothing to say").

Rosenzweig's version of the meaning of a speech which has enlarged its domain so as to speak by way of silence also merits attention:

> The tragic hero has only one language which completely corresponds to him: namely keeping silent . . . Tragedy casts itself in the artistic form of drama just in order to be able to represent speechlessness . . . dramatic poetry . . . knows only of speaking, and it is only thereby that silence here becomes eloquent. By keeping silent, the hero breaks down bridges which connect him with God and the world, and elevates himself . . . into the icy solitude of the self.[3]

The genealogy might be extended to Hölderlin's idiosyncratic reading of the caesura in his translations of Greek tragedy: the rhythmic break, which indeed inflects the notion of silence here toward what we have called the dialectic of the interruption. Benjamin's unwritten treatise may in any case be taken as an attempt to give figuration to some depersonalized mode of thought beyond judgment—the dialectic rather than some discovery of death, as in Rosenzweig, or some emergence from paganism, as with Rang. What is clear, however, is that in the Benjaminian scheme of things, tragic speechlessness marks the emergence from the mythic and the archaic—a different mode of overcoming the "irrational" than the peasant fairy tale, but one which is equally unavailable to us.

2

As for the academic framework of this work, it is logical and symmetrical enough: the "thesis" falls into two parts, the first on the genre of *Trauerspiel* as drama, the second on the theory and practice of allegory that is at work in it, particularly in its language and thought-modes. These are, if you like, the two dimensions of the baroque that Benjamin wishes to explore here, and they are related roughly as content to form, plot to expression.

---

3 Franz Rosenzweig, *Star of Redemption*, New York: Holt, Rinehart & Winston, 1971, 77.

Meanwhile, each of the two sections is then subdivided into three parts, which also have a logical rationale and a certain symmetry. In each, a first section examines the theoretical literature on the topic; the next two sections then study the thing itself and finally its subjective "equivalent"—melancholy in the case of the first section, on drama, and thoughts of death and dismemberment in the allegory section.

Obviously, there will be a good deal of spillage from one of these divisions into the others: the first chapter, a critique of the prevailing theories of drama (mostly Aristotelian in inspiration) will demonstrate error by way of truth and thereby expound much of the fundamental (objectively formal) distinction between *Trauerspiel* and ancient tragedy on which Benjamin's own reading of these plays will be based. Meanwhile, the prehistory of allegory will inevitably involve a specification of the Baroque form here under study. And obviously questions of affect arise again and again throughout both sections. It is a logically satisfying arrangement, which has only this disadvantage, that it brushes against the grain of Benjamin's genius and forces him to separate his materials out into groups and topics to be analyzed independently of one another. Yet the very spirit of the "dialectical image" or the "thought-picture" demanded similitudes, metaphorical combinations, paradoxical links and the intersection of only distantly related levels: figural monads, as he liked to call them, which could not be classed in distinct categories and under abstract topical headings, nor could they really be discursively developed either, inasmuch as each yields a unit only discontinuously related to what precedes and follows it. The academic requirements of the *Trauerspiel* thesis, then, blocked the movement of Benjamin's thought at every turn and made for a cumbersome movement as tortuous for the future reader as it must have been for the writer/collator of these materials.

Indeed, the very central division itself—between play form and allegory—offered the possibility of many rich and transversal flashes of intersection between these two levels which had to be repressed and degraded into hints and passing suggestions; while within each part, the pressure of the organization tended, for example, to reduce the official chapter on melancholy to a set of psychological observations; while the final chapter on allegorical dismemberment tended to taper off into the dryer discussions of script and hieroglyph (of interest, no doubt, only to the graphologist) when it did not reduce the phenomenon of allegory itself to a logic of fragmentation whose spirit had already been covered in the earlier melancholy/acedia discussion.

We will find, therefore, that the panoply of themes raised in the *Trauerspiel* book finds itself dispersed throughout his life's work and often more suggestively explored in other contexts. Thus, even those extensive discussions of allegory, which turn out for Benjamin to identify its exemplary form as personification, are more fruitfully pursued later on in the Baudelaire materials, whose discussions then prove to illuminate those of *Trauerspiel* in hindsight, just as the account of *spleen* will shed a more useful light on Baroque melancholy and that of modern (capitalist) "catastrophe" to characterize non-transcendent Baroque history in a more usable way as well.

I would therefore judge that the only topic in this work which is fully developed in its own right is the mapping of the "characters," the physiognomies within these plays, while in a way the most important sections, unresolved, point backward to that unwritten discussion of tragedy as such (as distinguished from *Trauerspiel*) which has already been mentioned. Indeed, I am tempted to say that Benjamin chose this topic of a properly German *Trauerspiel* mainly in order to be able to work out more directly an analysis of classical tragedy on which he had hitherto been able to write only a few notes. This topic is, as we have seen, essentially at one with the theme of silence and speechlessness, fate, and expressionlessness, scarcely related, save by dialectical opposition, to the ranting and verbiage, the Baroque bombast, the "expressive" and perhaps even operatic language of the plays which were to be his official subject.

In what follows, then, our job will be to separate out the various materials which will feed into Benjamin's work later on (in his, as it were, "secular" period), and we will here propose a disjunctive reading in the spirit of Benjamin's theory of criticism as destruction. This said, we should observe that even the corpus of seventeenth-century drama is here augmented by two further, related theatrical traditions: the grotesque political dramas called *Haupt-und-Staats-Aktionen* and various kinds of Romantic dream plays that attempt to revive such forms; to which must be added the far greater incarnations of *Trauerspiel* as such in *Hamlet* and in Calderón (*La vida es sueño*).

3

In a sense, then, the first section of the thesis implies a theory of "access" (or *Zugang*): a discussion of what for historical as well as purely philosophical or cognitive limits prevents us from distinguishing these baroque texts from that classical or ancient form for which Benjamin wishes to reserve the word "tragedy." Ironically, it is the misappropriation of Aristotle himself by Renaissance theorists which blocks this perception and encourages the assimilation of the *Trauerspiel* to tragedy as the moderns and even Nietzsche misunderstand it. Nor are they to be assimilated to Romantic dramas of fate either. It is, indeed, only in "theology" and more specifically in Rosenzweig's *Star of Redemption* (and the correspondence with Rang) that we will find hints toward that historically adequate grasp of genuine tragedy that allows us to return to *Trauerspiel* with fresh eyes and to grasp its genuinely historical originality.

For tragedy draws not on history (as with the *Trauerspiel*) but on myth: its actors are mythical heroes rather than the tyrants and martyrs of a bloody earthly history. And where the Baroque (coming after Luther's dismantling of the medieval universe) offered the last dying unearthly light in a world from which transcendence was vanishing, tragedy retained the gods if only to indict them: Nietzsche indeed thought (anticipating Artaud) that ancient tragedy was a spectacle of human suffering designed for their delectation. For Benjamin, the truer relationship of humans and divinities is captured by the realization "that in tragedy pagan man realizes that he is better than his gods." This is expressed in "expressionlessness": it is the moment in which the blind beauty of the immobile statue replaces the dying speechless hero. Benjamin's paradigm for this moment is taken from the *Oresteia,* rather than from standard Sophoclean situations: a trilogy which reasserts history in the overcoming of myth by law.

But here, as in the concluding section of the *Prologue* (T, 48–56; I, 288), a second theme or problem emerges simultaneously: it is once again that of historical access, of how to make contact with those monads that make up a past which is not a continuity, not a tradition, but which, as we shall see, "flits up" and offers itself "in a moment of danger." This one has the distinction of bearing a name—the Baroque: are we to take this named singularity as an index of absolute difference, of otherness, of what remains out of reach? The experience of the tragic would seem to have offered just such a lost moment, "to which we no longer have access," replaced by that of *Trauerspiel*, which is presumably more accessible to our time. The work on Baudelaire retrospectively confirms this, by way of spleen and allegory; are we then to assume that there is a further coincidence, a further astrological conjunction, which links both those now combined historical periods to a third one, that of Weimar, if not of the Hitlerzeit itself, or perhaps to yet an even more distinctive monad we can now name as the "phony war," the "*drôle de guerre*," a monad as doomed and ephemeral as human life itself? In that case, our job as readers is to determine whether we are not again in just such a period, which harmonizes with these stars realigned and which demands that we rethink our own ontology of the present; or whether our readings are not rather something closer to an archeological expedition into a vanished past, more closely resembling the now-sealed tomb of the tragic. Do we once again confront the hostile gods (the remorseless laws of planetary geology, the inevitability of Homeric warfare and the finitude and doom of myth), or something closer to the allegorical landscape of rubble and mangled bodies in the midst of which mad tyrants and usurpers rave, schemers scheme, and saints joyously accept their martyrdoms?

This is indeed the option at which Part I proposes a closer look, a kind of tour of the battlefield: it is, so to speak, Benjamin's version of the seemingly eternal question of whether modern tragedy is possible and what its hero would look like. The confusion between the forms, the identification of *Trauerspiel* with genuine tragedy, complicates this problem, which might otherwise raise a second question of whether modern *Trauerspiel* is possible either. Benjamin sometimes seems to follow Rosenzweig in identifying the saint as the modern avatar of the tragic hero, thereby answering the question in the affirmative: "The *Trauerspiel* is confirmed as a form of the tragedy of the saint by means of the martyr-drama. And if one only learns to recognize its characteristics in many different styles of drama from Calderón to Strindberg it must become clear that this form, of the mystery play, still has a future" (T, 113; I, 292).

The affirmation does not carry much conviction, and Benjamin turns to the fateful moment of the death of Socrates to refute his own speculation: "The martyr-drama was born from the death of Socrates as a parody of tragedy" (T, 113; I, 292). Nor can we forget the passion with which Nietzsche indicted Socrates as the very end and dissolution of the Greek spirit, its loss of the heroic in the birth of reason and philosophy. Like Nietzsche, Benjamin will be willing to posit its rebirth in opera, though for him it is *Trauerspiel* which will eventually bear this new form. But its other offspring will be the trial as form and historiography, and in a sense the two are the same ("*Die Weltgeschichte ist das Weltgericht*," ran Schiller's famous Hegelian motto, to which Benjamin would not have subscribed).

This heightened status of the trial, which constantly threatens to break through the seeming autonomy of theatrical drama, then accounts in retrospect for the privileged position Benjamin will accord Aeschylus in his meditations on tragedy. He cites Rosenzweig: "In Sophocles and Euripides the heroes learn 'not to speak . . . only to debate.'"[4] This process is a significant moment in Benjamin's ambivalent meditation on the law, as it reemerges in the essay on violence, for example: a unique statement on modern politics on his part and a commentary on Sorel which is sealed not by constitutions and the legalities of the Enlightenment, but rather by that "divine violence" he finds in Sorel and in Bolshevism. For "the most important and characteristic feature of Athenian law is the Dionysian outburst, the fact that the intoxicated, ecstatic word was able to transcend the regular perimeter of the *agon,* that a higher justice was vouchsafed by the persuasive power of living speech than from the trial of the opposing factions, by combat with weapons or prescribed verbal forms. The practice of the trial by ordeal is disrupted by the freedom of the *logos*" (I, 116; I, 295). I must feel that such a passage implies a dialectical identity between the "Dionysian outburst" and the stunned silence of the tragic hero: both affirm the priority of "living speech" over the dead norms of the law; both are formal breaks, interruptions, discontinuous and monadic moments within the "homogeneous time" of "normal" (or normative) social and institutional life. And both silence and ecstatic speech are canceled and negated by the bombast of *Trauerspiel* and its raving characters.

In such instances, we rediscover Benjamin's most characteristic attention to what he finds historical in history: the great moments of crisis and transformation. Dialectically, they reproduce the antinomy of the line and the point: like limits and boundaries, such moments can be mere

---

4   *Star of Redemption*, 77.

breaks, or they can take on their own autonomous value as monadic episodes, preceded and followed by meaningless befores and afters.

Here is another one: "Just as the transformation of history into natural history in the baroque drama was overlooked, so too, in the analysis of tragedy, was the discrimination between legend and history" (T, 120; I, 299). Tragedy brings history into being by emerging from legend, by overcoming myth; *Trauerspiel* is condemned to a history without transcendence, which it can only think by means of natural categories, cycles, organisms, the seasons, the eternal return. (This dialectic of history and nature is the subject of a remarkable proposal in Adorno's inaugural lecture [Frankfurt, 1932], in which he suggests that we read nature in terms of history and history in terms of nature.)

Meanwhile, the historical problem of the representation of history, which comes to a standstill in *Trauerspiel*, is then inevitably handed on down, first to the more purely theatrical spectacle of the *Haupt-und-staats-aktionen* and then to Romanticism, where, for the moment, it disappears from sight in Benjamin's work, only reemerging, in a far different form, in the work on Baudelaire and finding material, or materialist reconstruction and reproblematization in the technological media. Benjamin never really engaged the problem of the novel as such, which is to say that it never seems to have interested him except in the case of individual works like *Wahlverwandtschaften*, Gladkov's *Cement*, Dostoyevsky's *Idiot*, Keller, or Brecht's *Threepenny Novel*. We may assume that he felt satisfied by Lukács's *Theory of the Novel*, a fundamental problematization of the novel as *genre*, which even Bakhtin planned to translate. At any rate, we may certainly conclude that the form-problems raised by Lukács, and somehow solicited by the very structure of the novel itself, were not interesting for him—that is, they were not felt to be productive, despite their relationship to experience and its narratives, as those surfaced in "The Storyteller" and interested him centrally. Novelistic psychology constituted for him a falling off from the art of storytelling or "epic drama."

At any rate, this debate between *Trauerspiel* and tragedy breaks off with the demonstration that *Hamlet* is not a tragedy and shifts to the new subjectivity of *Trauerspiel* as a form by way of what he called its "physiognomic cycle" (IV, 209; B, 808). For subjectivity demands the medium of a character (if not exactly a point of view), and here suddenly the melancholiac will take the word, if not the stage: it is the figure I elsewhere identified as the *Grübler*, who is at one with the subjective physiognomy of the second part of the book, namely the allegorist. The *Grübler* indeed should be included in that list of Benjaminian physiognomies—*flâneur*, "collector, counterfeiter, gambler"—to whom we may now add those of this book—tyrant or usurper, schemer, martyr; these make up, as it were, the dramatistic cast of characters seemingly essential to his thought. It is in this fashion, rather than in some biographic and novelistic reading, that it seems best to confront a theme of melancholy that has unfortunately colored so much of the literature on Benjamin, who could also be sly, dogmatic, predatory, anxious, humorous, satiric, bumbling, incapable, workaholic and many other seemingly incompatible things. Indeed, one can only, today, deplore the inveterate association of Benjamin himself with that "left-wing melancholy" he himself so pointedly denounced in his essay of that name. (I count myself, in one of the earlier American studies of Benjamin, as responsible as anyone else for this misconception, which must be chalked up to the vividness with which Benjamin described this state and the kind of intellectual who dwelt in it, the allegorist, the *Grübler*, the reader of signs and portents. Benjamin was also that, *à ses heures*, but the characterization misses the aggressive conversationalist, the alert commentator and diagnostician of the zeitgeist, the ambitious scrivener and journalist, the lover and world traveler.)

In fact, this section of the *Trauerspiel* book presents itself as a purely historical catalogue of the theories of melancholy that have come down the ages from even before the era of the four humors. Baudelaire's spleen will offer him a better opening onto this interesting passion, in which melancholy will be related to history in a different and more productive way. Much of the potentially rich subjective material will here only begin to catch fire in the final chapter of the book, on the "allegorical attitude." Still, here and there, one can find sentences like this one: "In [melancholy's] tenacious self-absorption it embraces dead objects in its contemplation, in order to redeem them" (T, 157; I, 315). The collector hovers nearby, but also the *feuilletonist*, if not the poet himself; the dead landscape of a history without transcendence has here disintegrated into an object world of which items can thoughtfully be contemplated, as with the skull of Yorick which the *Grübler* Hamlet holds in his hand.

That artificial separation between the content of *Trauerspiel* and its form, which was forced on Benjamin by the requirements of a university dissertation, now results in an impoverishment of the account of allegory here in this second half of the book. Its first chapter repeats the plan followed in Part I, in which historical and traditional studies of the topic are reviewed. Here he will spend some time on Creuzer, the principal Romantic historian and theoretician of allegorical iconology, as well as on the more scant contemporary research, principally that of Karl Giehlow (1863–1913), which concentrated principally on the Renaissance and its fascination with hieroglyphs and other forms of symbolic script. Not only does this attention to language begin unduly to fascinate that graphologist which Benjamin also was, it tends to point him toward an essentially symptomological conception of allegory: "Any person, any object, any relationship can mean absolutely anything else" (T, 175; I, 350). This narrow view of allegory as writing will, Benjamin rightly observes, secure a conception of the world and history as script and, in the process, as emblem. It will fragment a reality (theatrically centered on the space of the royal court) and "subject it to the law of 'dispersal' and 'collectedness'" (T, 188; I, 364), thereby laying the groundwork for Romantic valorizations of the fragment as such.

But script necessarily demands a place for its reader; this enlarges Benjamin's physiognomic cast of characters beyond those of the allegorical play itself, to include its spectators, who are essentially its readers. Unsurprisingly, these are summed up in the figure of the melancholiac and its own intrinsic dialectic: "the profound fascination of the sick man for the isolated and insignificant is succeeded by that disappointed abandonment of the exhausted emblem" (T, 185; I, 361). But since Benjamin has already invested the essentials of his view of melancholy in Part I, he has little more to say here, where, in any case, the lack of scholarly attention to the matter leaves him with little enough to do (he has already, in Part I, drawn generously on the pioneering 1924 work on Baroque by the future national-socialist literary historian Herbert Cyzarz [1896–1985]).

The same skewed distribution of topics and materials will determine a kind of "set towards the form of the content" in this section, which deals essentially with the verse forms and their trappings (ghosts and dreams, but also emblems and staging). "This poetry was in fact incapable of releasing in inspired song the profound meaning which was here confined to the verbal image. Its language was heavy with material display. Never has poetry been less winged" (T, 200; I, 376). Yet "the written language of allegory enslaves objects in the eccentric embrace of meaning" (T, 202; I, 378). In the same way, it enslaves Benjamin's own interpretive imagination; what was viewed from the standpoint of plot and characters in Part I as sheer bombast here peters out in an appeal to "the self-indulgent delight in sheer sound" (T, 213; I, 384–5), a reduction which will of course eventually motivate Benjamin's perhaps Nietzsche-inspired suggestion of an evolution of *Trauerspiel* toward opera—a possibility which remains unexplored in Benjamin's mostly unmusical work.

This final section, still following the model of Part I, should mark the place for an analysis of the subjective dimension of allegory. However, the rich description of Baroque subjectivity in Part I has absorbed everything exciting in this interesting area, leaving the topic of allegorical subjectivity to the more lofty and abstract realms of theology (T, 216; I, 390), which is to say, inasmuch as it is a question in Baroque allegory of "corpse poetry" (T, 218; I, 392), to the vision of resurrection. Benjamin will find a tortuous path to this "happy ending," beginning with the Renaissance revival of the occult and the famous medieval demotion of the pagan gods to Christian devils (explored in a classical work by Jean Seznec) and culminating in the absorption of the fleshly and the material by the demonic realm and the cult of the devil himself (as in Shakespeare's Iago or Webster's Bosola).

Allegory has, of course, its own historical determinant: it "established itself most permanently where transitoriness and eternity confronted each other most closely . . . It was absolutely decisive for the development of this mode of thought that not only transitoriness, but also guilt should seem evidently to have its home in the province of idols and of the flesh. The allegorically significant is prevented by guilt from finding fulfilment of its meaning in itself" (T, 224; I, 398).

It is because Christian nature is fallen that it mourns: but this "mournfulness makes it become mute. In all mourning there is a tendency to silence" (T, 224; I, 398). Allegory as a linguistic form then compensates this silence with names, which themselves paradoxically signal the incapacity of a fallen nature to be named. "How much more so not to be named, only to be read, to be read uncertainly, by the allegorist and to have become highly significant thanks only to him" (T, 225; I, 398). This is the point at which the demonic becomes satanic: "just as earthly mournfulness is of a piece with allegorical interpretation, so is devilish mirth with its frustration in the triumph of matter" (T, 227; I, 401). At this point the illusion of evil appears, and with it a complex dialectic of good and evil and of judgment (both results, as we remember, of the "fall" of language), which will result in the reappearance of resurrection beyond this fallen world: the allegorical halo of that last historical transcendence beyond secularity which is the landscape of the Baroque and of the Counter-Reformation.

It is a frustrating conclusion which condemns allegory to the littered fragments of a world whose redemption is as illusory as a Baroque sunburst. Benjamin will not find a reconciliation between the body and the soul of allegory until he rediscovers Baudelaire and the secular ruins of modernity, where it takes the form of personification.

Still, Benjamin was proud of the concluding exordium of his treatise, in which the language of architecture is called upon to convey the effects of a sublimity projected upward by the sheer weight and gravity of earthly matter as such:

> Subjectivity, like an angel falling into the depths, is brought back by allegories, and is held fast in heaven, in God, by *ponderación misteriosa* . . . The powerful design of this form should be thought through to its conclusion; only under this condition is it possible to discuss the idea of the German *Trauerspiel*. In the ruins of great buildings the idea of the plan speaks more impressively than in lesser buildings, however well preserved they are; and for this reason the German *Trauerspiel* merits interpretation. In the spirit of allegory it is conceived from the outset as a ruin, a fragment. Others may shine resplendently as on the first day; this form preserves the image of beauty to the very last. (T, 234–5; I, 407–9)

Unfortunately, in purely formal terms, all this splendid eloquence can be reduced to an excuse to himself (as well as to the examining committee) for wasting so much research time on an unworthy object.

We are not reviewing Benjamin's works from any developmental perspective. Still, this unrewarded labor on the Baroque not only marked a break in Benjamin's exploration of his other and numerous interests; it also, by crystallizing some of them, marked a standstill from which he had to invent a breakthrough. Perhaps, then, a roadmap to future developments may not be out of place at this point:

Figure 4.1

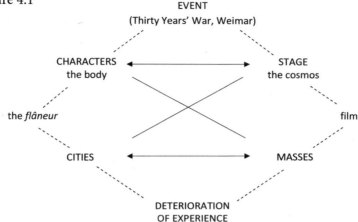

3

But we cannot leave the *Trauerspiel* book behind without some final word about its famous and enigmatic preface, the Epistemo-Critical Prologue. It will be a further elaboration of Benjamin's relationship to abstraction—this time of a historical variety. We have already seen that the famous "constellations" evoked in this prologue reproduce the formal categories of Benjaminian episodism: separation of one cluster of themes or motifs and its formation into a monad whose logic of discontinuities is reproduced within itself. But the prologue encourages us to believe that we are dealing here with something on the order of ideas ("ideas are to objects as constellations are to stars" [T, 34; I, 214]). The new figuration displaces the problem of universals by substituting the relations between them for the problem of the link that connects the abstract idea with the empirical object, a dilemma it then dispatches by transforming classification into the act of naming, and shipping the whole philosophical conjunction back into theology and the book of Genesis. "This introduction," he tells Scholem with no little pride, "is unmitigated chutzpah . . . my early work on language . . . dressed up as a theory of ideas" (February 19, 1925; C 261; B, 372). But what he omits even in this confession is that the ideas in question in this prologue are not the usual abstractions (themselves allegorically capitalized), but rather historical designations and the names of historical periods. The debate on universals, which will send Adorno off into a culture-critical theory of nominalism as the logic of late capitalism, here turns out to be a reflection on the idea of the Baroque.

With most of the German tradition, Benjamin saw human evolution as a movement from matter to spirit; yet the Platonic overtones in his figure of the constellation are meant not to emphasize the idealism implicit (and, I fear, inevitable) in his study of superstructures, but rather to emphasize that very different and far more original feature of his work (and his view of history), namely radical discontinuity as such.

Constellations are distinct groupings, necessarily separated from each other, and, from the modern standpoint, including a great diversity of points of light, some of them from very distant stars and galaxies, others up close cosmologically but with no relationship to one another in astronomical space. Benjamin's image does not emphasize the way in which an astrological picture is constructed by human subjectivity, but rather the intelligibility of the image and its distance from other stellar groupings (however much they may then be reorganized in an imaginary sequence like the zodiac).

Yet the association between things and names, once established, can work both ways; it is in this sense that in the Epistemo-Critical Prologue, it can return in a reversal in which things—in this case, the stars themselves—take the place of the names with which they were once at one. But there remains a secondary interference here between a terminology of "things" and the phenomena which for the most part interest Benjamin and which are social and historical rather than ontological: things still tend to project a static world of objects (such as the items surrounding Adam and demanding to be named or, rather, pleading to recover contact through their original names with their divine source). The *Trauerspiel* book, however, but also his more seemingly objective descriptions of cities and landscapes, for example, deal with humanly constructed objects, institutions and thoughts in time. They are historical, and their expression and figuration thereby demands renewed consideration: can an event, for example, be a star, let alone a constellation? How is a thought that emerges in a historical situation to be characterized in astrological language?

All of which requires further analysis of the famous prologue, which stands somewhere between the first "mystical" essays and the later reflections on media (and which also poses renewed questions about that issue of the theological in Benjamin which has always plagued his more attentive readers). The prologue, indeed, always repays rereading after immersion in any of Benjamin's other texts: the issue of breaks and interruptions, which will return in the course of this reading of the prologue as well, is at first lightly touched on by the idea of a "continual pausing for breath [as] the mode most proper to the process of contemplation" (T, 28; I, 208). Any number of other such veiled allusions to some properly Benjaminian thematics will assail us as we continue and cannot be followed up here, where, in the guise of an inquiry into the status of concepts like "the Baroque," the formula of the constellation will at length appear and seem to offer, if not a philosophical solution, then at least a usable code. For the Baroque is not a notion that can be ranged under any single conceptual category: an ostensibly periodizing instrument, it is historical and transhistorical all at once, but also stylistic and, finally, as Benjamin deploys it, affective and generic as well (*Trauerspiel* being a specific genre, as Benjamin defines it). Meanwhile, there is a Baroque cosmology, as well as a specifically Baroque linguistic or representational mode (allegory) and so on. This is, of course, why the Baroque is a constellation rather than a single star in the Platonic heavens, and it behooves us to see what this might imply on a conceptual level.

Three distinct elements or terms are at work here: concepts, ideas, and phenomena. That the idea, then (Platonic or otherwise), corresponds to a reality or a phenomenon, we can assume—that it names such a phenomenon then arouses a sense of imminent complexity. This sense is reinforced when we learn that "[i]deas are neither their concepts nor their laws" (neither the concepts of their objects nor the laws of those objects). "They do not contribute to their knowledge . . . they are timeless constellations."

So, the various individual concepts—the "conceptual elements" of a phenomenon—are then formed into a pattern, which we will call a constellation. These conceptual elements are, for all practical purposes, best derived from the most extreme forms of phenomena, its exceptions rather than its rules, its most extravagant versions—at the outer limits of a form, for example, such as the state, a drama, the human body, an emotion—rather than its average form, its Aristotelian "mean." So the concepts, which might otherwise have served science or the knowledge of an abstract genre or category, are here arranged and interrelated more dramatically, in such a way that they serve truth (rather than science or knowledge), thereby revealing themselves as names or essences.

To join a group of concepts together in a "constellation" is thus to name a thing and to discover its essence: to constellate is to name an idea and thereby recover its essence as truth; and this has little enough to do with logic or abstraction. "Ideas are displayed, without intention, in the act of naming, and they have to be renewed in philosophical contemplation. In this renewal the primordial mode of apprehending words is restored. And so, in the course of its history . . . philosophy is . . . a struggle for the representation of a limited number of words which always remain . . . a struggle for the representation of ideas" (T, 37; I, 217).

What first needs comment here is the peculiar evocation of "intention." The term returns in the more familiar context of the distinction between knowledge and truth: "The object of knowledge, determined as it is by the intention inherent in the concept, is not the truth. Truth is an intentionless state of being, made up of ideas." I believe that we cannot grasp the full import of these sentences without coming to terms with that notion of the "expressionless" which we have seen Benjamin borrowing from Rosenzweig in his characterization of tragedy. It is the blank eyes of Greek statuary, a state somehow beyond human psychology and even human subjectivity—Spinoza's third way, if you like, but certainly an ideal inherent in the dialectic and in contemporary attacks on "philosophies of the subject," a state beyond judgment (that is, in Nietzsche's sense, beyond good and evil, beyond the ethical binary and, I would even add, in the Althusserian mode, beyond ideology). This is the sense, then, in which Benjamin also uses the seemingly quaint language of the timeless or the eternal, and of the perhaps less lofty realm of essences. I therefore claim that the reassembling of empirical concepts in constellations rescues individual words from their fallen state and transforms them, as an ensemble, into a name: the constellation is a name, in this case "the Baroque."

Meanwhile, the crucial feature of this process, in our present context, is the separation of the names from each other, the "unbridgeable distance between pure essences" (T, 37; I, 217), the radical discontinuity between the constellations. It is this radical discontinuity which disqualifies philosophy as such (or, as we have seen, condemns it to perpetual struggles about names, words and spatial conjunctures). The fall of language into abstraction and judgment is the same as the emergence of philosophy as such; and this is why we must qualify Benjamin's thinking in a different way, as a kind of *pensée sauvage* or "tender empiricism," which we might today be willing to salute as theory or as the dialectic, but which determines a rigorously antisystematic form of thinking and writing. The semantic convulsions of the name "Baroque" in the *Trauerspiel* book are but one signal example of this general process.

Constellations are, in other words, a kind of montage (Deleuzians would call them *agencements* or assemblages) whose figural implication lies in difference rather than in identity. They are a visible argument against system or, if you like, against the systematicity of philosophy itself. This principle—which governs the construction and effects of what Benjamin sometimes liked, for want of a better expression, to call "dialectical images" (to which we will return later)—must also be invoked in order to understand the nature of Benjaminian form and its relationship to the Brechtian aesthetic.

The sequence of the Benjaminian prose piece is then precisely this discontinuity of the constellated groupings: gaps and blanks which solicit a continuity the reader can never really reestablish: they seem to constitute the broken pieces of what can never be "glued back together" (as he puts it in "The Task of the Translator" [I 260; IV, 18]), for in that sense the reader is also a kind of translator. But what must precede them is an initial act of destruction, and this is necessarily the reader/interpreter's first act.

As for Brechtian montage, it offers the same operations, whereby familiar continuities (the conventional understanding of an act or event, for example) are first broken up and then reconstructed in the form of something that looks entirely different—the two moments of the famous V-effect, *Verfremdung* or estrangement. What Brecht shares with Benjamin is this overriding insistence on the interruption, the separation, the gap. An ideal Brecht play is a series of autonomous episodes, each one a kind of monad whose reconstructed unity is presided over by a description, a song or a placard coming down: in short, its name.

This shared logic of discontinuity is what makes up the elective affinity between Benjamin and Brecht and likewise what governs their views of art and of history itself (as we shall see). It also confirms the reading we have given of Benjamin's assessment of "judgment" as a degraded form; here is Brecht's version:

Me-ti said: Our experiences usually change very quickly into judgements. We remember these judgements but we think they are the
experiences. Naturally, judgements are not so reliable as experiences.
A certain technique is needed to keep the experiences fresh so that
you can always reach new judgements based on them. Me-ti called
that kind of knowledge the best which is like snowballs. They can be
good weapons, but you can't keep them that long. They also don't
survive, for example, in the pocket.[5]

Brecht's emphasis on action here throws an interesting crosslight on the
same distinction in Benjamin, between the all-important "phenomenological" notion of (concrete) experience and that of judgments (which
normally alternate between negative and positive). Indeed, in Benjamin's
modus operandi, we can observe a primordial alternation in his versions
of the transition from the archaic to the modern: on the one hand, it is
valorized aesthetically as the New and as production; on the other hand,
it is the loss and deterioration of experience. This is very much a trans-
valuation of judgment in the Nietzschean sense: it resituates the ethical
binary and, depending on the historical context, "politically" reevaluates
the process as good (positive) or regressive (bad). Here, therefore, very
much in the spirit of Benjamin's antiphilosophical attack on abstractions
and system, history itself and its mobile and situational judgments replace
the old static philosophical ethics (and aesthetics as well).

As for ideology, it is a term no doubt used sparingly in Benjamin and
had not yet taken on the global proportions proposed by Althusser (where
it becomes an equivalent, on the one hand, for worldview and, on the
other, for a kind of Sartrean "originary choice"). But I think this prudence
is also dictated by Benjamin's keen sense that ideological identification is
not reliable in an immanent criticism or reading; this is why so often
Benjamin hesitates between negative and positive judgments. The famous
aura, for example, can characterize a precious survival of genuine or
authentic experience, or it can betray a suspicious regression to the logic
of the archaic, a spurious substitute and compensation for the latter's
impoverishment. Immanent analysis cannot resolve this ambiguity; only
the pragmatics of the situation can do that. This is why the Benjaminian
judgment—always pragmatic—sometimes seems perfunctory: it is always

---

5   Bertolt Brecht, *Me-ti*, trans. A. Tatlow, London: Methuen, 2016, 113.

political (his word! his recommendation!). It always depends on the situation, in which the "ideological stance" deduced from the text can be useful or not (energizing or fascist!). Usefulness of this situational or pragmatic, essentially political, kind cannot be deduced from the immanent analysis of the text—it is always extra-textual and thus, for purely academic purposes, always scandalous.

As for periodization, to be sure the age of Expressionism will find much to recognize in this bizarre mirror image of the Baroque, and we will only grasp the historiographic dynamics of that "recognition of the Now" when we come to Benjamin's unique conception of history as such. We must also understand the transitional nature of this period, for which Luther's revolution spells the end of transcendence, which, however, lingers as the occasional Baroque sunburst in a brooding and bereft mortal nature, littered with the corpses and the carnage of the Thirty Years' War, the most devastating European conflict before World War I and a profoundly durable Central European trauma. Secularization no doubt heightened that trauma at the same time that it caused it, and the motives for religious regression emerge far more starkly here than even in Weimar's appetite for myth and ritual. It seems appropriate, then, to juxtapose Benjamin's revival of a grisly and verbose theatricality, more akin to Webster among the Elizabethans than to Shakespeare, with Brecht's *Mother Courage*, a dramatization of a novella by Grimmelshausen, the greatest novelist of that same period.[6]

In fact, however, Baroque does not in Benjamin become the kind of transhistorical category which some Latin American writers and scholars sought to revive (under the term neo-Baroque) as an alternative to the "Boom" and "magic realism." Rather, Benjamin assimilates it to the twofold categories of allegory, on the one hand, and the melancholy of decay, on the other, making the first of these an ornamental expression of the second and, as it were, its visible or hieroglyphic language.

This is how it can reappear in Baudelaire's Paris as a matter of capital letters and personified abstractions: *la Douleur* or *la Mélancholie*. Nothing is more revealing of this dimension of Baudelaire's language than the remark of a contemporary: "His utterances, Gautier thought,

---

6   And see also, for an immediate postwar snapshot of this same seventeenth-century cultural moment, Günther Grass's *Das Treffen in Telgte*, Munich: Verlagsgesellschaft, 1994.

were full of 'capital letters and italics.' He appeared . . . surprised at what
he himself said, as if he heard in his own voice the words of a stranger"
(A, 248, J11, a3; V, 322). Like Rabelais's frozen language, these words
come out of his mouth reified and already transformed into allegorical
objects. It is a reification which saves Baudelaire from the sentimental-
ism of the Romantics who preceded him and lends his poems that jewel-
like objecthood which the poet may well have thought of as their classicism ("the one half of art").

But I would suggest that it is Expressionism, loathed by Benjamin
and Brecht alike as a sentimental and social-democratic humanism,
which—for good or ill, in the artistic atmosphere of the Weimar
period—opens the critic's eyes to Baudelaire's allegorical achievements.
For the *O-Mensch* effusions of the Expressionists were no less allegorical
in spirit than the abstract emotions of Baudelaire: both aimed to express
and at the same time reorganize and reconstruct subjectivity, and both
were responses to profound political and social crises. But where the
Expressionists aimed to conjure an oceanic feeling in which humanity
recovered its powers of goodness and fraternity and celebrated its ideals,
Baudelaire's evil flowers dripped cynicism and the paradoxes of ill will,
fateful misery and the multiple moods of disillusionment. Expressionism,
like the flowering of Baudelaire's poetry (in particular, the "Tableaux
Parisiens," dear to Benjamin), is the expression of defeat, the failure of
the Munich revolution as well as that of 1848. But where expressionism
sought to overcome that disaster by a forced optimism that Benjamin
will assimilate to his detested "progress," Baudelaire, like Flaubert, drank
the bitter cup of disillusionment to its dregs and sought to map out
psychically—*Angoisse*, *Mélancholie*, Destruction—a pessimism in the
long run more energizing and Nietzschean than the false hope and
idealistic "strivings" of the degenerate allegorists who were Benjamin's
contemporaries. Here it is revolutionary optimism itself which is regressive, and the bad-tempered and rebellious satanism of the "angry
Goethe" (Baudelaire!) which prepares some future revolutionary subject
for the rigors of a glacial age of reaction.

The Physiognomic Cycle

1

When the allegorical gaze strikes human faces, however, its classification systems invent types. Benjamin will excel in the small-scale storytelling of anecdotes, but at the level of the *event* he remains stalled at the pre-novelistic stage of the physiognomy, whose practice, encouraged by that new medium of the popular newspaper, one can observe in the early exercises of a Balzac or a Dickens. Still, it is mildly surprising, in a life's work that begins with a study of obscure plays and ends in a kind of partnership with one of the world's most nonconforming playwrights, that the formal influence of drama on Benjamin's work and thought has been so infrequently explored. At fault, perhaps, is a dialectical distortion whereby the actors are sundered from their stages, and withdraw into fates and destinies inspired by the ancient Greeks while their showplaces, rich in special effects, are abandoned to the empty category of space. The virtual absence of the novel from Benjamin's preoccupations stands as another symptom of this unusual dissociation of sensibility, as I have already suggested.

This tendency was already registered, as we have seen, in the *Trauerspiel* book, in which the formerly tragic actions, and indeed the plots themselves, the historical convulsions so avidly welcomed by the spectator, have retreated into the stereotypical character types: whatever the tyrant does, whatever the usurper or the intriguer plots, whatever

the martyr suffers, has now become a feature of the static type itself—
and in this withdrawal and reifying personification, we may witness
events becoming physiognomies.

The word long precedes Balzac's loving usage: oscillating from physiognomy to physiology it found its modern (or at least nineteenth-
century) notoriety in the obsessions of Goethe's sometime Swiss friend
Lavater; and can still be recognized under the theatrical trappings of
Benjamin's ally Brecht (in his concepts of *gestus* and *Haltung*). But the
Balzacian reference, mostly unnamed, seems to me the more permanent
association for Benjamin—and usefully designates the area in which its
repression of the novelistic and of psychology is most marked—who
would in any case have reveled in its antiquated flavor, like old prints
and tables of facial expressions unfolded by some Balzacian antique
dealer.

The concept, however, is not a trivial or decorative one, and it immediately betrays its philosophical depths in an early attempt ("Fate and
Character," 1919) in which Benjamin's most fundamental "theological"
doctrines are rehearsed, and above all that, of "predicting the future,"
which will, fatefully enough, return in Benjamin's ultimate meditations
on History.

Character is no doubt the form taken by fate in the world of a Daumier
or a Balzac. Yet neither fate nor character, which share an essentially
hermeneutic existence, are immediately present—or accessible, to use a
charged keyword: both must be read through the intermediary of external
signs, and they must be distinguished from one another in order to reach
a more "fateful"—which is to say, a more historical—understanding.

Most significant of all, in this respect, is Benjamin's decisive separation of the notion of fate from ethics, from notions of guilt and innocence, and the "moral accent" or what in the 1916 language essay he calls
judgment. This is where "fate" is ultimately identified as the fundamental speechlessness or expressionlessness of tragedy, of the moment in
which "pagan man becomes aware that he is better than his god" (I, 203;
II, 175); in other words, the moment that distinguishes genuine tragedy
from *Trauerspiel*: "the paradox of the birth of genius in moral speechlessness, moral infantility, is the sublimity of tragedy." It is probably the
basis of all sublimity, in which genius, rather than God appears: "the
natural innocence of man" (I, 203–4; II, 175); at which point fate is
degraded into law and guilt, and comedy—the realm of character and

physiognomy as such—finally appears. These complex reflections are thus elements in Benjamin's downgrading of judgment (good and evil), abstraction and psychology, in favor of some new dialectical "third way" or, in other words, of genuine historical and situational assessment. They have their family relationship with the even more enigmatic essay "The Critique of Violence" but, in our context, can be grasped simply as the emergence of that category of the character which will be given its form in the work on the *Trauerspiel* book and then flourish in his more familiar portraits of the *flâneur*, the collector, the gambler, the story-teller, the insurrectionist, the child and the characterologies of Daumier and Kafka, to which we are about to turn.

But why not start with individuals—the two great literary figures in Benjamin's life, for example—Baudelaire and Brecht? Here, surely, we find a ready-made typology at work, but one which, in Brecht's case, leads us rather into the cast of characters of Benjamin's own life story: Brecht the master, Scholem the friend, Adorno the disciple, Horkheimer the holder of the purse strings (would it be impertinent to compare him to Baudelaire's Anselle?) and the women, Acjis the Beatrice, and so on. This certainly blocks out a stage and a drama, a theater for us, one more dramatically organized than in most biographical materials; but it does not necessarily correspond to the typology of Benjamin's own imaginary, nor do the categories into which these figures fall necessarily have much to do with the organization of his own thinking and writing.

2

We have already met Baudelaire as the cosmological meteorologist, who announced the overcast ceiling and the shutting down of the stars. Now it is as the star of Benjamin's life work that he appears, not merely as poet and stylist, not merely as the allegorist whose voice was full of "capital letters and italics," but the very pivot of what was to have been a pano-rama of Second Empire Paris, itself a metonym for nineteenth-century bourgeois culture as a whole. That this project began to divide itself under its own momentum into two batches—the notes on Baudelaire and the notes for the *Arcades Project*—is only one symptom of its profoundly Benjaminian logic of separation and discontinuity, and only

one consequence of Benjamin's Hamlet-like characterological "procrastination." It is also the projection of an inability to confront the *event* as
such, a hesitation which leaves his cast of characters to bide their time
idly, waiting for a cue that never comes, while the empty stage, in multiple and varied settings, will, as Baudelaire puts it in another context,
tantalize the reader, "*haïssant le rideau comme on hait un obstacle*"
("Rêve d'un curieux," 129).

We will therefore need two separate discussions of Baudelaire, the
one on the early *Arcades* notes and sketches—the physiognomy of the
poet as such—and the other taking shape from the later "motifs" essay,
in which Baudelaire serves as the Geiger counter for the city (and which
will therefore take its place in another chapter).

But even as a portrait, there are many different views of Baudelaire to
be sketched, and not a few are missing from Benjamin's account (and
from the record of his interests). He duly notes the eccentricities of
Baudelaire's gait—mincing and mechanical, like a marionette—and of
his voice—strident, prompt to tirade "as if the words were capitalized,"
but does not particularly dwell on that related (and seemingly for
Baudelaire himself, essential) hatred of nature (which Sartre registers
extensively in his Bachelardian analysis of the poet's fascination with
metal, glass, and ice—substances Benjamin himself would certainly
have tended to read differently, akin to the modernity of Corbusian
architecture). He notes the striking and unexpected impression of
Baudelaire's facial expression—"an angry Goethe" (A269, J23, 2; V,
345)—without noting its kinship with that duality of the modern and
the classical which the poet attributed to his aesthetic of "modernity."
Above all, he fails to theorize the provocations, the delight in scandal,
the flaunting of excess and immorality, which so struck his contemporaries, friends as well as enemies. "It must be admitted," remarks a
contemporary observer, "that his women and his sky, his perfumes, his
nostalgia, his Christianity and his demon, his oceans and his tropics,
made for a subject matter of stunning novelty" (Eugène Marsan, A248,
J11, a3; V, 322). Or, if one prefers a more psychological and Dostoyevskian
inventory: "nervous irritability of the individual devoted to solitude . . .
abhorrence of the human condition and the need to confer dignity upon
it through religion or through art . . . love of debauchery in order to
forget or punish oneself . . . passion for travel, for the unknown, for the
new . . . predilection for whatever gives rise to thoughts of death

(twilight, autumn, dismal scenes) ... adoration of the artificial ... complacency in spleen" (Edmond Jaloux, A288, J33, 4; V, 366). It is an attractive menu, but Benjamin adds a stern cautionary remark: "Here we see how an exclusive regard for psychological considerations blocks insight into Baudelaire's genuine originality." And it is clear that Benjamin's physiologies oppose psychology at every step of the way. Not that they show any of that fascination or complicity with behaviorism with which the young Brecht flirted, but they register psychology's interference with a historicity to which Benjamin was always faithful (even in his language mysticism, which needed to draw on the primal history of the Garden of Eden). Psychology and the subjective lead off into that Platonic world of essences and human nature (from which his version of theology saved him), if not into aestheticism and fascism as such.

But his attention will be captured by Jules Lemaître's (hostile) mention of *contradictions* in Baudelaire (A255; J15a, 1; V, 329–30). Nor was it an accident that the first translations of Baudelaire he undertook (in World War I) centered on the "Tableaux parisiens," the city poems, added by the poet in the 1850s after the judicial condemnation of *Les Fleurs du mal* and the failure of the revolution of 1848. The contemporary social scandals—prostitutes and lesbianism, syphilitic chancres and trash in the streets, beggars, blind men, arthritic old women, hymns to revolt, corpses—have largely died down half a century later; if anything, these are now read for what they meant biographically, as provocations to bourgeois decency and impotent rage at an ungrateful social order. The lesbianism gives Benjamin a rare chance at feminism and an appreciation of emancipated women; Satan offers two choice and antithetical roles, the rebel and the victim, which cancel each other out in blasphemy. Benjamin has little interest in some putative Catholicism (leaving that to T. S. Eliot); he takes the Eros for granted but revels in the cityscape (the "Tableaux Parisiens," the first poems he translates, are precisely those Stefan George left out of his stunning versions). Above all, he will read these multiple provocations as political, provided we understand that it is a politics of the period, introduced into the heart of language as such (and not a political strategy in its own right).

What this politics was we will see in a moment, but we must also note Benjamin's persistent materialism, his interest in the status of *Les Fleurs du mal* as a book, its readership, the decline of the public in a society in which Hugo's verses were the last bestsellers (all this resonating with his

rediscovery of Joachim's essay on the decline of poetry in Romantic
Germany). Very little attention to Baudelaire's art criticism, surely as
pathbreaking as any of his other novelties (it is interesting to see how
many of Benjamin's citations include the expression "he was the first
to . . ."); the first to salute Wagner as well (for whom, quite unbidden,
Baudelaire served as a guide to Paris during the *Tannhäuser* visit); the
first, finally, to use the words modern and modernity ("modernism" as a
noun came late to France, but the adjective, thanks to Baudelaire,
appears earlier there than in other languages—it will however, never be
one of Benjamin's basic concepts). Still it is worth noting, particularly in
light of Benjamin's own translation work and his early attachment to
Baudelaire's texts, that much of the classicism of this poet is that he
uniquely represents French literature—perhaps, alongside the Chinese,
the premier literary history in the world—in a situation in which no one
reads foreign languages any longer.

We may add a second contemporary deficiency to this first one: an
obsolescence of the classical languages in our own era, in which they are
all well and truly dead a second time, after their long survival as school-
room texts. The status of Baudelaire as a classic is thereby something of
a substitute for the vanished classics of the old Greco-Roman era; it is
therefore interesting to find Benjamin ruminating on the poet's relationship to that classical past: Baudelaire having affirmed a belief in the
persistence of an eternal, classical, historical half, alongside a modern
ephemerality, in his poetry ("the transitory, the fugitive, the contingent . . . the one half of art, the other half being the eternal and
immutable").[1] The strict forms, the rhyme (he will break out of them in
his experimental prose poems), the anti-Romantic self-control even of
his most passionate outbursts ("Baudelaire is as incapable of love as of
labor," one critic writes [A249, J12, 3; V, 322]), whose emotional turmoil
is effortlessly mastered by the sentence itself. In fact, the "classic" most
invoked in Benjamin's scraps and notecards is neither Virgil nor
Sophocles, but Dante; and the curious assimilation (by the fin de siècle)
of this classic to the very archetype of decadence must have intrigued
the Riegl side of Benjamin, for whom the medicality of that period
concept had cooled into the outmodedness of fashion.

---

1 "Le peintre de la vie moderne," *Oeuvres complètes, II*, Paris: Pléiade, 1976,
683–724.

So, it is essentially in style that we will discover the deeper sources of Benjamin's allegiance; the American reader can take some pride, not merely in Baudelaire's own allegiance to Poe, but also to Laforgue's rather remarkable evocation of the "Americanisms" of Baudelaire's metaphors. We modern Romans may wonder whether this simply reflects the Greek's cool perception of vulgarity and excess, brash awkwardness; at any rate, we need blame neither Baudelaire nor Benjamin for this epithet, inasmuch as neither of them showed much interest in or curiosity about the New World, and we have ourselves tended to treat Poe as something of a Europeanizing loner. (On the other hand, Jules Laforgue, born in Montevideo, might well be considered something of an American himself.)

Yet these "readerly" attentions should not shoulder out the properly writerly ones; the Barthesian distinction also serves to underscore Benjamin's own passions and to explain in another way his strategic fixation on Baudelaire. For of few writers can it be so unremittingly affirmed that they have been the object of writerly attentions: the writerly makes one want to write, no doubt, but it also makes one want to write about writing itself, and in that sense it can also be said that Baudelaire's style has fascinated his critics to the point at which they find themselves forced to reflect on the nature of style (which, as Barthes is close to claiming in his *Writing Zero Degree*, had not hitherto existed as a phenomenon in its own right). This is obviously erroneous when one has a look at the Romantic generation in general, from Kleist to Victor Hugo, from Keats to Hölderlin or Mickiewicz; but somehow Baudelaire, by repressing everything which is grandiose and operatic about the Romantic production of style, leaves the thing itself visible in all its simplicity, if indeed a style can be truly plain and simple without vanishing from sight (as in Wordsworth). A "will to style" cannot wish to pass unnoticed, it cannot be hidden or secret. In the same spirit one might observe that Baudelaire has often been counted as a dandy—but was it not Beau Brummell's ideal to wear clothes of a slightly worn elegance? Is it this elegant wear that we admire in Baudelaire's style (the two halves, the eternal and the everyday)? At any rate, his quotability strikes a particularly sensitive nerve in Benjamin, as does Baudelaire's fascination for poets and translators in many languages. Nor does the affinity for the visual distance him much from the taste for hieroglyphs and graphology (it has been argued that Baudelaire's "painting of modern life" missed its mark; the poet's antipathy to photography blinded him to the more truly Benjaminian identification of this medium as his deeper subject).[2]

But I would argue that what makes Baudelaire an archetypal subject for Benjaminian physiognomical demonstration is the comparison with Blanqui that runs through the latter, beginning with a youthful sketch by the poet which is alleged to resemble the great conspirator (A255; J15, 6; V, 329). What should be noted, however, is that the comparison singles out but one supreme aspect of Baudelaire's multiple identities: that of the versifier. He has been compared to a rag picker (IV, 48; I, 582), a crucial physiognomy in Benjamin's view, a kind of detective of the detritus of the commodity universe, if not a day trader and profiteer (as in Dickens's *Our Mutual Friend*). Then it is to a duelist that he is compared, whose rhymes are so many deadly strokes (*"ma fantastique escrime,"* *Le soleil*, B83), yet of an outmoded weapon (are there any fire-arms in Baudelaire?). Finally, to the black-suited figure of Blanqui, already discredited in his putschism by Marx, who compares his insur-rectional strategies to the fantasies of the alchemists. "This almost auto-matically yields the image of Baudelaire," Benjamin observes, "the enig-matic stuff of allegory in one, the mystery-mongering of the conspirator in the other" (IV, 7; I, 519). But the true putschism lies in Baudelaire's verse line (and not only in his melodramatic "Americanisms"): the *mot juste* slashes like a knife-thrust, like the seizure of arsenal, radio station, post office, in an insurrection. The verse line is definitive, no turning back, no flood of alternate formulations as in Hugo: it is there once and for all, like a marble statue which is also the unerring drone-strike of a targeted explosion.

This idea of the Baudelairean verbal "insurrection" completes the methodology of *Stilstudien* with an unexpected and extralinguistic flourish which would not be inconsistent with any properly modern revival of genuine philology: it identifies words and syntax, the sentence in action, as a bodily act, as what Brecht called a *gestus*. What is compared is not the political strategy of Blanqui with the "Realpolitik" of Baudelaire (according to Valéry), although those are broader historical likenesses which emerge from this first, seemingly more minute and situation-specific similitude (they are its allegorical levels, if you prefer). The

------

2   See Timothy Raser, *Baudelaire and Photography*, Cambridge: Legenda, 2015.

gestus is indeed neither exclusively bodily nor exclusively linguistic; the concept has something of the multidimensionality aimed for theoretically by a now aging semioticism and is at one and the same time a building block of that narratology with which the former is conceptually at war.

For the Brechtian *gestus* suffers all the ambiguities of the dialectic of point and line: it is the outcome of a divisibility of action and scene which might, however, be susceptible to further divisibilities, to the emergence of smaller intelligible units yet: it is at one and the same time a fragile unity which threatens to disintegrate larger narratives on the one hand and yet to be reduced to empirical fragments on the other. Only Benjaminian similitude can rescue it by asserting its intelligibility as a legible act.

Yet the event remains absent; and why this is so may be suggested by a final emphasis Benjamin finds in his poet, a sonnet on which he intermittently broods and which has indeed a unique splendor among so many illustrious specimens fashioned by this sonneteer:

"À Une Passante"

La rue assourdissante autour de moi hurlait.
Longue, mince, en grand deuil, douleur majestueuse,
Une femme passa, d'une main fastueuse
Soulevant, balançant le feston et l'ourlet;

Agile et noble, avec sa jambe de statue.
Moi, je buvais, crispé comme un extravagant,
Dans son œil, ciel livide où germe l'ouragan,
La douceur qui fascine et le plaisir qui tue.

Un éclair . . . puis la nuit! — Fugitive beauté
Dont le regard m'a fait soudainement renaître,
Ne te verrai-je plus que dans l'éternité?

Ailleurs, bien loin d'ici! trop tard! jamais peut-être!
Car j'ignore où tu fuis, tu ne sais où je vais,
Ô toi que j'eusse aimée, ô toi qui le savais!

(Baudelaire, vol. I, 92–3)

"A Passerby"

The deafening street roared on. Full, slim, and grand
In mourning and majestic grief, passed down
A woman, lifting with a stately hand
And swaying the black borders of her gown;

Noble and swift, her leg with statues matching;
I drank, convulsed, out of her pensive eye,
A livid sky where hurricanes were hatching,
Sweetness that charms, and joy that makes one die.

A lightning flash—then darkness! Fleeting chance
Whose look was my rebirth—a single glance!
Through endless time shall I not meet with you?

Far off! too late! or never!—I not knowing
Who you may be, nor you where I am going—
You, whom I might have loved, who know it too![3]

I pick Roy Campbell's version on account of its energy (which regrettably led him politically in another direction from Benjamin) and because it rhymes, as Baudelaire's translations into English surely must; the classical version by his greatest translator, Clive Scott, is a little too grotesque for my purposes here; German readers should consult the remarkable version of Stefan George, and readers of Scots should look at that of the immortal Tom Scott. And, of course, there is Benjamin's own version:

"Einer Dame"

Geheul der Strasse dröhnte rings im Raum.
Hoch schlank tiefschwarz, in ungemeinem Leide
Schritt eine Frau vorbei, die Hand am Kleide
Hob majestätisch den gerafften Saum;

---

3   Roy Campbell, *Poems of Baudelaire*, New York: Patheon, 1952.

Gemessen und belebt, ihr Knie gegossen.
Und ich verfiel in Krampf und Siechtum an
Dies Aug' den fahlen Himmel vorm Orkan
Und habe Lust zum Tode dran genossen.

Ein Blitz, dann Nacht! Die Flüchtige, nicht leiht
Sie sich dem Werdenden an ihrem Schimmer.
Seh ich dich nur noch in der Ewigkeit?

Weit fort von hier! zu spät! vielleicht auch nimmer?
Verborgen dir mein Weg und mir wohin du musst
O du die mir bestimmt, o du die es gewusst!

(IV, 41)

Some commentators identify this "passerby" as a prostitute, a characterization which seems to me prudish and quite unnecessary, even in an already Victorian, Second-Empire Paris, where I assume that at least a few bourgeois ladies, not only those in mourning, were able to move about on foot. The overcast look in the eyes certainly promises the stormy relationship Baudelaire had with Jeanne Duval but does not otherwise implicate this unknown woman; a prostitute, one assumes, (and there are admittedly many of them in Baudelaire) would want to project a more alluring gaze. Benjamin expressed his fascination with the poem in at least two major essays; and the chance encounter, placed squarely at the midpoint of the "Tableaux Parisiens," certainly catches a fundamental feature of the modern city as a place of cruising and of sexual freedom—an added dimension of the Luft der Stadt, the medieval freedom of the city where serfs need no longer fear recapture by their masters, a liberation frequently enough passed over in silence.

The dual question of why this woman is in mourning, on the one hand, and the poet's ironically spastic account of his own reaction, on the other, both perhaps hold some clues for us. Meanwhile, one truly "extravagant" reading of the poem enlists the late Althusserian theory of the "rencontre," to tease out its deeper meaning, and the unexpected reference may well be more suggestive than one might at first think. For Althusser's theory was in a way a reprise of his earliest thoughts on the "overdetermination" of an event, which can never be thought to have but a single cause or line of determination, yet whose multiple causes are frequently bypassed in favor of the pseudo-idea of chance or contingency.

But that event, for Althusser, is revolution; and it comes with all the shock of a genuine historical discovery to find Dolf Oehler reinserting this poetic moment into a long and well-nigh codified iconography, from "Marianne" to Delacroix's great painting of "Freedom mounting the Barricades"—the personification of revolution as a woman. What if, indeed, this also turns out to be a level of the poetic allegory, in which not only the city and the spirit of l'amour but also the revolutionary event were signifying investments?

Both Flaubert and Baudelaire, those two hardened reactionaries (the former's reaction to the Commune is only comparable to Luther's fury at the peasants in revolt), were in fact, as we now know, enthusiastic supporters of the July Revolution and of its promise of radical social transformation and the destruction of the hated Restoration. Both were then disabused by the inevitable betrayal that followed; we thus need to take into account the possibility that their reactionary political views were not reasoned convictions but rather affective reactions in time, a rage at the collapse of hope and a loathing for the new bourgeois authorities who built something even more distasteful in the place of the ancien régime.

This is to underscore the other face of the poem, not the encounter as such, but its failure, its power and existence as a missed opportunity. This is, then, at the very heart of Baudelaire's work, a figure for the absence of the event as such and the boredom and ennui of its omission, the emptiness at the heart of this temporality which blocks narrative in Baudelaire and transforms Flaubert's *L'Éducation sentimentale*, for all its teeming detail and movement, into a uniquely anti-novelistic experiment, of which Lukács said that there could only be one of its kind (*Theory of the Novel*) and which Henry James loathed as the gigantic manifestation in flesh and blood of that narrative futility he may have feared for his own work.

3

But the experience of defeat is not to be thought of in the vulgar commercial terms of success and failure; Benjamin tells us so himself, and it is this strange state of the revolutionary event—a presence even in the midst of the most thoroughgoing defeat—which he must himself have felt in the thirties and, above all, after the Stalin-Hitler pact— and whose paradoxical manifestation he felt to be incarnated in another obsessive figure of his characterology, namely the gambler. We do not know what role gambling played in Benjamin's own life (nor in that of Baudelaire either), but he clearly had enough sympathy with this passion to be fascinated and willing to deploy his own understanding of it in various places in his work. Gambling is, for the medicalized thinking of today, an addiction, and it is also a metaphysical passion for other thinkers of the past. It plays a central role in Pascal's notion of *divertissement*, for example (it is the very basis for his conception of the misery of the human condition), and its most eloquent modern analysis is to be found in Benjamin's contemporary, André Malraux (a figure strangely analogous to Benjamin in many ways, if we omit the political role-playing and the passion for lying and "mythomania," of which the novelist himself gave a lucid analysis in *La condition humaine*). For Malraux, the instant of the bet marks a suspension of reality in time, in which both wealth and poverty are momentarily abolished: gambling, in other words, offers the satisfaction (if not the excitement) of a unique temporal moment in which neither riches nor poverty exist, and a present of time which risks destroying temporality altogether.

It is on this temporal dimension of gambling which Benjamin, in some of his most extraordinary pages, concentrates. A variety of "similitudes"—indeed, a dazzling bravura listing of the various forms of modern "shock" (Simmel's term) in which the temporal instant of gambling can be glimpsed and identified—is followed by the decisive identification of gambling with factory work: it lies in a form of repetition which is better described as a time without a future:

> The jolt in the movement of a machine is like the so-called coup in a game of chance. Since each operation of the machine is just as screened off from the preceding operation as a *coup* in a game of chance is from

the one that preceded it, the drudgery of the laborer is, in its own way, a counterpart to the drudgery of the gambler. Both types of work are equally devoid of substance . . . the time of hell, which is the province of those who are not allowed to complete anything they have started . . . This process of starting all over again is the regulative idea of gambling, as it is of work for wages. (IV, 330; I, 633)

The nontemporality of repetition here—in which the very logic of proletarian labor, of the production of exchange and surplus value, is revealed in the unrelated figure of the gambler—is preceded by a disquisition on the radical difference between the satisfaction of a (Freudian) wish and the desire to win: "a wish fulfilled is the crowning of experience [*Erfahrung*]" (IV, 331; I, 635). Benjamin's figuration is thus an enlargement of the Marxian notion of alienation, but one which makes it available not to psychology but to the philosophical investigation of temporality as such. A Marxian transformation of the labor process would then result in a transformation of *Erfahrung* or, rather, to use Benjamin's theological version, its fulfillment, its redemption. The allegorical notion of fulfillment is thus hidden away inside this figure (much as the shrunken dwarf is hidden inside the militant chess-playing Turkish-warrior automaton).

But there is another mode of escape from the radical alienation and dissatisfaction of this kind of temporality interruptus, and that is to be found in the figuration of what psychoanalysis calls its sublimation. Here we met another fundamental Benjaminian character: the collector. This is a passion—and like Molière's obsessive types, Benjamin's characters are also figures of monomania—about which Benjamin knew something personally and which we feel authorized to enrich with biographical information. (It should, however, always be understood that such biographical references are not psychological; they are at best phenomenological and at worst psychoanalytic, but at all times philosophical.) Benjamin collected books, with a special emphasis on children's books: his interests thereby included two kinds of nostalgia within itself, inasmuch as the historical books also exhale the ontic nostalgia of childhood, above all in their materiality, their incarnation of origin: the sumptuousness of the first printings of the classics in Venice or Nuremberg, their typeface and rich bindings, all of this combines with the classicality of their dead languages to summon up an object of passion no less peremptory than the child's attachment to a unique if tattered text.

Yet Benjamin's peculiar and recurrent association of the figure of the collector with that of the gambler reminds us that we have to do here with a perversion and not an innocent hobby (but perhaps there are no innocent hobbies!). The book collector is in that sense to be ranged alongside the foot fetishist; the gambler alongside the stalker or pathologically jealous lover; just as the cast of characters of the *Trauerspiel* approximate the inhabitants of Charenton or Bedlam who offer Benjamin some of his choicest anecdotes ("Shuvalkin . . . Shuvalkin . . . Shuvalkin . . .").

It may not be inappropriate to quote Jacques Lacan here, whose example makes the link between collecting and the constructional dimension of toys, the physical delight in removing the object from use and in incorporating it into a higher (we might even say transcendental) unity. Lacan identifies the psychic structure of collecting with an object, in this case, a set of interlocking wooden matchboxes, claiming that for the collector, "the box of matches is not simply an object, but that in the form of an *Erscheinung*, as it appeared in its truly imposing multiplicity [united, as he also puts it, "with a copulatory force"], it may be a Thing [or Ding, in Lacan's vocabulary]."[4] This is, as he says, one of "the innocent forms of sublimation"; but from a philosophical perspective, we may also transcode the phenomenon into the endowment of an inner-worldly thing with a metaphysical dimension, a transcendence.

The analogy with gambling now introduces the dimension of time (which is, in fact, virtually the only link between these two "passions"). Obsessive gambling, indeed, has fascinated literary representation since the feudal era (when, with hunting, it was virtually the only pastime—a word to be taken literally—of the dominant, or "leisure" classes). Probability theory began with Pascal (it has never been explored, I think, whether it has some deeper link with his theory of the two kinds of character or intelligence—"*esprit de géométrie, esprit de finesse*"). A vice, not quite over the line from the unmentionable and the obscene, gambling fascinates all the way down to the period of Benjamin, when it shows signs of being overtaken by drugs (both exist simultaneously in

4   Jacques Lacan, *Le Séminaire VII*, Paris: Éditions du Seuil, 1986, 113–14.

Baudelaire's repertoire) and then seemingly effaced altogether (perhaps the passion for computer games marks a return of the repressed).

Like drugs, gambling operates on the future: a temporal dimension drugs suspend, but one which is in gambling used to exacerbate the present and to heighten it to a synchronic and total identification with the world itself, a moment which, sadly, does not last, at least until the next bet (which may in some ways approximate Deleuze on alcoholism and "*l'avant-dernier verre*").

But in collecting there appears the other side of temporality, which is memory itself: "every passion borders on the chaotic," Benjamin says, in a self-consciously memorable phrase, "but the collector's passion borders on the chaos of memories" (II, 486; IV, 388). It seems unnecessary at this point to gloss the term "chaos" with all the anthropological, if not cosmological, associations Benjamin developed for it (primarily out of Bachofen, as we have seen). What is more important is to depersonalize the memories at stake here, which, to be sure, include the obscure little antique store in that small French town in which the collector discovers a unique volume at a specific moment of his own life, the memory of which here at once, however, introduces history, at first chronological and homogeneous, but which may well, owing to the materiality of the volume in question, become obsessively enlarged into a dialectical image, the eruption into heterogeneous time, the time of the Now.

For intellectuals, books are no less life records than old photo albums, documenting stages of ideological development, literary passions, philosophical and literary discovery; as theoretical fashions change, some becoming as rare as officially rare books, if not as valuable. How much the more, then, were not Benjamin's various libraries—some lost in exile, others boxed and preserved by friends, working batches sent off to Denmark or England, a veritable trail of displacements and the intertwining of research and changes of address—a bibliography of exile and misery?

The valuable items, officially collected, have however their own relationship to history, fanning out beyond mortal ownership. Authentication in such collections involves what the police procedurals call the chain of custody, in which the passage from hand to hand, the record of ownership, even for the time spent at the dealer's, is an essential part of the record, verification being a history in its own right. Nor should we neglect a different set of paths, namely those the ever-restless Benjamin pursued across Europe, from Moscow to Ibiza, from Denmark to the Riviera, punctuated by solitary promenades in obscure stops and towns in which the discovery of an antiquaire is often as thrilling as that of the unexpected volume itself! "I have made my most memorable purchases on trips, as a transient. Property and possession belong to the tactical sphere. Collectors are people with a tactical instinct; their experience teaches them that when they capture a strange city, the smallest antique shop can be a fortress, the most remote stationary store a key position" (II, 489; IV, 391). And there follows a loving evocation of all the cities in which he has had the memorable experience of a discovery, an appropriation, a bibliophilic jouissance!

At this point the figure of the collector begins to morph slowly into neighboring physiognomies: not for nothing do we recall the deliberately dusty strategy of the *Arcades*, for he pointedly notes that book collecting also is going out of fashion, that it is yesterday's passion. But behind this outmoded character lies the child, who is one more fundamental form of the collector, as we shall see. And alongside the child, but utterly distinct, from another layer of time, mature and even cynical, world-weary, the collector, whom one famously imagines in the henceforth legendary act of "unpacking my library," begins a slow mutation into the restless and curious, well-nigh homeless, pedestrian called the *flâneur*, to whom we will come in a moment.

4

The child, however, is not, I venture to say, a character in the Benjaminian universe, even though its point of view is endlessly appealed to and interpreted, as when Benjamin explains how ignorant are today's manufacturers of children's toys, under "the influence of psychology and aestheticism" (II, 118; III, 128), of the child's most spontaneous interests. The essay "Toys and Play" (1928) is not only the sketch of a whole philosophical treatise on the latter ("play . . . is the mother of every habit" [II, 120; III, 131]), it is also a little handbook for precisely those manufacturers on how to do it right. One hesitates to characterize children's position in Benjamin's various worlds as one of innocence ("children are insolent and remote from the world" [II, 101; IV, 515]). His interest in them is neither paternal nor pedagogical, although Asja's revolutionary reeducation of Soviet wild or homeless children through theater was certainly a fundamental marker for him. The child constitutes for Benjamin one available and even privileged standpoint or viewpoint for a fundamental estrangement (or V-) effect. It yields, for instance, a wholly different experience of color (I, 442; IV, 613) and a resurrectional or transcendent version of the humdrum mortal adult collector. Through it, something of a radically different relationship to objects, activity and even production becomes available. As we have seen, one of Benjamin's great lessons is his suspicion of what we generally call psychology, whose effects (although not necessarily its positivist motives) result in a subjectification of all its objects (perhaps Nietzsche was the last to use the term "psychology" as the sign of a triumphant conquest of the historicity of the subject rather than of its reification). At any rate, here is an instructive example, speaking of the "mustiest speculations of the pedagogues":

> Their infatuation with psychology keeps them from perceiving that the world is full of the most unrivaled objects for children's attention and use. And the most specific. For children are particularly fond of haunting any site where things are being visibly worked on. They are irresistibly drawn to the detritus generated by building, gardening, housework, tailoring, or carpentry. In waste products they recognize the face that the world of things turns directly and solely to them. (I, 408; III, 16)

If there is psychology here, it is a Marxian kind, for which production is always the most satisfying feature of that stream of events, changes, metamorphoses, which is the world itself. To be sure, his example—that of rubbish (from which he will also derive collecting as a specifically children's activity)—also lends itself to the counter-psychological doctrine that children's first impulse and delight lies in destruction, in tearing the already formed and produced objects of the adult world into a joyous heap of broken pieces, in some first naive and even natural upsurge of revolt, culminating in those orgiastic moments of chaos which are in many ways the ontological climax of the best children's films. But destruction is simply the other, the dialectical, face of production; and Benjamin's account has the additional merit of rebuking that specifically bourgeois version of production which is the philosophically valorized concept, from Schiller on, of play as such: "In using these things, they do not so much imitate the works of adults as bring together, in the artifact produced in play, materials of widely differing kinds in a new intuitive relationship" (I, 408; III, 16). Not only is play, then, a form of production, but the very emphasis on heterogeneity, which is one of the leitmotiven of contemporary—dare I say postmodern?—doxa, is itself in advance revealed to carry a secret libidinal charge of the productive impulse as such.

Much more transpires in the context of this seemingly innocent book review of a now-forgotten work on children's books by Karl Hobrecker: in particular, I must also single out a remark crucial for that other feature of children's mentality which touches on color as such, and that is the virtually offhand remark that the pictures in these books "usually exclude any synthesis of color and drawing" (I, 410; III, 18). Predictably, then, the book review hereby becomes a genre in which philosophical analysis can be exhaustively developed in a very different discursive context than in traditional philosophizing or in the treatise. A whole systematic view of childhood is here unobtrusively inserted into a modest account of a commercial product—description imperceptibly passing over into phenomenology. Meanwhile, this determines a different receptivity to events (fairy tales, "The Storyteller").

5

But the one place in Benjamin's work where something akin to children's experience seems to open up and to crystallize is to be found in another writer, whose work's meaning for him, however, is strictly nonliterary, and that is Kafka, who can also therefore, in that spirit, be added to Benjamin's characterological collection.

Now that Kafka has been canonized by the academic reading lists and pronounced a modern classic, it becomes even more difficult to assess his meaning for Benjamin, for whom literary history was not a matter of establishing a canon but of gauging effectivity in the present situation, and who rarely wrote about "masterpieces" for their own sake: there is a short essay on Dostoyevsky's *Idiot*, a long meditation on Julien Green's *Adrienne Mesurat* (not exactly a canonical work, at least from the present standpoint), an extensive celebration of the unclassifiable Gottfried Keller, a homage to Proust and numerous reflections on the avant-gardes and the contemporary literary situation in France and Germany. With poetry we fare somewhat differently, for Benjamin duly registered the impact of the rediscovery of Hölderlin and consistently affirmed the preeminent if ambiguous status of Stefan George—that there was no reason for him to write about Rilke or even about Valéry (except for the latter's prose), and every reason to write little commentaries on some of Brecht's poems, gives one a fair idea of his pragmatic conception of literary criticism. To write on Goethe's *Wahlverwandtschaften* (a literary curiosity if there ever was one) is best assessed in terms of methodology; to write on Karl Kraus was an intervention designed to measure literary usefulness in the contemporary public sphere and also to transform the values of literature into those of writing as such and, more privately, to promote his own conception of "destruction."

As for Kafka, Scholem certainly wanted to believe that it constituted proof of Benjamin's lifelong commitment to a tradition of Jewish mysticism; and he certainly abounded in Scholem's sense in their correspondence (and showed an equal diffidence about the text in his discussions with Brecht). But I would range his Kafka interests and loyalties in another "tradition" altogether, one which runs from his commitment to children's books all the way to the weird science-fictional fantastic of Scheerbart's *Lésabendio*, from fairy tales to oral storytelling. We cannot follow Deleuze in calling this "minor literature," but that it is anti-novelistic we can affirm without hesitation, in a sense rather distinct either from Lukács's or Bakhtin's theories of that "modern" anti-form.

Here Benjamin's McLuhanism avant la lettre is prominent and definitional: indeed, his account of Kafka's unique vision (particularly as he expresses it in the important letter to Scholem of June 12, 1938) underscores the way in which, in Kafka, the technological forms of perception of the new industrial city intersect, capture and distort the remnants of an ancient village culture of wisdom, law and tale. Yet inasmuch as storytelling is necessarily oral, it precedes all the linguistic subjectivity and "inwardness" stimulated and released, produced, by the printed text. In such storytelling (of which the I-novel is a kind of *Umfunktionierung*), *Erlebnis* is already by definition *Erfahrung*, for there does not yet exist a "psychological" realm into which the former can be translated and assimilated by the latter. *Erlebnis* is still, as he likes to put it, "*einverleibt*," bodily experienced, absorbed by the physical in the static form of character, the dynamic forms of *gestus* and habit. (Brecht's theater—a storytelling theater—returns to these tangibilities, which are neither naturalism or *neue Sachlichkeit*, and just as little "expressionist.")

Are they then archaic, and the survival of or regression to some reality which preceded the modern, Enlightenment, technology and which, in that case, would seem dangerously related to that zone of "myth" Benjamin was always concerned to denounce? Kafka will be the extreme test case and the laboratory in which this crucial problem will be explored.

But the Kafka essay, its superb anecdotal prologue aside ("Shuvalkin . . . Shuvalkin . . . Shuvalkin . . ."), turns out to be an exercise in characterology. If character is destiny, then its obverse signals a compression of any number of narratives in time into an equal number of what Benjamin called physiognomies, shading over into types and even stereotypes. These are static images; they are not, as I have just argued, nonnarrative, but perhaps described as postnarrative. This is the sense in which I have claimed that Benjamin was no storyteller, however much he values that gift. He simulated the art of the anecdote, as in the prologue to "Kafka" just mentioned. But if he never made his way into the novel (not even by way of the elaborate Proustian detour of the *Berlin Childhood*), he also theorized that "failure" by affirming the novel to be little more than a by-product and even a substitute for the faculty of storytelling in decay.

Meanwhile, as far as mysticism is concerned, yes, to be sure, the Kafka essay gets there, too, but by way of assigning Kafka's cast of characters to the various ontological, angelic, diabolical, or chthonic spheres from which they emerge, thereby allowing them by implication to trace out a whole metaphysics, from the archaic realm of myth, through the fantasy realm of oral storytelling, to the law and its emissaries. And it is this superimposed set of levels or realms which constitutes the mystical kernel projected by the characterology rather than the other way round (very much as with the stories of the Kabbalah itself, which, a compendium of Blakean legends, passes itself off as doctrine).

Still, the movement of this essay, from "burden" to "burden," has as much to tell us about Benjamin's mental processes as it does about Kafka's. In fact, this is one of the rare essays in which Benjamin surveys the totality of a writer's work, so that the character system he posits is as much a way of unifying that work as it is a random set of perceptions, with their own hermeneutic logic.

The list begins, as it must, with fathers and sons, the assistants, bureaucrats with decisions to make—"as shy as young girls"—who, in their slutty innocence, form the next group, passing over to the actors of the Nature Theater of Oklahoma. This backdrop not only then introduces the matter of backdrops as such, the "context" against which a character becomes a type, but also that of acting and the point at which "Jewish mysticism" meets Brecht on theater, and the vital notion of the *gestus* appears. Only then do we "come to the certain realization that Kafka's entire work constitutes a code of gestures": gestures in and of themselves, rather than any "symbolic meaning for the author in advance." The latter, too, must search for the meaning of these gestures in their "ever-shifting contexts [backdrops] and experimental groupings. The theater is the logical place for such groupings" (II, 801–2; II, 418–19).

This cast of characters goes on to include Kafka's animals, who stand as gestures without backdrops in a sense, but, at the same time, put us on the track of a great secret of Kafka's creative process, namely that he does not know their context, either: each of the "experimental" stories attempts, by way of variation in the backdrop or background, to ferret out their meaning. It is this persistent inquiry of the narrator, the puzzled innocent and bemused observer (in that, Kafka the writer begins his own metamorphosis into the Benjaminian *Grübler*), which finally turns these observations, these gestures that seem to form an event, yet an incomprehensible one, into parables, except that they are parables without doctrine, which teach nothing we can see, which allude to meanings out of our reach, yet which ought to have all the rigor of the bureaucratic society, the real world which the insurance adjuster finds all around him.

Such parables cry out for interpretation, but not even he—especially not he, Kafka!—can say what their interpretation might be (Camus's famous image of the man in the phone booth, making incomprehensive movements with his hands and mouth, is a banal reduction of this situation). This is why attention swings back to the backdrops, the contexts, that ought to make these gestures comprehensible; it is here that we encounter the Benjaminian "prehistoric world" from which all such parables arise, guilt and the forgotten, the archaic, the reduction of *gestus* and character to a veritable abstraction of spools and tangled thread—Odradek: the ultimate figure of an observer for whom the most familiar things (the family and the home themselves!) are incomprehensible. But the innocent must preserve this burden of oblivion and incomprehensibility; if his surroundings become realistic, then everything unique in this world experience vanishes on the spot. The solution is that of the concluding fable of Sancho Panza, who turns out to have invented Quijote and his illusions precisely in order to "enjoy great and profitable entertainment to the end of his days" (II, 816; II, 438). Parables without doctrine, the inexhaustible mysteries of the bureaucratic world system, Kafka's not-at-all fantastic narratives, are his mode of enjoyment.

6

At this point we may return to that figure who is certainly the most famous character in Benjamin's physiognomic cycle and, at the same time, one of the most ambiguous: the *flâneur*. Now virtually indissociable from Benjamin himself, this loan word was borrowed from Baudelaire, where it is also omnipresent, without, for all that, applying to Baudelaire's own person, who was emphatically not, Benjamin assures us in a curious afterthought, a *flâneur* in his own right. Often synonymous with other figures such as the dandy and the *Grübler* or allegorist, the *flâneur* comes the closest to a character who fades into his very background, or he is revealed as something like the genius loci of the boulevards themselves as historical sites.

Benjamin was himself very much a traveler and a travel writer, as the great essays on Moscow and Naples testify; in a sense, his survival strategy posited the attempt to translate exile into travel and exploration (in Paris, it will be exploration in time, along with a stroll around the current literary situation, understanding the future Sartrean word, in the intensive sense of a militarily assessed landscape, whose traps and possibilities you map in advance, a "city of words" whose suitability you investigate for guerrilla warfare). This is not yet the modern industry of tourism, with its reified monuments and prepackaged trajectories: we are here essentially talking about walks and walking, and about cities, still a fresh topic, where his thinking is guided by Simmel's great essay "Metropolis and Mental Life." Walking also has its history, as Rebecca Solnit has shown, with interesting pages on the bad eyesight which Benjamin shared with Joyce and Nietzsche, and which determined a particular gait, in thought as well as in bodily movement, and a particular close-up mode of peering as observation.

Still, the *flâneur* is not a traveler, as Baudelaire's unhappy adventures with his aborted "voyage to India" instruct us; nor is it at all certain that Baudelaire himself loved masses of people or shared the *flâneur's* delight in mingling with the multitude, which he loathed in any case, in principle. Still, Benjamin assures us that "the masses" haunt every page of *Les Fleurs du mal*, even where they remain unmentioned and unthematized (and there is a sense in which the same is true of Benjamin himself). Clearly, however, whatever his affective relationship, he was aware of the deeper category at work. As we have seen, he quotes *Fusées*: "The pleasure of being in a crowd is a mysterious expression of sensual joy in the multiplication of number . . . Number is in all . . . Ecstasy is a number . . . Religious intoxication of great cities" (A 290, J34a, 3; V, 369). To which Benjamin adds, rather enigmatically, "Extract the root of the human being!" One assumes that this is meant to refute the idea that the individual, added up, makes the foundation of the mass; rather, it is the other way around—the collective is the constituent part of the individual (when the latter exists).

Other features of the *flâneur* deserve emphasis, in particular his aimlessness: his refusal of purpose and utility makes of him a hero in the struggle against commodified labor and in particular against wage work as such (he is often, like Benjamin and Baudelaire themselves, penniless); and it is worth remembering, in this context but also in our own situation of mass unemployment and post-work, that Marx's son-in-law, Lafargue, wrote a whole book in praise of laziness, thereby inscribing himself in that alternate tradition of Marxism which wishes not to glorify labor and productivity, but to abolish it altogether.

Nonetheless, I think it is also appropriate to remind ourselves that Benjamin's explorations of (mostly European) cities were not altogether disinterested. He had aims and interests, motivations, directions and goals, if not exactly touristic ones. A hint is furnished by an exasperated letter (to Scholem) by his wife, Dora: "all he is at this point is brains and sex," to which we may append the reminiscence of his son, Stefan: "I just saw him in between trips, when he would bring me toys."[5] So if by what Dora calls "brains" we substitute books, either to be written or to be collected along with the toys, and if we speculate that gambling was another feature of Benjamin's secret life, we can add up some of the features about which Benjamin was reluctant to say I.

To be sure, prostitution is also everywhere in his work as theme or topic, and we must note in passing a remarkable mutation of Lukács's central theory of the proletariat in *History and Class Consciousness*. The latter there defines the proletarian (and the privileged standpoint of proletarian consciousness and experience) as a human being completely reduced to the commodity form, an individual whose condemnation to the sale of labor power leaves no place for the obfuscation of other ideological and personal identities.

In Benjamin, however, and in the context of Baudelaire's Paris and the *Arcades Project*, it is the prostitute who enjoys this unique privilege of being nothing but a commodity (and thereby gaining a unique view of the real nature of capitalist society). Perhaps this is what Benjamin has in mind when in his correspondence with Adorno he enigmatically evokes an "empathy with exchange value," that is, with commodity reification. The formula offers a new perspective on what we have come to call "cultural studies" (a field of which Benjamin is certainly a totemic ancestor), suggesting that the apt student of culture in late capitalism must necessarily bring a certain feeling, if not a fondness, for commodification, consumption, cultural reification, what we nowadays call "desire."

As for prostitution itself, perhaps we are too little mindful of the immense role it played (particularly since the development of the capitalist city) in the life of young males, even beyond the twenties and as far as the invention of the pill. This is an existential dimension of nineteenth- and twentieth-century male life, which, along with the terror of syphilis (and tuberculosis), is too frequently passed over in silence in literary and cultural study before the postmodern; of course, it finds a sublimated expression in such works as "À une passante," of which Benjamin was particularly fond (see above) and which focuses on the fleeting existence of the Look, the sexual glance in city life, an

---

5   See Walter Benjamin, Howard Eiland and Michael W. Jennings, *Walter Benjamin: A Critical Life*, Cambridge: Harvard University Press, 2014, 316.

experience Benjamin himself transfers to his visit to Asja's hometown in the segment called "Ordinance" in *One-Way Street* ("had she touched me with the match of her eyes, I would have gone up like a powder keg" [I, 461; IV, 110]). But we cannot mention prostitution without reminding ourselves that the work of the professional journalist, writing on command and given commissions he is not particularly suited for—Benjamin's situation, even with respect to the Frankfurt School and their journal—is also a kind of prostitution, and that of a kind of commodity-physiognomy.

We must therefore demystify the omnipresent reference to the *flâneur*, without which no essay on Benjamin would seem to be complete. The figure is certainly an unmistakable symptom of the spatiality that pervades all of Benjamin's thought and writing; for the moment, we simply follow it into the more general category of the walk and of walking—to be distinguished from Deleuze's not quite so well-known (schizophrenic) *balade* or stroll in space, and even from the "*promenade surrealiste*" that inspired the latter's use of it, or the situationist "*dérive*" that followed (and that did not yet know Benjamin as a predecessor). These last seem motivated by the look for something, if only the *inconnu*; in principle, Benjamin's *flâneur* is not, with the exceptions noted above. In his Baudelairean avatar, he makes his way through a crowd, or leans against a wall to observe its multiple features and physiologies. But this epistemological function is itself ambiguous, and we can best grasp its relationship to action by juxtaposing the two sources of Baudelaire's figure in all their difference from each other.

In the one, E. T. A. Hoffmann's "My Cousin's Corner Window" (1822), the protagonist is reduced to the purely epistemological by paralysis: he gradually becomes nothing but a pure gaze and sits at his window observing the holiday crowd in the square beneath him. It is known that Baudelaire deplored the lack of the demonic in Hoffmann, something he found in abundance in his other great source, Edgar Allan Poe.

For in the latter's text, "The Man of the Crowd" (1845), the *flâneur* not only redoubles himself—his avatar develops from pure observation into the most violent action. The sketch, hardly even a tale, begins with one *flâneur* (the narrator) observing another, the eponymous man of the crowd. He follows him. Little by little his target is seen to transform himself into a violent figure, analogous to the transformations in *Dr. Jekyll and Mr. Hyde*, even if Poe does not bring it to outright murder as such. Would it be far-fetched to compare this development with that from the verse of *Les Fleurs du mal* to Baudelaire's prose poems, in which, for a famous example, the almsgiver beats his unfortunate beggar, in what the Freudians would call a *passage à l'acte*, an exteriorization of all the boiling resentment repressed by a situation in which he has been reduced to mere observation?

It is but a glimpse, after which the *flâneur* subsides into that figure virtually without content, whose function is to absorb the outside world without himself participating in it. But there remains, in Benjamin, a final shadowy position in which such observation may itself be said to be productive.

This is an impersonal "character" through whom Benjamin does not even speak, but whom he quotes (perhaps another layer of motivation for his practice of quotation), and to whom he attributes urgently significant things—methodological imperatives fully as much as alternate explanations—but who is somehow not present, nor does he really "represent" (for it is not the party who speaks through him, although the party is no doubt the destinatee of his corrections). This is "the historical materialist," the figure who "will know that," who "avoids," who "understands that—." This authoritative figure, the source of perhaps a somewhat more philosophical wisdom than that, practical-political, of Brecht's Herr Keuner, is not a big Other in the Lacanian sense (closer to that of the "analyst"). The historical materialist (or the dialectical one; Benjamin does not seem to have respected the distinction as sharply as we might today) is, of course, from one standpoint simply "the Marxist." Anyone can assume this position if they like, but perhaps out of politeness for his non-Marxian readers, Benjamin avoids doing so, just as he refrains from endowing "Marxism" with some absolute truth inaccessible to anyone else, thereby evading the exclusionary in-group consequences of the "we."

The "historical materialist" is no longer an actor, even anecdotally; he is, like the child, something like a medium, a vehicle for contemplation, perhaps the final form of that *Grübler* immobilized before his now "scientific" allegorical emblems. He is perhaps also the avatar of what Hasidic storytelling called the wise man, the "man of counsel," as Benjamin called him in his essay on Leskov and the storyteller. And every practiced reader of Benjamin will have come upon sentences which, duly avoiding the stigmatized first person (the named actor or actant), gravely warn us how "the historical materialist" will understand the matter.

So it is that in the absence of an action that could unit both terms, the former character becomes a rather static physiognomy and the former scene of action becomes a space as such, indeed, a veritable typology of spaces (and in particular the spaces of cities). There then appears, in the absence of praxis, a kind of medium of pure contemplation which will include the child on the one hand, the very locus of estrangement effects, and the "historical materialist" on the other, the place of the scientific understanding of history. So it is that the final form of depersonalized contemplation becomes a seemingly technological kino-eye, and the character function gives way to a function tout court, both returning us, paradoxically, to art and the aesthetic (one which will have to be secured and sheltered against fascist and aestheticizing appropriation). I want to emphasize, before we explore these new developments, that deperson-alization is here not to be misunderstood as some psychological trait or flaw in Benjamin himself, but that it is part and parcel of a generalized crisis of action and of the act as such, in a modernity which has evolved into mass political confrontation. The dissolution of the act is one of the privileged forms of that dissolution of experience which was Benjaminian Erfahrung par excellence; now we must examine that empty stage it leaves behind.

Figure 5.1

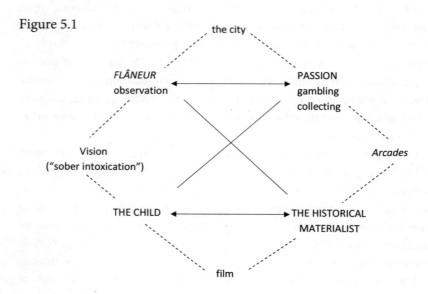

6

Space and the City

So we need to disengage Benjamin the traveler from the stereotypical image of the *flâneur* that his work has (perhaps unwittingly) promoted. A pity Michel de Certeau did not exercise his tropological analyses of the practices of space on Benjamin (a late lecture betrays his interest, rather in the latter's "angelism"). En revanche, I have already reminded us of Rebecca Solnit's suggestive pages on him (and on de Certeau himself, as well). It will now be necessary to approach the matter more formally and deal with Benjamin's travelogues as a genre, one ultimately deployed in the service of a vision of history.

No account of Benjamin's relationship to space can, however, be complete without some mention of the shadowy, legendary figure that often haunts his pages (and those of many of his contemporaries), namely that of Alois Riegl (1858–1905), whose pathbreaking *Late Roman Art Industry* (1901) seems to have been decisive for at least one aspect of Benjamin's aesthetic. With Simmel, Rosenzweig, Scheerbart and Roger Caillois (and we should probably also include, alongside Carl Schmitt, the far better known but today scarcely read Paul Valéry), his is one of the names that block out as it were a whole intellectual secret society within which Benjamin's originality can alone be appreciated.

The Victorian (or Wilhelminian or Third-Republic) period is, as

Marc Angenot has shown,[1] one in which a medicalized ideology of health and disease (or degeneracy) flourished and extended to the most important political as well as ethical issues of the age. Max Nordau's *Degeneration* (1892) is only the most striking expression of an ideologically selective mentality debating the tension between "civilization" and "culture" at the same time that it is seeking to affirm the legitimacy of bourgeois values and the bourgeois state over against the inroads of unionization, socialism, anarchism and anticolonialism (Multatuli's *Max Havelaar* dates from 1860, *Heart of Darkness* from 1899). The ideologies of modernity depend absolutely on a distinction between the civilized and the premodern, in which essentially medicalized notions of the irrational and the abnormal play an important role. Riegl's book strikes a blow against that ideological framework in the world of visual and spatial culture.

There are two basic points to be made about Riegl's position in Benjamin's thinking. The first is the familiar one: Riegl's choice of a much-maligned period in art history (and it should be pointed out that neither Riegl nor Benjamin really believes in "art history" as such) is already an act of defiance and a notice of the intent to disprove the conventional idea that late Roman art, with its clumsy, weird, childish and misshapen forms, is a period of decadence (and beyond that, indeed, that such periods exist in the first place). This could be seen as a logical implication of Ranke's famous dictum that "all ages are immediate to God," but in practice, and not only for art historians, the idea that some ages are more immediate than others is a long-standing prejudice. Benjamin will read Riegl's move as support, not only for his Baroque project (which involved work with a good deal of mediocre literary production), but even for the *Arcades Project*, in which secondary material of all kinds is dignified in ways which do not become legitimized in historiography before the Annales school, or in culture before cultural studies.

The importance for him of Riegl is documented by an untranslated 1929 note on four "books which have remained alive" (III, 169–71): they stake out a grid of what Benjamin thought was the fundamental problematic of "modern" thinking in the Weimar era. Besides Riegl, he included A. G. Meyer's book on iron buildings, *Eisenbauten* (a

---

1   See *1889*, Quebec City: Le Préambule, 1989.

forerunner of Giedion and one which marks the significance of Corbusian architecture in his conception of modernity); Rosenzweig's *Star of Redemption* as a new theological summa which goes far beyond current philosophical, Jewish or theological issues in its historical sweep; and Lukács's *History and Class Consciousness* as a fundamental advance on orthodox or nineteenth-century Marxist theory. These twin materialist and theoretical pairs—architecture, space and history on the one hand, redemption and class consciousness on the other—oddly omit what is for him the decisive breakthrough of Surrealism, which will find its place in another basic characterization of the age:

> To encompass both Breton and Le Corbusier—that would mean drawing the spirit of contemporary France like a bow, with which knowledge shoots the moment in the heart. (*Arcades Project*, N, 1a5, 459; V, 573)

Still, the exemplary significance of Riegl's book, which Benjamin was not alone in appreciating, may well be heightened by his sense that Riegl's choice of objects was an unconscious harbinger of the new sensibility of Expressionism as such (a word which, like its opposite number, Surrealism, he often used as a signifier of "modernism" in general).

This emergence of a new aesthetic sensibility is, however, at odds with Riegl's view of history; quite different, as we shall see, from Benjamin's, but perhaps no less contradictory. It involves the identification of historical periods with the dominance of this or that specific form of what he called a *Stilwollen*, which we may translate as a "will to style": this influential concept opens the door to the exploration not merely of period styles (such as the Benjaminian Baroque), but also of a thoroughgoing characterization of the base-and-superstructure of individual historical moments, a procedure for which I fear I must evoke as its most striking elaboration the historicism of Spengler, whose ambitious cultural syntheses are still worth reading. What will differentiate Riegl's efforts, however, from some garden-variety history of ideas is his emphasis on the forms of spatial perception which inform such moments of period style.

Here Riegl mobilized the perceptual categories already being explored by contemporaries such as Wölfflin and, later on, the Gestalt school: touch and vision, opticality and tactility, figure and ground. These categories develop independently but in a determinate play of forms, a configuration which would later on be characterized as a perceptual structure and which can also be grasped as the embodiment of a specific "spiritual" worldview, or, in other words, a distinctive metaphysical coordination of body, spirit and world. But there is also a Hegelian movement in what might at first seem a simple variety of perceptual *agencements*.

> [Riegl's conception of] artistic development would be incomprehensible without a basis in specific formal devices by which Riegl thought the work of art made manifest signs of touch and vision. The most important is the pattern-ground relationship. In the *Grammar*, touch and vision correspond straightforwardly to pattern and ground. Egyptians in the time of Ramses omitted ground, crowding their patterns together on the wall to represent solidity; classical Greeks used only enough ground to set off the pattern, and monotheistic Christians disguised the difference between pattern and ground, in their metalwork the viewer sees the glittering lights and shadows of an optical surface, representing the most immaterial (*unwesentlichste*), ungraspable (*unfaßbarste*) reality, "as ungraspable as the spiritual world power."[2]

When we come to built space, however, this interplay of sensory categories will become a differential of perceptions in which the longitudinal experience of the basilica will stand in dialectical contrast to the centered spaces of buildings like the Pantheon or the extraordinary temple of Minerva Medica, until both are united in the Christian structure of nave and transept. It seems to me likely that it is this differentiation of perceptual experiences, like the operation of distinct bundles of muscles and nerves beneath the surface of the skin, which must have initially fascinated Benjamin: their differential interplay, indeed, forms the basis for the reading of his "spatial sentences" I proposed in an earlier chapter. I also like the conjecture that he would have been fascinated by Riegl's later work on collective Dutch portraiture, such as Rembrandt's *Night Watch*, for a formal innovation in which the then-novel bourgeois

---

2   Margaret Olin, *Forms of Representation in Alois Riegl's Theory of Art*, University Park: Penn State University Press, 1992, 137.

portrait is itself "*aufgehoben*" into a pathbreaking new formal expression of the collective, the revolutionary Dutch democracy.

What is inconsistent in Riegl with Benjamin's view of history, however, is the rather Hegelian progression of his moments of perceptual combination (or *Stilwollen*) toward some Renaissance "synthesis" in which all their distinctive features are subsumed. Here, what Benjamin may have taken as an emphasis on the uniqueness and exceptionality of the "late Roman *Stilwollen*" turns out rather to be a conception of this period as a transition in a sequence: a conception of historical time which Benjamin would not admit, substituting for its horizontality his own suggestion of the dialectical kinship (or "elective affinity") between the late-Roman moment and Weimar Expressionism, a vertical and disjunctive echo or similitude.

2

He traveled a great deal, but often to spaces in which he could live cheaply and write (Ibiza) or talk (Capri; Svenborg). The cities, however, were places one could explore, on the model of the "*promenade surréaliste*" (crystallized in the historical figure of the *flâneur*), or which one could provisionally organize in local sorties—the search for rare books, the strategic setting of interviews (Gide, the meetings of the Collège de sociologie, Koenigstein), the hunt for prostitutes (an omnipresent figure in his works). He lived, however, in two major capital cities, Berlin and Paris—and the daily experience of such environments is quite different from the flash visit, it demands other forms of representation. With Berlin, the city in which he grew up, he made two attempts, the final one opting for the unique spectrum of childhood to sort out the relevant moments. With Paris, whose perceptual experience is complicated by innumerable historical and literary layers, it was eventually by way of the choice of the historical level that he sought to grasp its essence as a city, each archival probe widening out further and further, their expectations remaining among the most impressive things he ever wrote. Two other cities, however, stand out in particular—Moscow and Naples (the Marseilles piece and other sketches remaining a series of notes).

These cityscapes are not easy reading: masses of detail assault the reader with a precision that demands a response at the same level of concentration or *Geistesgegenwart*. Nor is the term "masses" chosen innocently, either: it is one of those Benjaminian code words which alerts one to subterranean and categorial activity. As we have seen, Baudelaire anticipated him in this discovery of sheer number as a category. Number in Benjamin encompasses the masses, mass production, abstraction (allegory) and the multiple as well as multiplicity. Yet just those masses of sensory, even empirical detail—items of watchful perception—represent hours of material labor to be taken into account in the assessment of Benjamin's "production." To be sure, they mark the alertness of the *flâneur*, at least in his Benjaminian appearance, but they are not merely idle looking or the practice of curiosity, they are observed *in order to be written down*; and this distinguishes them from the contents of a leisure hour. Each directed gaze is a sentence in the making, a formulation already virtual and implicit; the writing is already being done with the movements of the eye.

At that point, they are consigned, fully formed, to the long-held notebook in which they are stored. But that implies a second round of labor, a second commitment of labor time, in which they are to be sorted out and reclassified. For, in fact, each of the paragraphs of the two great essays in question has a thematic unity, all the beggars here, all the items for sale on the street over there, before the ordering of the paragraphs can take form.

As for the essays themselves, however, I must feel that we cannot adequately approach them without realizing how many tripartite sequences lie hidden away in Benjamin's works, intentional or not. I have often insisted on the tripartite relationship between "The Storyteller," "On Some Motifs in Baudelaire," and the essay on technical reproduction. These sketch out a periodization, thus setting in place—in a work that openly denounces "homogeneous time" and in one way or another imposes an attention to the present—a deeper periodization scheme: the latter unobtrusively reestablishing that longer temporality of the past/present/future, the before and after, that the emphasis on the phenomenological present rebukes and indeed seeks to discredit. But the tripartite periodization is not merely chronological, it has its own internal logic, which may well be a survival of older cyclical schemes.

Peu importe! The essays on the city also fall into just such a sequence, as we shall see below: Naples, Berlin and Moscow are not just swarming experiences each in their own right, they are moments in the rise and fall of urban individualism, which is also to say in the use of the first person, something Benjamin always advised against. Yet it is in the most harshly judged "bourgeois" city culture of the three—Berlin, with its nineteenth-century interiors and overstuffed furniture—that Benjamin most fully deployed a well-nigh Proustian rhetoric of the self and of personal, even private, experience.

3

We have two versions each of the essays on Berlin and Moscow: one is the *Berlin Chronicle* of 1932, whose distinction from the *Berlin Childhood* (1938) lies in the latter's exclusion of any material beyond that of "childhood" as such. The other is the fortuitous survival of the personal journal Benjamin kept during his 1927 stay in Moscow and from which he culled the definitive published essay.

In fact, the surviving notebook[3] offers a useful working demonstration of that supplementary labor required to remove all traces of subjectivity. (Is this the real meaning of Brecht's "Verwisch die Spuren"?) The trip to Moscow, in all its lived and existential reality, was obviously a hectic experience of frustration, frantic scheduling, obsessive love in all its desperation, professional obligation (the play to be seen tonight, locating a translator, finding time to write up the notes): a schedule as exhausting for the unintentional reader as for the subject himself, here disclosed against his will. Indeed, nothing is quite so shocking as the contrast between the seemingly neutral catalogue of impressions that constitutes the published essay and the frenzied and desperate private journal, which affords a glimpse into his relations with Asja (she is in a clinic) and her husband (with whom he is obliged to lodge), a whole misery compressed by an urgent schedule of meetings and cultural events, exacerbated by the traditional Muscovite indifference to punctuality. This Benjamin, sweating, in full anxiety, scrambling to catch buses or tramways back and forth across the city, has been utterly effaced from the essay—and Asja, his reason for being there, has also vanished. It is true that for Benjamin himself, Asja and Bolshevism are somehow one and the same; to underscore her role, however, is not to psychologize or

---

3   *Moscow Diary*, Cambridge: Harvard University Press, 1986.

depoliticize his motives or his essay, which remains a historical and political intervention, as we shall see.

But in the finished essay "Moscow" (II, 22–46; IV, 316–48; VI, 292–409), this harried experience—which one hesitates to assimilate to the *Schockerlebnisse* of the Baudelairean city but which is here transformed, not into the wisdom of *Erfahrung* but into the saleable commodity of the journalistic "copy"—becomes an objective analogon: it is transferred to the Slavic but also the revolutionary temperament (Benjamin is cautious here and clearly does not want to deal in culturalisms) and becomes the well-known "*Seuchas!*" (Right away! In a minute!) of any self-respecting waiter in a Soviet restaurant; it becomes the long lines of the shoppers, the hours passed in the waiting rooms. But they are not empty hours, that futile waiting; they are here and elsewhere in Benjamin transformed into an aesthetic of filled space. One searches the stylistic handbooks for the usable term for this, the very space of the Chirrugueresque, that Baroque so handily adopted by its Aztec workmen in the first churches of the Conquest and scarcely at all theorized in the Baroque book, unless we range it under the heading of the irreversible decay of nature and its temporality, an uninterrupted ephemerality observed without sympathy by the now-absent transcendent divinity of the Counter-Reformation. For here, truly, time becomes space, and this Moscow daily life lived from morning to night without a moment's respite becomes, for the reader of this spatial essay as well as for the foreign visitor, the city itself. The temporal theme and focus, the topic of Soviet temporality, becomes the very space of the written object and of what one cannot hesitate to call the Benjaminian work of art.

Politically, however, it means something else. To be sure, Benjamin has some critiques, some lessons, for his Soviet hosts, and they mainly consist in a warning about the Western aesthetic ideas they have imported along with Western technology, imagining the former to be as equally "advanced" and "progressive" as the latter, whereas they turn out to be nothing quite so dusty and boring as yesterday's outdated academic dogmas and clichés. Don't try to catch up with an antiquated traditionalist West in this area, he warns them; in reality, here, as elsewhere, you yourselves are the future, with your new notions of popular production and workers' writings (theorized by Tretyakov).

As far as daily life goes, however, Benjamin's essay (if not his journal) maintains its aloof dialectical stance, beyond all banal judgments of good and evil. He probably senses how unattractive this regimented life will strike his bourgeois readership back home. No matter! He is not interested in the cheap Utopian propaganda of the future, of the promises of the "*lendemains qui chantent*." He wants his despised German compatriots to feel what a post-individualistic life will look like; how radically different it is from their complacencies and luxuries. That is indeed the message here, the meaning of this so patiently and painstakingly pieced-together mosaic. This is the meaning of the text, the moral of the travelogue. It is the painful breaking, resetting, of the bone of habit, unpleasant work on the changing of habitual perception, the production of a new consciousness, the construction of a new subjectivity, a virtual cultural revolution, in which time and space alike are transformed.

But if that is the case, then what is Naples doing here? For it is this same Asja who is credited with the coauthorship of the essay on Naples (I, 414–21; IV, 307–16). Perhaps her name is the sign for the absence of an earlier version of this essay, the mark of an achieved synthesis of subjectivity and objectivity. Yet the answer is virtually given in the question itself: Naples is then the pre-bourgeois life, juxtaposed with the post-bourgeois life of Moscow and the revolution. The famous Neapolitan "porosity" (on which so much ink has been spilled, a rather un-Benjaminian theoretical concept, perhaps to be attributed to Asja herself) means a collective life before individuality, its essence being theatricality, a life in front of others (as in ancient Greece), in which public and private have become indistinguishable: promoted into a theoretical concept its very concreteness is unable to sustain.

Like "aura," indeed the term "porosity" summons the spatial to the service of the cognitive and the historical; but aura belongs to the philosophical and indeed to the more narrowly aesthetic realm, while porosity tends toward social relations. "[So] dispersed, porous and commingled is private life . . . [that] the true laboratories of this great process of intermingling are the cafes." This sense of the overlap, the interpenetration, the fading of boundaries, is perhaps the optical illusion of the Northern visitors, who need their differentiated categories in order to perceive and articulate their absence in Naples. Thus, paganism flourishes within Catholicism in the great religious processions (as in Rossellini's *Journey to Italy*), where there is everywhere "interpenetration of day and night, noise and peace, outer light and inner darkness, street and home." The porosity of the stone is thus a material in which matter and emptiness meet and mix, just as already figural openings in the walls permit a mingled vision of inside and outside.

I believe that this evocation of a new kind of de-differentiated space is calculated to summon up, for the modern or bourgeois tourist, the feeling of an epoch before individuality, in which, as Riegl might say (but reversing his own progression), the freestanding object is not yet isolated from its background and context, and it is the sheer fabric of the latter, filled space (the aesthetic of "nature abhorring a vacuum") that reigns supreme. The masses of people who fill exterior as well as interior spaces are no doubt ancestors of Baudelaire's modern nineteenth-century Parisian crowds, who play so crucial a role in Benjamin's aesthetic and political imagination; but they are, so to speak, the real thing, collectivity as it existed before modernity, a glimpse into the premodern past.

This is why the Neapolitan excess must be so sharply distinguished from the Muscovite experience—equally a filled space of populations and activities which interpenetrate each other and offer a stream of life, day and night. The silence of winter no doubt adds an escapement, a pause, an empty space of cold, to the Muscovite plenitude; but "the eye [remains] infinitely busier than the ear." Meanwhile winter brings green ("the supreme luxury of the Moscow winter") to the city: it marks the presence of the forest within the urban, the interpenetration of land-scape and built space, of the medieval, no doubt. It also awakens new dimensions of existence: sweets, but above all the sharp zakuska, no doubt accompanied by vodka, "Moscow's most secret winter lust," which enriches life "by a dimension."

What differentiates the Russian overpopulation from that of Naples, however, is the suffusion of this space by time, by temporal urgency. It is not only that socialist "existence . . . requires that a stand be taken a hundred times each day": "one is tempted to say that minutes are a cheap liquor of which they can never get enough, that they are tipsy with time." What does not exist in Naples is the Plan: "Bolshevism has abolished private life." "Indoors one only camps, and usually the scanty inventory is merely a residue of petty bourgeois possessions that have a far more depressing effect because the room is so sparsely furnished." If "Naples" was the record of an encounter with the past, "Moscow" is the experience of struggle to emerge into a post-bourgeois, post-individualistic future: it is not always lovely or picturesque but always exciting, and

Benjamin's sentences, from which quotable aphorisms here emerge incessantly to dizzying effect, record the stimulation of the encounter (nor is the text without its criticisms, particularly of the attempts to imitate Western culture; but its cool objectivity lifts it, if not above good and evil, then at least above propaganda and the partisan judgment). Naples, meanwhile, offers the stage on which the body retains its characteristic repertoire of "expressive" Southern gesturality in private as well as in the street (as though the "private" here were not the street in the first place), the exhibit of the emotions of what will only later on become bourgeois subjectivity (Adorno's "intérieur"), retaining their initially operatic theatricality: a society of the spectacle indeed, but this time (unlike Debord's somber inventory of a well-nigh postapocalyptic capitalist simulacrum-society) a joyous chaos, a denser time and space, but of a radically different type than Moscow's snowy version, yet both sharing this: it is not bourgeois life, it is not the silence of the privileged bourgeois city streets, the absence of crowds (or masses!), the individualism of the isolated citizens or bourgeois subjects as they go about their private business: Nothing private! No poetic solitudes! No empty time or unpeopled space!

4

At this point, then, it becomes clear where Berlin itself gets positioned: it is that space of individualism between precapitalist, well-nigh archaic life and this clamorous Soviet future. It is the silence of petty-bourgeois individualism, the empty streets of bourgeois life, the overstuffed furniture and wall-to-wall decorations of the bourgeois apartment and family, a type of space already anticipated in *One-Way Street* and celebrated in the detective story as a genre: "The bourgeois interior of the 1860s to the 1890s—with its gigantic sideboards distended with carvings, the sunless corners where potted palms sit, the balcony embattled behind its balustrade, and the long corridors with their singing gas flames—fittingly houses only the corpse. 'On this sofa the aunt cannot but be murdered' " (I, 447; IV, 89). One is reminded of Oscar Wilde's description of a fashion ad for a lady's hat whose caption read, "With this style, the mouth is worn slightly open." Bourgeois individualism seems to reach its apogee with the disappearance of the individuals themselves. Berlin can be adequately conveyed only through its objects, a spectrum which demands the view of the child. But what can be the image of a city consisting of so many stacked interiors, like something postmodern constructed entirely of shipping containers? Is there then some second kind of city poised over against that of the first two cities, which both mean something, albeit antithetical moments of a historical process? Sometimes it is simply emptiness, silence, streets without people but as snow-covered and as cold as Moscow? Can a city of words like *One-Way Street*, through which one can carve a street of symbolic storefronts, constitute a meaningful montage of attractions, despite the fact that the crowds, the masses, of the other two cities have here dwindled simply to the statistical and sociological dimensions of "Germans in the great inflation"?

How to characterize this alternate city form in which no one seems to live? The first image is that of the *étui*, the plush-lined case in which you carry a precious item, such as an antique watch, a pen, an expensive pipe, perhaps, and whose lid you close to protect it. But these *étuis* are empty, they are precisely the plush-lined apartments, themselves full of Victorian (we might here say Wilhelminian) furnishings, but (as so much later in Georges Perec's *La Vie: mode d'emploi*) emptied of their previous inhabitants, who have only left their traces, the outlines of their forms, on the velvet lining.

This would be the place to insert a disquisition on rooms in Benjamin. Rooms are unsurprisingly a fundamental element of human experience, the problem being that there seems so little to say about them—whence Benjamin's admiration for Adorno's famous "intérieur" chapter in his Kierkegaard book. Their significance is only heightened by the lowered ceiling of the Baudelairean sky, which, at its most oppressive, turns the very out-of-doors into a vast room in its own right. The *flâneur* feels this, whose "'perfected art' . . . includes a knowledge of 'dwelling.' The primal image of 'dwelling,' however, is the matrix or shell, that is, the thing which enables us to read off the exact figure of whatever lives inside it. Now, if we recollect that not only people and animals, but also spirits and above all images can inhabit a place, then we have a tangible idea of what concerns the *flâneur* and of what he looks for" (II, 264; III, 196). Yet, like everything else, this primal category of the room and of the building made up of its nested habitations is menaced by the transparency of light and glass stridently heralded by the architectural modernists. One may even go so far as to maintain (Benjamin does not) that Le Corbusier sought to abolish the very category of the room with his "free plan" (just as his *pilotis* aimed to repeal that of the street). At any rate, the mixed feelings this development is bound to have aroused in Benjamin go a long way toward explaining his fascination with rooms for good and ill alike: Goethe's "cell" in Weimar (II, 150; IV, 354) and the bourgeois apartment or *étui*—that plush-lined container in which "*étui-menschen*" dwell like so many pieces of jewelry or expensive cigars.

Yet these are modern city-dwellers, and surely their existence could be expressed less metaphorically? Despite its immense influence, not least on Benjamin's "Motifs in Baudelaire," Georg Simmel's vision of a big city, whose inhabitants are reeling with the minute shocks of daily industrial life, is less appropriate than these hives made up of separated compartments—a true estrangement-effect for a condition in which, collectivity having disappeared, the forms of the alienated adults can only confuse the picture and offer an ideological appearance, a mask, behind which the truth of such existence is concealed. Benjamin's hatred of the family, perhaps of his own family and his paterfamilias, is far more openly captured by the French literature of the period, in which a genuine bourgeoisie has come into full existence, and in which Gide's great cry, "*Familles, je vous hais!,*" is the omnipresent echo and leitmotif. In Germany, the lateness of the *Gründerzeit* makes for a flowering of corruption only momentarily dispelled by inflation, with the result that the nostalgic German must return to an earlier period, its space epitomized by the simplicity of Weimar, with its productive silence ("To think that today the quietness of such hours can be found only at nights" [II, 149; IV, 353]). Benjamin dedicated his *German Men and Women*, a collection of letters from those older years, to the evocation of this other Germany, which the *Nazizeit* had virtually effaced: a fourth Utopian space, perhaps, and a handicraft bourgeoisie (as in Keller's Swiss novellas), honorable and free from class guilt. The Berlin sketches propose two different directions for underscoring these paradoxes. The first is the hidden triptych, of which there are a number scattered throughout these texts; it would be Benjaminian to invent a game for finding them, like faces hidden in a landscape (here it is, Berlin, which is the midterm of the series of city portraits that include Naples and Moscow).

But the two Berlin series—*Chronicle* and *Childhood*—also offer a different material for interrogation: a vertical or superimposed one, which it would not be a good idea to study chronologically, in a scholarly project, as first draft and definitive revision (an analogous warning to the one extended for the other pair—the *Moscow Diary* and the definitive essay simply called "Moscow"). It is true that the *Chronicle* is filled with topics which will be elaborated more fully as episodes in *Childhood*, sometimes four or five of them in a single paragraph of the earlier work (as with the trip to the grandmother's apartment). It will be more instructive, however, to read them as work in two different and distinct genres, two types of discourse. The *Chronicle* begins by proposing four or five distinct ways of mapping a city (and also—a characteristically Benjaminian superimposed and, as it were, secondary motivation—the guides who led him through each map). But the text, even as it begins with that intention (and perhaps precisely because it begins with that intention), at once lapses into chronology and the continuity of a life or, better still, of a Bildungsroman.

The second text (and we have several versions of that as well!) settles on the *One-Way Street* format: a series or sequence of formally independent and thereby autonomous items, about which we must not say they are fragments; nor really episodes, either; glosses too finished to be described as sketches; "phenomenological exercises" is the cumbersome formulation I would have preferred; or numbers in a montage of attractions perhaps too hastily juxtaposed. What comes to mind, wrongly but irresistibly, is that they are all meditations on objects and thereby themselves become something like separate objects; whereas the *Chronicle* keeps trying (fitfully) to tell something like the story of a life, a set of events. This last impulse is deliberately blocked by Benjamin's new title, which restricts these exercises to the realm of childhood, about which it then has suggestive things to tell us insofar as childhood, as subject and object alike, will fade in and out of Benjamin's writing career. We might, however, observe that both kinds of texts steer toward a common ending, a common conclusion (that of the section called "The Moon," in *Childhood*, of which a version is also to be found in the *Chronicle*) and which occupies a place not dissimilar to that of "To the Planetarium" in *One-Way Street*.

But perhaps we can make a more pertinent beginning with this observation, namely that the *Chronicle* is again and again interrupted by moments of literary reflexivity, in which, as though repeatedly questioning its own generic status, it raises issues of style and discourse. (These will only recur, in *Childhood*, on the mode of an acting out, as we shall see.) The very opening, on maps and guides, might already figure here (and has) but can be restricted to a single enigmatic comment: "the two forms in which alone this [the cityscape] can legitimately—that is, with a guarantee of permanence—be done had I not forsworn the attempt to equal the first as firmly as I hope one day to realize the second" (II, 597; VI, 467). The first form is immediately identified with Proust (whom he translated); the second remains obscure—it may be the map (which we might want today to identify with Franco Moretti's work), but a number of alternatives are also given, including a mysterious designation ("the fourth guide," in which not a person, but rather the rare ability to get lost in a city, is evoked), to the point at which it seems fruitless to theorize these possibilities further.

But if these texts remain, in reality as at the outset, merely twofold alternative strategies, then a later reflection proposes itself for our clarification: "Reminiscences, even extensive ones, do not always amount to an autobiography. And these [he means the topics of the *Chronicle*] certainly do not, even for the Berlin years that I am exclusively concerned with here. For autobiography has to do with time, with sequence and what makes up the continuous flow of life. Here [again, in the *Chronicle*], I am talking of a space, of moments and discontinuities" (II, 612; VI, 488).

It is once again the dialectic of the line and the point, whose paradoxes and incommensurabilities go back at least as far as Zeno. As might be expected, this is an asymmetrical dialectic, whose continuous term is easier to nail down than its opposite, as indeed he does here. Continuity is narrative, it is autobiography and what will come to be defined, after Bergson, as "homogeneous time." But the form taken by its opposite number is less clear-cut, even though it is here called on to define the (new) aesthetic Benjamin: break or cut, gap between the texts or the sketches, the routine between events, boredom, nonhistory—none of these noncontinuities holds the key to what will in *Childhood* become the content and the form of a different kind of writing. Nor is it hard to see why: the point is an entity without linear content—it cannot define a form without taking on linearity, albeit a unique new linearity of its own without much in common with what has been attributed to its opposite number. Here, the word that tends to impose itself—far from the Romantic term, overused to exhaustion, of the "fragment," let alone the "sketch," the "impression," the "memory," which all carry their own ideologies with them—the term that seems most appropriate for the moment turns out to be again the "episodic," and at once it awakens its kinship with the analogous problems of the Brechtian aesthetic and the latter's "epic" or narrative drama, the separate numbers of the music hall series, the vignette, whose logic extends not in the direction of the story but rather in that of the anecdote, the *fait divers*, the quip, the twist, the pratfall, the Jolles "simple form." Still, are these not to be considered narratives of some kind as well, and do we not here confront once again the great divide between the tale and its scenes, the story of a life and its incidental peripeties, the philosophy of history and the swarm of individual events that make it up and inflect its meaning and its direction?

Benjamin in fact uses none of these terms; his is a far more idiosyncratic word, with its own logic and destiny within his work as a whole and whose untranslatability has systematically misled his commentators. I mean the word *Bild*, for which the term "image" is utterly unsatisfactory, nor does the simple "picture" do much for us, either. Still, the reader will already have begun to guess what is at stake here, when the much-debated keyword "*dialektisches Bild*"—"dialectical image," "dialectic at a standstill"—comes to mind. We will return to it. *Bild* would indeed be to the Brechtian episode what the freeze-frame of the tableau was to those eighteenth-century dramas that reveled in it, the plot on stage suddenly immobilized into the lineaments of a famous painting. But is that then what *Berlin Childhood* wants to be, a picturebook, an album of well-chosen photos?

The Proustian reference in this same paragraph refutes it, which describes the procedure of the master in some detail, however enigmatic it may remain:

What Proust began so playfully became awesomely serious. He who has once begun to open the fan of memory never comes to the end of its segments [the German says "*neue Glieder, neue Stäbe*"]. No image satisfies him for he has seen that it can be unfolded, and only in its folds does the truth reside—that image [*Bild*], that taste, that touch for whose sake all this has been unfurled and dissected; and now remembrance progresses from small to smallest details, from the smallest to the infinitesimal, while what it encounters in these microcosms grows ever mightier. Such is the deadly game that Proust began so dilettantishly, in which he will hardly find more successors than he needed companions. (II, 597; VI, 467)

The two footnotes required here would first brush off any knee-jerk recall of Deleuze's Leibnizian folds and mediations (to which, to be sure, in the fullness of time and mature reflection, it might be interesting to return), and would gloss Benjamin's nontrivializing characterization of Proust as a dilettante with the reminder that much of Proust's style and even content was first developed and perfected in his gossipy letters to the various society ladies of his *connaissance*. The temporal warning, however—out of this playful banter a "deadly game" will inevitably emerge—is surely an encouragement to himself and a prediction of the emergence, from these scattered memories, of the *Berlin Childhood* as such.

But this is not a bad place to pause and reevaluate Benjamin's relationship to the great predecessor; nor is "The Image of Proust" a bad text on which to perform such an exercise, inasmuch as Benjamin now carries about him a slight odor of Proustianism, as a token of his translation of this work. (In fact, he felt increasingly distant about Proust, resented the time spent on the rather mechanical labor of translation, and feared contamination by Proust's style as well as of his ideologies—involuntary memory, aestheticism, and so on.)

The essay itself will no doubt disappoint Proustians, especially recent converts, who are full of enthusiasm about the concrete detail, the experience of reading, the characters themselves and their destinies. But Benjamin's is little more than an "appreciation" (something like an obituary, but for the work itself rather than its physical author) and is content to isolate two or three distinct impressions—or "images"—the essayist has formed of the novelist.

What we can first select is a long concluding paragraph to the first section (of three), in which, for those alert to them, virtually all the themes of the Benjaminian corpus make their fleeting appearance. A note on happiness and the past—a strangely atemporal, "Eleatic" happiness—recalls the mechanism of dreams, which turn on the fundamental Benjaminian category of similarity. Children know this—the Benjaminian interfolded stocking appears as evidence—and Surrealism is not far behind; all of which culminates in the *Bild*: Benjamin has used a pertinent observation about Proust to put his favorite themes and issues through their paces.

In a second section, we observe an extraordinary, and characteristic, conversion process at work, in which ideas are gradually transformed into characters. From the "physiology of chatter" (*Gerede*—at any rate, gossip)—and physiology itself would lead us on to character, the hidden theme of class that will emerge as full-blown class struggle at the very end of this section—we seem to move into psychology proper: "the vice of curiosity"—which impels this outsider's often malicious, often humorous, voyeuristic "observation" of a specific closed social group into which he has managed to insinuate himself. This character trait comes up abruptly against another, unrelated one, namely flattery, the Proustian speech act par excellence, particularly intolerable and even eventually insupportable in the writer's letters. Two distinct sides to Proust's character or his "physiognomy"? No, for Benjamin they will combine and produce a specific character formation: the writer as the domestic servant—and suddenly a whole new side of Proust's work is illuminated (like the forgotten staircase in the "Overture" to *Swann's Way*). Will it also become a Benjaminian character? Probably not: he himself was much too abrupt for flattery, except, perhaps, for a seductive reinforcement of ties to his closest friends (or his most necessary ones) and too proud to be anyone's servant. He deals with the characterization poetically, however, substituting for his own characteristic figural flourish one of Maurice Barrès: "un poète persan dans une loge de portière"—the Arabian nights of the concierge.

Still, the domestic servant, however magically embellished by this association, has another metamorphosis in store: that of the detective, a figure Benjamin associates with the *flâneur*. And it is as detective that Benjamin himself will return to this aristocratic remnant into which he has introduced himself, in order to deliver the final diagnosis: they are pure consumers (parasites) whose unconscious stylistic and existential effort lies in concealing the traces of production. Here we have the historical materialist speaking.

In a brief final section, then, having begun the essay with an insistence on the crucial role of forgetting in Proustian remembrance, he now, in passing, associates it with rejuvenation, before concluding on style and illness, the relationship of the Proustian sentence to asthma and suffocation. This leads us to a "physiology of style" in which the image itself undergoes a radiography: its memory, at first visual and throwing up a catalogue of faces, proves in fact in its bodily depths to harbor smell as "the sense of weight experienced by someone who casts his nets into the sea of *temps perdu*" (II, 247; II, 323): not a novel insight for readers of Baudelaire, but one strikingly reabsorbed—*umfunktioniert*, might we say?—into a more properly Benjaminian stylistics. Predictably, the latter will fulfill its final obligation—the concluding flourish—by identifying Proust's sickbed with Michelangelo's scaffolding in the Sistine Chapel!

Still, we have not yet, with this lesson in micrology, come to the end of the formal thoughts that intermittently punctuate the not-so-early unfinished text which is the *Berlin Chronicle*. We have not yet, for example, touched on the august category of the event as such—but it is there, patiently waiting for us. First in the form of catastrophe: "the most remarkable of all the street images [*Strassenbilder*] from my early childhood . . . was (this must have been about 1900) a completely deserted stretch of road upon which ponderous torrents of water continuously thundered down" (II, 597; VI, 468). The notion of catastrophe will, however, undergo a good deal of refinement in the next decade of Benjamin's life.

Then, too, there is the question of childhood itself (and its accompanying and still Proustian problem of memory as such). Leaving aside other considerations—such as collecting and fatherhood—it is, in the Benjaminian context, above all to be considered an estrangement-effect, indeed the most fundamental estrangement-effect of them all, and perhaps the deepest affinity to Brecht. Not the latter's children, whom Benjamin liked, not the theme as such (in which Brecht himself had little or no interest); rather, above all, the supreme value attributed to a mode of transformation which had the power of revealing history itself at work. In the dedication of the *Chronicle* to Stefan, if not in the far more tortuous justification of *Childhood* which I have already discussed, one is entitled to recognize a simple Baudelairean project of retaining the "image" of a city first lost to history, and then, far more definitively and irrevocably, lost to *them*. But the V-effect is something else, and it is scarcely some mere instrument for manufacturing souvenirs.

This can serve as a kind of analytic instrument, like an X-ray machine, a mechanism of demystification that, above all else, turns objects back into processes. So it is that over and over again the life of the child is revealed to be a superimposed series of treasure hunts, in which the longed-for object proves, when found, to be nothing at all (the fable of the socks rolled up onto themselves). This is not to be confused with appropriation, "possession in memory" (II, 632; VI, 516), or annexation "to my domain" (II, 634; VI, 518; I), something perhaps closer to Marx's distinction between possession and property. No, what happens here is the substitution, for the object as such, of the desire and search for the object or, in other words, for life itself. This will be, as we shall see, the achievement of *Berlin Childhood*, to have dramatized this substitution in the very movement of the sentences themselves.

As with Proust's experience of the great actress la Berma (Sarah Bernhardt), this revelation is also associated with the theater, but with conclusions that seem to me to be utterly distinct from those of the master. In Proust, the dissatisfaction with the "real" performance of the great actress is ultimately called upon to drive home the lesson that there is no "real" first time of experience, but that reality happens only a second time—and not in the memory of it, but in its writing.

In Benjamin, on the contrary, expressing the experience does not result in the disintegration of experience altogether—a category that, for all its vicissitudes, remains central to Benjamin—but only in its restructuration. What the young theatergoing Benjamin discovers is that the value of the experience lies in expectation: not the final achievement of the desire, but rather the time of waiting, the time of anticipation itself, as though the point and its rupture led back to the reality of the line as such, rather than its dissolution. I learned, he tells us (II, 625; VI, 506), "how much more significant and enduring the anticipation of an event can be than what actually ensues." Benjamin's modernism is condensed and concentrated in this phrase, and it teaches us to approach the moments of seeming fulfillment in his work with some suspicion, suggesting a new option: not breaking through time with the static instant, but rather introducing into that bad "homogeneous" time of Bergsonian fabrication an altogether distinct and more secret time of waiting and of boredom ("boredom is the dream bird that hatches the egg of experience" [III, 149; II, 146]). Now *Bild* as a static image or picture is called into question, and as for aura itself, the perpetual distance it maintains even at the very heart of proximity may well turn out to be what gives it its value, by forever forestalling some absolute possession or identification. It therefore seems possible that the overt condemnation of narrative in his early warning against autobiographical discourse may not rule out another (storytelling) way of handling

the rather different temporality embedded in all these folds and perceptions of childhood experience.

Before we identify the discursive prerequisites of this other kind of
narrative time, it is worth preparing our reception of it by once again
warning against psychology as such, and in particular of observing the
ways in which *Chronicle* must divest itself of the urge to psychologize
what we may be tempted to think of as effects of memory. It is telling
that his one philosophical effort (the Bergsonian formulas of "our
waking habitual, everyday self" . . . "our deeper self" [II, 633; VI, 516])
breaks off in recognition of its failure as writing; and is then reconstructed more successfully as the room which owes its immortality to
the father's news of a family death. Perhaps Benjamin meant this to
serve provisionally as an ending and conclusion: the reported death that
ends childhood? It will be rewritten twice again in *Childhood* but there
removed from this terminal function. For it is a death twice told, and the
second version of this second version tells us why (he had already
blurted out the punchline in the *Chronicle* version): the father's omission of the cause of death, namely syphilis. The bourgeois security of the
house, apartment, room is here demonstrated to conceal, hypocritically,
the grown-up reality of prostitution, or in other words sexuality as such.
That demonstration keeps the memory (the image, the *Bild*) of the room
alive, through many different childhood *déménagements* (it is a revelation which will also, along with childhood itself, put an end to family
and Judaism).[4]

But this virtual allegorization of the room—not only by way of the
father, but above all through the dead cousin and his unmentionable
disease—puts us on the track of a final distinction between *Chronicle*
and *Childhood* which takes us back to the very beginning of this discussion and the difference between autobiographical narrative (homogeneous time) and that enigmatic *Bild* which will be called upon to
replace it.

For all of this culminates in a discovery of which Benjamin was proud
enough to have repeated it in a correspondence in much the same terms:
"If I write better German than most writers of my generation, it is thanks
to twenty years' observance of one little rule: never use the word 'I'

---

4   See II, 629; VI, 512 and also, in *Berlin Childhood*, "Sexual Awakening" (III, 386;
IV, 251).

except in letters" (II, 603; VI, 475). It is a peculiar remark to introduce into a text whose saturation by the first person is extreme and warrants, as we have seen, no little discomfort about the "autobiographical" qualities which, in the very spirit of this recommendation, he seeks to deny. And I must admit that in my own experience of the twin texts of *Chronicle* and *Childhood*, it is the latter which first struck me as the more objective account, while the former's fidelity to the personal and the intimate justified the subjective aura of its title. My initial impression, then, aroused a perverse suspicion that it was precisely by way of this omission of the "I" that the more mature text achieved its subjectivity, and that Benjamin's discovery lay in the unexpected power of the impersonal to convey the intimate which became an inert, dead letter in subjective and emotive hands.

Such is indeed the very ambiguity of phenomenology itself, which has here several times been associated with Benjaminian Impressionism. For if in an epistemologically oriented, scientistic context of neo-Kantianism, the phenomenological project could stand out so sharply as a regression to the subjective and to that "experience" recovered and valorized by Dilthey,[5] it is perhaps paradoxical to realize, at one and the same time, that Husserl's efforts were nothing if not "objective" in these senses and aimed to bring the most rigorous impersonality to bear on what had hitherto been abandoned to the merely subjective and to experience in its most personal, if not irrational, forms. The truth, however, as so often, does not lie somewhere in between these contradictory judgments but stands resolutely on both sides, in antagonistic mirror images: phenomenology was part and parcel of the reaction against late nineteenth-century forms of scientistic Enlightenment at the same time that it pioneered a postsubjectivistic attention to what had until then been considered merely psychological.

But it will be observed that I was wrong in my characterization of Benjamin's two texts, for the first person appears—statistically—in ever greater quantities in the sentences of the second, finished text than in its first, more narrative and autobiographical version. For the proud warning against first-person discourse is followed by a muddled explanation that finally clarifies everything: it turns out that what Benjamin actually discovered was the more intimate relationship between "self"

---

5   Unfortunately he called it *"Erlebnis."*

and place, and that it was not by insistence on the former, but rather by way of a bias through space and locale that his childhood experiences could most authentically be conveyed. (The inseparable relationship between experience and the notion of authenticity was also a fundamental, if equally paradoxical lesson of a phenomenology on its way to existentialism.)

Let's review these findings concisely. The protagonist of a truly autobiographical narrative—the hero of continuities—is a character among other characters. These last—essential to all such narrative discourse— are rigorously to be omitted, as the prefatory paragraph of *Childhood* has already reminded us: "certain biographical features . . . altogether recede in the present undertaking. And with them go the physiognomies—those of my family and comrades alike" (III, 344; VII, 385). (Whence, as we have already seen, the apparent loneliness and isolation of a child who had a true gift for friendship and could be as gregarious on occasion as one likes.)

What remains then, after this well-nigh phenomenological epoche or "reduction," is place and *Bild*, its actors vanished, its streets as empty as a movie set ("Atget's photographs," as we well remember, "seem to register the scene of a crime"). What is the truth sought for in such documentation? What is the crime whose forensic evidence is here assembled and presented? And what does it have to do with experience, childhood or otherwise? The answer lies in the place of Berlin in the cityscape trilogy: the crime is that of bourgeois security, the class privilege of a place of greater safety, the phenomenological or eidetic essence of bourgeois culture itself, which looks a good deal different under this pitiless gaze than it did when an autobiographical voice recounted it. Let a single example suffice:

> For even if the products of the 1870s were much more solid than those of the *Jugendstil* that followed, their most salient trait was the humdrum way in which they abandoned things to the passage of time and in which they relied, so far as their future was concerned, solely on the durability of their materials and nowhere on rational calculation. Here reigned a type of furniture that, having capriciously incorporated styles of ornament from different centuries, was thoroughly imbued with itself and its own duration. Poverty could have no place in these rooms, where death had none. (III, 369; IV, 258)

Even more than the muffled prognosis of the obliteration of this promiscuous nineteenth-century historicism, this wealth of ornamentation from all the styles of history, by the great cleansing of a Giedion iron-and-glass modernism to come, there sounds here the deeper prophecy of the sinking of this whole class under its own weight, and under the blows of the Great War and the Depression that followed it, into the oblivion of deep history and the end of the bourgeoisie and its "civilization."

Benjamin has already denounced the foreshortened perspective of mere style in his own earlier effort, whose pre-Hitlerite wit passes judgment on itself fully as much as on these overstuffed objects:

> The inventory that filled these many rooms—twelve or fourteen— could today be accommodated without incongruity in the shabbiest of secondhand furniture shops. And if these ephemeral forms were so much more solid than those of the *Jugendstil* that superseded them— what made you feel at home, at ease, comfortable, and comforted in them was the nonchalance with which they attached themselves to the sauntering passage of years and days, entrusting their future to the durability of their material alone, and nowhere to rational calculation. Here reigned a species of things that was, no matter how compliantly it bowed to the minor whims of fashion, in the main so wholly convinced of itself and its permanence that it took no account of wear, inheritance, or moves, remaining forever equally near to and far from its ending, which seemed to be the ending of all things. Poverty could have no place in these rooms, where even death had none. They had no place for dying—which is why their owners died in a sanatorium, while the furniture went straight to the secondhand dealer. Death was not provided for in them. (II, 621–2; VI, 500–1)

But it is the worldly and frivolous autobiographical first person who mentions death so often and so blithely; only in the impersonal voice-over of the later text can the hissing of the gas chambers actually be heard. As he rounds out his trilogy with this autobiographical account of a "Berlin childhood," you find yourself regressing, very much in the Surrealists' program, to the descriptions of the way in which the child, unforewarned and not yet an "individual," tries to turn this forbidding space into landscape of play, thereby discovering that Schiller's very aesthetic of play is itself predicated on the Weberian *Entzauberung* of an already bourgeois space.

And Paris? Would not the *Arcades Project* have constituted some monstrous third to Moscow and Naples, some strange monument to the golden age of Offenbach (or at least to Karl Kraus's Offenbach) and a nostalgic Heaven which is also (like Brecht's Hollywood) Hell? Well, yes—and perhaps this explains the secret of its historical emplacement in the past as the "capital of the nineteenth century," the emergent bourgeois century par excellence. Perhaps Baudelaire and his solitary *flâneur* in the midst of the pre-bourgeois crowds is, after all, the perfect figure for the transition from a pre-bourgeois France of the life of the streets to a deserted and monumental Berlin of the childhood condemned to capitalism.

7

The Foremost German Literary Critic

Le but ... c'est d'être considéré comme le premier critique de la littérature allemande.

The goal is that I be considered the foremost critic of German
    literature.

(To Scholem, January 20, 1930 [C359; B505])

1

This status is, in the last instance, a social and institutional one: to be a critic in this (now extinct) sense implies the existence of newspapers with cultural pages and feuilletons, journals with a nonspecialist following (like Gide's *NRF* in France) and other outlets (in Weimar and in the postwar BRG, the state radio stations also reserve a place for cultural commentary). The term also excludes academic status (although some of the George Circle, like Gundolf, would seem to have reached this level by way of scholarly work on the heritage—in the latter's case an influential study of Goethe, which Benjamin detested). Meanwhile "German literature" presumably excludes debates on German-Jewish identity, and on the Hebrew literature and Zionism of the type Scholem constantly presses on him. It must be added, for foreign-language readers, that Benjamin did do his bit for some purely German "tradition" with a number of important texts on Goethe, a long article on the relatively neglected Swiss novelist Gottfried Keller (also a significant figure for Lukács) and work on Romantic criticism and aesthetics. But the one deliberately antifascist intervention here was a collection of letters from the classical period, *German Men and Women*, published in Switzerland in 1936, which sought to promote the image of an alternate German humanism in the face of the new national-socialist revision of the past, by then already thoroughly institutionalized in the schools.

But it cannot be said that he undertook the wholesale construction of a new German tradition as such, which was one of Lukács's ambitions and most noteworthy pedagogical achievements, undoubtedly because, among other things, he harbored the gravest doubts about literary (and art) history as such, as a form and a mode of thought. These perpetuated a notion of historical continuity which, under various guises (the social-democratic notion of progress was a favorite one), furnished him with frequent polemic targets.

The result is that, although his vast learning presupposed an extensive archive of (Western) classics from antiquity to the George School, the last in date of the German literary movements that he was willing to acknowledge, his own private canon was thoroughly unorthodox and could not be characterized as "modernist" in any current sense, even though it betrayed the keenest interest in all the latest literary and cultural developments. But he does not theorize about the history of literary form—no great interest in the novel (he interviews Gide but catches fire only on reading *Adrienne Mesurat*), no historian's eye for the future of poetic language, not even a historical view of the evolution of drama, despite Brecht, despite Asja, Piscator, the Expressionists, Eisenstein, Cocteau, theatrical Berlin, theatrical Paris, Berg's *Wozzeck* and so on. Instead what he found time to write about are what we would today call the margins and the fringes: fairy tales (what a pity he left so little in the way of notes on this future project!), the occult (whether the Kabbalah, dear to Scholem, or astrology and graphology, in which last he counts himself an adept), the old-fashioned tale, from Hebel to Leskov, the fantastic (Scheerbart) and cultural curiosities (like the food fair, see above). Kafka was not, for him, as we have shown, the canonized figure of modern literary culture but a writer of weird and dream-like oddities, a secret hobby you might share with a few friends; while Baudelaire was not a classic, but rather a lifelong intellectual partner, along with Brecht.

I think he would have been happy to consider himself a philologist (his contacts with Auerbach have recently attracted interest), but neither the academic status of this discipline nor the inevitable antiquarianism of its subject matter held any interest for him. To call him simply a writer is to attempt to separate his passionate practice of style from the absence of "creative works" and, indeed, of any ambition to produce them. To call him a cultural journalist is simply, in our present context, to trivialize and vulgarize his work and the centrality of it in his well-nigh metaphysical concern for language as such.

Today he would be characterized (and has been, extensively, in EU propaganda) as a European, and it is certain that he thought in terms of (a few) national cultures. Yet in a letter to Florens Christian Rang (himself the promoter of a German humanist tradition), he observed of a colleague, "he carelessly dedicated himself. . . to what was European . . . For me, on the contrary, circumscribed national characteristics were always central: German or French" (C 214; B 309). But those were his languages, and one's impression is not only that it is language which was central for him rather than literature, but also that this seemingly restrictive "Eurocentric" focus in reality corresponds far more adequately to what one hopes for in an age of globalization than the weakly canonical and classicizing values and categories of a "world-literature" type revival of Goethe's much misunderstood formula. Yet he was a true internationalist, even though his observations center largely on the differences between Germany and France. (To understand how complex these differences then were and how they included everything we now debate under the opposition of West and East, or modern and traditional, the reader is directed to Thomas Mann's voluminous, fraternally internalized debate in the *Reflections of an Unpolitical Man*, another book Benjamin himself detested.) Globalization, world literature and all the rest are already present in these Benjaminian approaches; he took very seriously his role as an analyst of contemporary French developments; and as a sweeping observer of the intellectual and cultural life of his own country, he is matched only by Gramsci.

At any rate, he had very little interest in things English or American; the Soviet East was for him an immense laboratory whose experiments were always historically vital, if not necessarily exemplary, while the Mediterranean world, in which he lived so long (another German tradition, compounded by affordability), only makes its appearance in his work in the person of Calderón and the Baroque. He never managed to acquire a working knowledge of Spanish or Hebrew; although those were for him an existential and not a merely academic matter. We must be very careful to qualify any temptation to use the words modern, modernity and modernism in relationship to Benjamin; they were not particularly in use in this period, except in Baudelaire himself, where most of Benjamin's mentions are to be found. He had, to be sure, all the trappings of the orthodox modernist's fetishization of the New, and the experimental certainly concerned him. But as we shall see, his hostility to the aesthetic and to aestheticization shut him off from what it is now conventional to characterize as the telos of modernism—as one finds it in sequences that lead from Manet through Impressionism to Cézanne; from Mallarmé or Pound to Olsen or Ashbery. Yet he had an unshake-able commitment to the conviction that the present, and history itself, has a logic: "To encompass both Breton and Le Corbusier—that would mean drawing the spirit of contemporary France like a bow, with which knowledge shoots the moment in the heart" (A 459, N 1a,5; V, 573). If Benjamin can be said to have had an "aesthetic," it would be this one of the current situation, which obliges us to inquire into the presupposi-tions involved in the evaluation of French culture as more "advanced" than the German, and also to account for the place of Brecht in this notion of the "advanced."

Another crucial topic that must be postponed has to do with the status of the intellectual as such, a problem of interest to Lenin, and about whose urgency Gramsci (yet another philologist!) was as convinced as Benjamin himself. But what we cannot omit—and what appears wholly unexpectedly in the midst of a discussion of that seem-ingly epiphenomenal matter which is literary criticism—is the question of violence.

2

Literary criticism—critique in general, in its German ambiguity—destroys the work as such; this is the practical basis of Benjamin's hostility to what Adorno will, on the contrary, fetishize as "the auton-omy of the work of art." It will be dramatized over and over again in Benjamin's language as he characterized it as the "wrenching out" (*herausreissen*) of passages, quotations, themes, ideas from that organic context conventional literary criticism admonishes us to respect at all costs. "Destruction" is the keyword here, and Benjamin over and over again emphasizes the very reading of the work as a process of destruction.[1]

The concept, derived from Friedrich Schlegel and Benjamin's early work on German Romantic criticism, in fact posited a two-stage process (the terms of which varied over his career), in which some first stage of textual commentary—the more narrowly philological moment—was followed by a second moment of Kritik in the larger philosophical sense: one of evaluation and ideological judgment (an adjective he almost never uses). Time and history thereby "destroy" the period trappings of the work, leaving its inner core or "truth content," its moment of truth, free of access; the process will be simplified and codified by his Frankfurt School successors. But it is the moment of destruction that interests us here; and it surely has its family likeness with that moment of radical simplification exemplified in contemporary architecture: Adolph Loos's attack on "ornament as crime" and bourgeois degeneracy, Le Corbusier's destruction of wall and street, and the transparency of the latter's deployment of glass, the monumental anti-monumentality of his steel frameworks. Something profound about Benjamin himself might be sensed as we witness him, armed with this militant aesthetic of unadorned purification, plunging into the rank verbiage and flamboyant proliferations of the Baroque.

But violence and destruction, if, as I believe, they take their origin in his linguistic and literary preoccupations, are not without more general consequences for his work and thought. Among Benjamin's early works, indeed his notes and sketches, two more fully elaborated statements stand out in this respect: "On Language as Such and on the Language of Man" (1916, already discussed) and the "Critique of Violence" of 1921, apparently planned as part of a systematic work of political theory (or political theology), unfinished in his lifetime (it has come in for a great deal of postwar interpretation, particularly by Jacques Derrida and Judith Butler).

---

1   Of the commentaries I have read, only Michael W. Jennings's *Dialectical Images*, Ithaca: Cornell University Press, 1987, gives this omnipresent "violence" the kind of attention it deserves.

What characterizes both of these seemingly unrelated and relatively complete essays, and what has rarely been taken into account by their commentators, is that they are neither of them doctrinal statements in their own right but rather textual commentaries, each one an exegesis of another, more central text. This means that both essays must be considered repositories of figures and figural language rather than philosophical texts designed to produce an affirmative terminology. The language essay, for example, is in fact part of an unfinished commentary on the Book of Genesis: it can thus authorize a figural use of the terminology of the Fall, as well as that of the opposition between divine and mythic violence to be found in the second essay.

The latter, meanwhile, is to be read as a meditation on Georges Sorel's epoch-making *Reflections on Violence* (1904), which deals with the central ethical issue in both late nineteenth-century anarchism, where the word terrorist first comes into general circulation, and in Bolshevism and its differentiation from Menshevism and later on, from social democracy. The most durable contribution of Sorel's book was the conception of the "general strike," projected as a new and energizing myth for working-class action. Comparable to Gramsci's distinction between wars of movement and wars of position, it sought to distinguish different kinds of revolutionary actions from the triumphant Leninist kind; in the French syndicalist context, however, its focus was not on an already formed communist base but rather on the situation of labor and its unions, where it seemed urgent to differentiate a different kind of action from the wage-oriented local strike in this or that individual industry. "Strike" here then takes on a different and heightened significance—that of a strike against the whole social order itself, a suspension of all production, comparable to May '68 or to the flash mobs and riots of our own time (and thereby of renewed interest for us as the articulation of a strategy).

Meanwhile, it is important to understand that the term "violence" in this general period (or at least in the one that runs from the late nineteenth century to the Bolshevik revolution) has to do with what was also then called terrorism, but of the then "anarchist" kind, as its anxieties spread across Europe from the various political assassinations and insurrectional attempts to literary versions like Conrad's *Secret Agent*. For Lukács himself, indeed, in the immediate period before the Soviet revolution, the reflection on Dostoyevsky (projected as the culminating chapter of *The Theory of the Novel* but never finished) was to have been a meditation on the unwritten second part of *The Brothers Karamazov*, in which Alyosha, the saintly young protagonist, becomes a "terrorist," assassinates the czar and is executed. But Lukács also wrote at length on violence in Bolshevism, already synonymous, in contrast to the socialist and Menshevik politics from which Lenin had differentiated it, with its already notorious slogan of "armed struggle." (It is known that during the period of the Hungarian Soviet, Lukács, as political commissar during the civil war, bore the responsibility for the execution of a number of deserters.)

Benjamin's text registers this preoccupation obliquely, by strongly affirming his dissent from all ideologies of "nonviolent struggle" of the future Gandhian type (I, 233, 243; VI, 107). But his emphasis is elsewhere, principally on the differentiation of state violence from that of revolutionary groups: it is a well-known distinction, reaffirmed in the 1960s by way of a philosophical distinction between force and violence and a reaffirmation of the inherent violence of the state as such, not only in its foundational act but in its very structure and existence. It is this affirmation which will lead, in recent times, to a preoccupation with state power and an inclination on the left to dismiss all forms of state organization as necessarily repressive in their very structure. This is not the place to renew this far more contemporary left polemic, but I will interrupt my commentary on Benjamin to express the opinion that the concept of violence as such is an incoherent and ideological one, politically demoralizing and best replaced by an emphasis on economic issues rather than those of this or that "Foucauldian" power. Benjamin's essay confirms me in this position by one of its most original assertions, namely that violence only appears as a nameable and thereby theorizable issue after the fact. It is only after the "violent" act has taken place that we are able to identify it as an example of the pseudo-universal called "violence": indeed the "critique" of violence announced in Benjamin's title is meant to warn us that it is, in this sense, violence itself which performs its own auto-critique and unveils itself as ideological in the very moment in which its concept is then able to appear in time as though it had always been present, presiding over the political realm like some eternal Platonic warning.

But Benjamin has other ways of slyly undermining this ideological concept, which always serves as the monkey wrench with which to disrupt political action and commitment of every kind—which is, in other words (as the concept, the very name, of violence), always antipolitical in function. The fundamental move is evident in his opening pages, in which the framework of the analysis is oriented in advance by the radical separation between a philosophical realm of ends and one of means. Benjamin seeks—and it is a radical move which may not at first be apparent in its consequences—to suspend and bracket any consideration of ends as such. He thereby neutralizes all of the judgments on violence which seek, either positively or negatively, to defend or denounce it in terms of ends, results, overarching values and the like, in order to examine what is called violence as pure means, in its own internal structure.

The result is that at once two very different types of violence become visible which may well prove to be two different species of action. These can now be defined by way of their relationship to the law as such: they are lawmaking and law-preserving on the one hand and law-destroying on the other; this grounds the force–violence distinction in a more fundamentally political and structural fashion, inasmuch as law is at one with the very existence of the state (and its destruction is not inconsistent with the Leninist formula of the state's abolition).

But this analysis and clarification is then immediately complicated with another one—namely, with Benjamin's "theological" preoccupation with myth and fate, with mythic violence and so-called divine violence, the punishment for hubris (the examples are the classical punishment of Niobe and the biblical destruction of Korah [I, 248–50; II, 197–200]). To simplify a complicated and obscure discussion, I will propose to read mythic violence as being essentially law-founding (and -preserving) and divine violence, on the contrary, as the punishment for an approach to what the existentialists will call human finitude or, in other words the limits of human life and the boundary drawn by the gods—the domain, in other words, of what Benjamin calls fate and associates with Greek tragedy (as opposed to the Baroque *Trauerspiel*). If so, then a radical disambiguation of the problem is possible, in which the social and political—collective—repressions of the law (and the guilt associated with them, which Nietzsche was among the first to diagnose as a political instrument) can be separated from the purely-individual and existential fate reserved for more purely "natural" issues of finitude and death, of the fact of life and existence in general. To put it in Benjamin's own private

language (language not being an issue in this cycle of essays except insofar as lawbreaking includes fraud, a verbal phenomenon):

> The dissolution of legal violence stems . . . from the guilt of more natural
> life, which consigns the living, innocent and unhappy, to a retribution that
> "expiates" the guilt of mere life—and doubtless also purifies the guilty, not
> of guilt, however, but of law. For with mere life, the rule of law over the
> living ceases. Mythic violence is bloody power over mere life for its own
> sake; divine violence is pure power over all life for the sake of the living.
> The first demands sacrifice; the second accepts it. (I, 250; II, 199–200)

It becomes clear enough that if mythic violence is that of the state and
the law, of the social order and its institutions, then divine violence can
only be the rebuke to these attempts to impose a substantive and normative form on history and time itself. Benjamin thus associates revolutionary violence with that of the divine, insofar as it is intent on destroying the archaic and its regressive continuities: he will insert the image of
the revolutionaries firing on the clock tower in his final theses. And he
reads Goethe's enigmatic *Wahlverwandtschaften* as the return of the
repressed, in which the breaking of the marriage vow releases all the
destructive forces of the archaic.

"History," said Lukács, "is the perpetual breaking of form." This is the
sense in which Benjamin's theological and political figures emerge from
his linguistic ones, and all find their origins in a violence exercised fully
as much on the literary text ("the autonomous work of art") as on the
state or the law. Violence becomes the very condition of possibility of
the Now-time, the "now of recognizability" in which Sorel's myth of the
general strike, God's vengeance on tyrants and archaic forces, and all the
revolutions of human history, come together in an energizing and multi-
dimensional "dialectical image."

3

We are today too far away from the shattering impact of World War I—
technological and collective alike—on the emergent bourgeoisie of what
was once called the *belle époque* to appreciate the violence of the artistic
avant-gardes that emerged from it—Dada in 1915, Surrealism in 1924.

Meanwhile, the word "Surrealist" is itself ambiguous in Benjamin's usage, ranging from a sense of experimentalism (and even "modernism" in our current usage) so generalized that he could characterize his own *One-Way Street* as a Surrealist production, to the historical movement itself, the small group of young Parisian troublemakers we must be careful sharply to differentiate from the German dreamers and pacifist idealists ranged under the looser banner of Expressionism.

Certainly Benjamin was extremely attentive to the formation of literary movements and avant-gardes as such, to local debates and experimental practices. But we do best, I think, to grasp these interests as focusing not so much on the phenomenon of the avant-garde as such, as rather on what Lenin called "the current situation"—that is, the state of intellectual life and production at a given synchronic cross-section of national life. This will, to be sure, produce a certain kind of literary history: his own view of Weimar, for example, expressed again and again, can largely be summed up in the following passage:

> Expressionism is the mimicry of revolutionary gesture without any revolutionary formation. In Germany it was overcome only through a change of fashion, not as the result of criticism. This is why all its perversions have managed to survive in a different form in the New Objectivity [*Neue Sachlichkeit*], which succeeded it. Both movements base their solidarity on their efforts to come to terms with the experience of the war from the standpoint of the bourgeoisie. Expressionism attempts this in the name of humanity; subsequently this was done in the name of objectivity. (II, 405; VI, 175)

He adds that both are the products of intellectuals, even the class bias of Expressionism is revealed in its idealistic humanism, while the New Objectivity is the work of radical leftists. But the ideologies of these intellectuals are no guarantee; the path they project, he tells us in the same fragment ("False Criticism"), is "a road from which a left or a right turn can be taken at any moment." This passage then constructs a situation—the war and the collapse of the imperial state—to which two dialectically opposed positions prove to be politically the same—in other words, to have the same political consequences.

Meanwhile, Expressionism cannot be said to have been an avant-garde or vanguard in the sense in which political movements (with their "manifestoes") took the term from military organization. Perhaps it was as much a new experience of the vanguard group, so different from these earlier artistic movements or coteries, which accounts for the sheer excitement of the opening page of Benjamin's 1929 "report" on Surrealism (significantly subtitled "The Last Snapshot of the European Intelligentsia" [II, 207–18; II, 295–310]).

A new character appears on these opening pages, perhaps the forerunner of the one we have identified as "the dialectical materialist": this one is "the German observer." We are back in the days in which the German latecomer wistfully gazes across the Rhine at the productivity of the West and in particular of French culture. But unlike Thomas Mann, who managed to persuade himself, against his Westernizing brother and in the middle of the deadliest of world wars, of the cultural superiority of the classical German tradition, Benjamin's observer sees all the rushing energy of a mighty waterfall pouring down into the otherwise uneventful flatlands of a placid and still bourgeois German daily life.

He is under no illusions as to its origins: "what sprang up in 1919 in France in a small circle of literati . . . may have been a meager stream, fed on the damp boredom of postwar Europe and the last trickle of French decadence"; but the German critic can "install his power station" on its momentous Europe-wide results. There is here a more concrete instantiation of that uneven development of "world literature" as the relation of very different national situations with one another that Goethe himself had begun to pioneer at the beginning of the nineteenth century (and that we now need to confront, in all its novel complexity in globalization and the world market—also sensed by Benjamin in his insistent thematic preoccupation with sheer number, with the masses and multiplicity itself).

It is the Great War which opened this fissure. Benjamin does not have to tell us that the emergence of Surrealism is an event that changed his own life: the would-be organizer of the prewar youth movement here suddenly confronts a real avant-garde (indeed, virtually the archetype of all later avant-gardes, complete with a "manifesto" to match). This particular avant-garde has been summoned up "at a moment of danger," the postwar lapse of European culture into a reactionary "*rappel à l'ordre*," if not a frivolous never-ending celebration which ignores the vigor and satiric venom with which Karl Kraus is investing his public readings of Offenbach at much the same time. Surrealism is characterized by its simultaneous discovery of two still academically ostracized bodies of intellectual work: Marxism (already denatured by social-democratic orthodoxy and revisionism) and Freudianism, whose scandalous topics the new movement will sublimate into an unexpected juxtaposition of the arcane conventions of "*l'amour courtois*" with the Marquis de Sade. As a politics, Surrealism remains locked in the more general contradiction "between an anarchistic Fronde and a revolutionary discipline," but its true originality lies in its attempt to square this circle from within "the poetic life," as Rimbaud, for example, led it, and to explode poetry's aesthetic categories. This fits well with Benjamin's own proposal "to transfer the crisis into the heart of language" (C 84; B 131), but adds a dimension of collective action which he missed in Weimar Germany (and had only briefly glimpsed in the earlier youth movement).

But to convey the excitement of his discovery of Surrealism and its immense and energizing possibilities, he needs to overcome a number of reservations, reticences and objections. Some of those will be historical and the result of an unfamiliarity with the movement's "heroic phase," which is now over. In that period, Surrealism touched and transformed "everything with which it came into contact." Its discovery of "the threshold between waking and sleeping" transformed language into a realm beyond "the penny-in-the-slot called 'meaning.'" And beyond "the self" as well: it was able to find access to an experience—related to religion and mysticism no doubt, but—of "a materialistic, anthropological inspiration" which could only be identified and named as *profane illumination*.

At this point, the account converges on one of Benjamin's most ardent interests and ideals, namely the identity of opposites to be forged between intoxication (drugs, for example) and that sobriety whose very name is associated with the newly discovered poetic realm of Hölderlin and his famous swans, so different from those, lost or frozen, of Baudelaire and Mallarmé:

> ... *trunken von Küssen*
> *Tunkt ihr das Haupt*
> *Ins heilignüchterne Wasser.*[2]

---

2   Friedrich Hölderlin, "Hälfte des Lebens," *Gesammelte Werke*, Düsseldorf: Bertelsmann, 1956, 231.

... as drunk with kisses
you dip your brows
in the sacred sobriety of the deep.

The Surrealists also knew this identification of opposites, however, and sought it in their "research," which is to say in their daily life. This is why it is an error to identify the movement with those trappings of spiritualism and the occult, red flags to the rationalist and seemingly inescapable in the schizophrenic pages of Breton's masterpiece *Nadja*, along with the more vulgar bourgeois misapprehensions of sexual obsession and adultery. All this is to be transformed by the well-nigh theological sublimations of *l'amour courtois*, as Auerbach expressed it and Lacan will explore it, himself a late product of an omnipresent, essentially Surrealist thirties culture ("The lady, in esoteric love, matters least").

But at this point we discover an important Benjaminian secret, the secret of the outmoded. He owes it to Breton and the latter's strolls in the flea market, and to Aragon's exploration of the last seedy, *louche* arcades: "the first iron constructions, the first factory buildings, the earliest photos, objects that have begun to be extinct, grand pianos, the dresses of five years ago, fashionable restaurants when the vogue has begun to ebb from them"; and why not add silent films, old roadsters, the hits of an older yesteryear, black-and-white photography, hairstyles of the 1930s and even character types from that era, and so on and so forth? "Breton and Nadja are the lovers who . . . bring the immense forces of 'atmosphere' concealed in these things to the point of explosion." The whole project of the *Arcades* is here, to convert the outmoded styles of the Second Empire into "revolutionary experience, if not action."

How can it be done? Or at least how does Benjamin think it can be done at this stage of his work (he has already assembled a first mass of material)? The figure of Blanqui—who haunts this period like a desperate yet serene specter, just as he haunts Weimar and will reappear in the "eternal return" that haunts the Nazi triumph of 1940—will not be enough to convert these archives into dynamite. What will do so, he thinks, is "the substitution of a political for a historical view of the past." Let's be clear: "historical" here means chronology, the continuous history of Lyotard's grand narratives, homogeneous time, bourgeois progress, the inexorable movement of the past into an inevitable future. "Political" means history in a different sense, the discontinuous history of the great uprisings, of the experience of defeat no less than the over-throw of the masters, the irresistible right to revolt, apocatastasis.

But the outmoded can be found in a very different way in space, and in particular the space of the city, and of the archetypal city itself, Paris, of which Atget's empty and immortal photographs register "the scene of the crime": "crossroads where ghostly signals flash from the traffic, and inconceivable analogies and connections between events are the order of the day." Even the interiors are here the public space of Paris, he tells us, "places where what is between these people [Breton and Nadja? The Surrealist avant-garde? The Parisian masses themselves?] turns like a revolving door." Another buried spatial metaphor estranging the surface account of space itself (like the swerving army column beneath the winding road of *One-Way Street*): who disappears in this revolving door? And who unexpectedly emerges (like the Messiah of the final theses)? This "is the space on which the lyric poetry of Surrealism reports."

So it is that art becomes a strange kind of documentation, and the first misleading impression of spiritualism and the arcane in reality harbors a "belief in a real, separate existence of concepts whether outside or inside things" which "very quickly" crosses over "from the logical realm of ideas to the magical realm of words"; impossible here not to think of that whole youthful linguistic mysticism that culminates in Benjamin's notorious "Epistemo-Critical Prologue" (to the *Origin of the German Trauerspiel*), but to which we are now enjoined to add Apollinaire's characterization of the newer art which creates "new realities whose plastic manifestations are just as complex as those referred to by the words standing for collectives"!

In his enthusiasm (read the word literally!), Benjamin sweeps all of his passions together, finds them all concentrated in the Surrealist project. So it is that at once technology makes its unexpected appear-ance—"the uncomprehended miracle of machines," leading Benjamin to recommend comparing "these overheated fantasies with the well-ventilated utopias of a Scheerbart"—futurism versus glass buildings, perhaps, or intoxication versus the sobriety of Le Corbusier.

It is a reservation which has all the earmarks of an internal dialogue, if not a self-criticism. This is, after all, the same Benjamin who, as we remember, opined: "To encompass both Breton and Le Corbusier . . ." (A, N1a5, 459; V, 573). But it is a tension which also leads to the either/

or of political assessment: revolt or revolution? Surrealist politics, like that of Benjamin himself, clearly springs from a horror and disgust with the bourgeoisie and thereby bears the traces of its origin, in "the boundaries of scandal," which are those of insurrection—in other words, of Blanqui himself, and of Baudelaire.

All the more reason, then, to return to the denunciations of "left-wing melancholy" and of social democracy, the "so-called well-meaning left-wing bourgeois intelligentsia" and to unmask its politics as sheer moralism, thereby identifying the very target of Surrealist scandal as such, which still finds something "usable" (a sturdy Brechtian word) within the "romantic dummy" of Satanism, "the cult of evil as a political device." To think that we have today, in a West in which Sade and Lautréamont are published and widely available, largely left a moralizing condemnation of their works behind us is to ignore the recurrent puritanisms of the American left and right alike as political forces. Indeed, Benjamin himself provokes it, as though by anticipation, with his explicit celebration of the episode of child rape in Dostoyevsky's notorious "Testament of Stavrogin." The Surrealist commemoration of such "vileness," which rebukes the "optimism" of the petty-bourgeois and social-democratic belief in the essential "goodness" of human nature, thus unexpectedly confirms the Russian orthodox writer, for whom "all these vices have a pristine vitality," in his politically energizing pessimism—something one can understand better if, like the Brecht of the *Caucasian Chalk Circle*, one counts "the temptation of the good" as yet another in that sink of vices which is human nature. This is why Naville's "organization of pessimism," which echoes that of Sorel, turns out to be "the call of the hour." Absolute mistrust: "Mistrust in the fate of literature, mistrust in the fate of freedom, mistrust in the fate of European humanity, but three times mistrust in all reconciliation: between classes, between nations, between individuals. And unlimited trust only in I.G. Farben and the peaceful perfecting of the *Luftwaffe*."

This wholesale profession *de foi* culminates honestly enough in an intellectual's bemusement at his own calling: should we then not give up art itself, is that not the implication of Surrealism's revolt against aesthetics? "Might not the interruption of his 'artistic career' perhaps be an essential part of [the Surrealist artist's] new function?" The anarchist confusion of revolt and revolution will be recast as the tension between intoxication and sobriety. Benjamin will end his essay with a reaffirmation of the body, with the qualification that "metaphysical materialism" (the materialist revolt) must give way to "anthropological materialism"—a term and a program which remains unclarified and is not, for Benjamin, a definitive solution or formulation either. But, significantly, this affirmation leads to another, more familiar one: "Only when in technology body and image space so interpenetrate that all revolutionary tension becomes bodily collective innervation, and all the bodily innervations of the collective become revolutionary discharge, has reality transcended itself to the extent demanded by the *Communist Manifesto*." And by the Surrealist manifesto as well? "Profane illumination" thereby becomes science fictional, if not post-auratic. All of this will be further hashed out in the three versions of the "Work of Art in the Age of Technological Reproducibility."

For now, however, the essay on Surrealism, which has been gradually transformed from a report on French cultural developments to an aesthetico-political manifesto in its own right, needs to end on something more than a garbled call for a new aesthetic politics. So, characteristically, the writer rises to the challenge with a sentence that is itself an event: [The surrealists] "exchange, to a man, the play of human features for the face of an alarm clock that in each minute rings for sixty seconds."

Perhaps he remembers here that anecdote about revolutionaries firing at a clock tower to stop time and begin time anew (it will resurface in his late theses); at any rate, this new clock will do two things simultaneously. It will be a perpetual call to arms, but it will also convert daily life into a filled time of the Now, where each minute truly lasts sixty seconds. The existential will not be overlooked in the fulfillment of the political: the body, which has become a kind of mechanism if not a machine, will have transcended empty time—a demand not unfamiliar to the Surrealists themselves, as the first pages of Breton's *Manifesto* attests.

4

One feature of Benjamin's fraternization with the Surrealists, however, demands closer and more critical attention; this is the language of the oneiric and of phantasmagoria which begins to drift through Benjamin's discourse after this momentous encounter and which (in my opinion) vitiates extensive portions of the *Arcades Project*, or at least a certain conception of it ("waking up from the nineteenth century"). If the word "surrealism," used very loosely, can often simply designate what we (equally loosely) call modern or modernist—*One-Way Street* as a "Surrealist" text—then, by the same token, this same term, taken very narrowly indeed, can include a wholesale endorsement of the movement's enthusiasm for dreams.

Both Benjamin and Adorno thought it worthwhile to capture their own dreams in writing, indeed to spend a good deal of their productive energy in doing so. My sense is that consumer society today, the publics of late capitalism, are far less interested in the effects of the oneiric, which have lost their sensory density in spectacles such as Robert Wilson's *Einstein on the Beach* and in stylistic codifications such as magic realism. It seems clear that even garden-variety postmodern film considers the "modernistic" effects of dream sequences (like those, stunning!, of Buñuel) as outmoded as the flashback. Even psychoanalysis, abandoning the terms of Freud's great discovery that the dream is wish fulfillment, has exchanged the phenomenological complexities of the concrete wish for the metaphysical sublimities of desire. Does this mean, as Baudrillard sometimes thought, that in our time, the Unconscious is as extinct, as a domain beyond the commodity world and independent of it, as nature itself?

At any rate, the predilection (in the *Arcades* fragments) for the language of "phantasmagoria" might well be framed by a more general argument about the conceptual problems raised by notions of the "irrational": a pseudo-concept produced by a Reason which can only designate what it cannot assimilate by a name without content. In an era like the eighteenth-century Enlightenment, in which reason is very narrowly construed as a confrontation with a whole environment of religion and superstition, the reproach of irrationality retains some force, its manifestations still have the objectivity of appearance, not yet medically codified and identified by the appropriate specialized terminology; irrationality is still a whole world out there, against which reason requires fortifications. But secularization means that, little by little, that world is colonized, its "dark places" explored and mapped; its otherness dissolved into the familiarities of the analyst and the anthropologist, its energies reinvested in advertising and fascism. Magic can longer be explained by recourse to the term "magical," as the founder of modern sociology tried to do with his reinvention of the term "charisma." In the consumer society of late capitalism or, if you prefer, of big data and thoroughgoing informational inventory and classification, very little remains that can be called irrational—in other words, that escapes the forcefield of what Habermas called "communicative reason." Dreams are assimilated to special effects and magic to new media technology; and for insanity and the psychotic, we have only to consult the new Book of the World, the DSM or psychiatrists' dictionary.

But this poses a unique problem for analysts of capitalism's superstructures. Marx himself, when he came to define the commodity (in his 1872 rewritten version of the opening chapters of *Capital*, I believe), found himself obliged to take recourse in the language of religion:

> The commodity . . . is a very strange thing, abounding in metaphysical subtleties and theological niceties . . . The mystical character of the commodity does not . . . arise from its use-value . . . It is nothing but the definite social relation between men themselves which assumes here, for them, the fantastic form of a relation between things. In order, therefore, to find an analogy we must take flight into the misty realm of religion where the products of the human brain appear as autonomous figures endowed with a life of their own, which enter into relations with each other and with the human race.[3]

He calls this relationship fetishism, drawing on the anthropological materials collected and named by *le président* de Brosses, in the eighteenth century. From one standpoint, then, the problem stands as a specific instantiation of the more general question of the relationship of superstructures to the base or to production, a question scarcely resolved by Benjamin's overhasty pronouncement that "the superstructure expresses the base" (*Arcades*, 392; A, K2, 5, 392; V 495). At any rate, with this famous passage, Marx inaugurates a specific tradition in which capitalist daily life will be characterized as being at best somehow ideological and at worst a realm of enchantment. As long as the nature of the commodity and of superstructures generally remained a secondary matter for the left—partly because modernization and its superstructural colonizations remained incomplete, partly because left politics

---

3   *Capital*, Vol. I, 163.

continued to draw its power from the mobilization of working-class people or, in other words, from the conditions of "the base"—the issue was not a particularly urgent one, and Marx's theological characterizations remained effective.

But when, in the 1920s and '30s, world revolution begins to recede and capitalism's production of the lifeworld is tendentially universalized, then—particularly in so-called Western Marxism—the problem of the theorization of superstructures returns in full force, and with Lukács's epoch-making *History and Class Consciousness* (and quite against his own political intentions), commodification becomes a political issue. Indeed, after World War II, it takes center stage as a crucial problem of political strategy and mobilization. The dangers of Americanization were recognized long before decolonization and the Cold War. Lenin could speak of the bribery of the working classes in a formula which will continue to be invoked as an explanation for their support for Hitler in the German elections of 1932, but which will come to seem inadequate (even if true) for answering the now hoary question of "why there is no socialism in America?" (whose better answer would seem to be "race").

This is, then, the moment in which Marx's characterizations undergo significant metamorphoses: after World War II, we may argue that commodification in the Western or "advanced" countries is complete and can be renamed consumerism (at the same time that colonialism is dissolved and reconfigured, and capitalist modernization, spreading over the entire globe, approaches the condition of what Marx called the "world market," and today we call globalization). It is under these conditions that, beginning with Lefebvre, something called everyday life begins to be identified as a new object of study, along with space itself, and theorized in its own right. It is characterized as a kind of second or parallel realm, in the sense in which (as Ford understood long ago) the worker is himself already a split personality: a wage earner on the one hand, a consumer on the other. Daily life is the shadow world of the worker's second personality as consumer; and it is this dimension which is the most visible and accessible to sociologists, writers and indeed the subjects themselves (labor, like sex, being unrepresentable, as Godard declared in a memorable moment).

The temptation therefore arises to find an independent language and figuration for the representation of what now seems a magic or enchanted realm. Benjamin was already aware of the problem, which he grappled with in an early (1921) essay called "Capitalism as Religion" (I, 288–91; VI, 100–3). Writing without the benefit of the Lukácsean theorization of commodity form, Benjamin articulates his sense of capitalism in terms of sheer saturation, filled time, "*natura non fecit saltam*," an omnipresence which does not even allow for the separation of work and "leisure," a temporality utterly given over to capitalism's rituals, of which he only identifies guilt. In a later, not often repeated formulation, he will observe that people think of crisis as an event, whereas "the catastrophe is that it just goes on like this" (IV, 184; I, 683). This early note seems related to the later one: there is a temporal dimension to the absolute saturation both guilt and capitalism affirm; yet not just time is at stake. "Guilt" is surely not just a subjective or psychological experience, but rather a return of the archaic, an enchantment waiting to be named as such.

Presumably, that name will be phantasmagoria; yet this new addition diverts us into a duality, a world of false appearances behind which the real world continues to exist with all the tenacity of the *Ding an sich*. Or, to shift to another key of this formulation, it is a dream which presupposes a different realm into which we can wake up. Neither of these formulations seems very apt, either for capitalism or for the Paris of the Second Empire. Does use value persist under or behind capitalism as a reality into which we can reawaken? And what is the real life into which the subjects of the Empire can awaken? Surely not the Third Republic. Benjamin's formulations hesitate between the figural and the phenomenological or even existential; they threaten to puncture his historical notes, to drain them of their historical reality.

Meanwhile, it is worth pursuing the fate of such representations in a later moment of capitalism. I think, for example, of Guy Debord's influential *Society of the Spectacle*, in which the emphasis on visuality includes a contemplative distance from the Real. It is a characterization which overlaps the far more widespread critique of the overemphasis on epistemology that has developed out of the reaction against neo-Kantianism in modern philosophy (Bergson, pragmatism, phenomenology, existentialism, dialectics, and so on). This larger critique emphasizes the narrowness of the Kantian tradition and its restriction of philosophy to knowledge as such, and the exclusion of other modes of relationship to reality. Still, Debord's version leaves room for a disembodied and contemplative knowledge, conveniently restricted to sight and spectatorship, which, however, includes production and makes a place for agency, at least in the staging of a reconstructed pseudo-reality. This is, as it were, the paranoid dimension of such representations, whose figurality necessarily posits a place beyond the spectacle from which its nature can be observed and can be seen to have been constructed (if not by history, then at least by this or that ruling class). Debord, of course, believed in the convergence of the US and the USSR in this well-nigh universal phantasmagoria; at the same time, his (anarchist rather than Maoist) denunciation of "revisionism" seems to limit its relevance to special events (spectacles) while, at the same time, his insistence on visuality productively develops the theme of commodification (the image, he observed in a memorable formula, is the final form of commodity reification).

Baudrillard's version of this theory of capitalist "enchantment" lies in his conception of simulation and presents at least some theoretical advantages over the spectacle–society thesis. Simulation is first and foremost a general process which does not particularly emphasize events but which certainly encompasses spectacles of all sorts; it does not require the existence of agents or an agency which is immediately responsible for its effects, but offers the picture of a deterioration of the Real that is far more inward and all-encompassing than that of a spectacle one could, in a pinch, leave, slamming the door behind one. Simulation can thus also be imagined as a mental process or congenital disease of some kind—a baleful enchantment!—which drains reality from everything including ourselves, our own individual or collective identities (if in fact those ever existed in the first place). This representation is thus far less political than that of Debord and approaches the status of a metaphysical proposition.

It is a proposition that would then seem to find its final form in what we might call the *Matrix* or *Truman Show* syndrome, in which reality is a pre-prepared illusion from the outset, and in which the existence of stage directors or simulation-operators is thus also overtly dramatized and a more general paranoid picture of things made inescapable. If it be absolutely necessary to retain the notion of the "phantasmagoria," then we may retranslate Baudrillard's process of simulation more productively back into what Benjamin called aesthetization.

Indeed, this later formulation will lead us to what, in Benjamin's own thinking, proves to be a more satisfactory substitute for cultural diagnosis than this rather facile characterization of "phantasmagoria": namely, the opposition between regression and "advanced" productivity. For regression has already put us on the track of what he calls "aestheticism" and what is surely a more adequate account of what was beginning in his own modern culture and has reached a climax in ours. Consumerism and the triumph of the commodity form over epistemology and ethics, let alone politics itself, is surely the more telling description of a social life saturated with images and reorganized around the consumption of commodities, the mesmerization by *schöner Schein* or aesthetic appearance as such. Benjamin's own association of it with fascism was perhaps historically limited by the emergence of the great Nazi spectacles, like Nuremberg, or the propaganda deployment of Germanic myth. We are today, however, in a better position to observe the way in which the aestheticism of spectacle society transforms our consumption of information itself, with a subsequent deterioration of traditional aesthetic experience as such and a reappearance of tribalisms that have a family likeness to the traditional fascisms.

5

But we must also resist the temptation to approach Benjamin's concept of the "advanced" by way of that fetishization of the New that has come to characterize modernism generally in the now-conventional definition of this style or period. For Benjamin, not all forms of the New are advanced; there is, for example, the fascist version of aestheticization. And there is also his own historiographic predilection for the no longer quite new, the just slightly outworn and outmoded: Breton, he observes, "was the first to perceive the revolutionary energies that appear in the 'outmoded' . . . No one before these visionaries and augurs perceived how destitution . . . could be transformed into revolutionary nihilism" (II, 210; II, 299). When one reflects on the relatively unusual historicity of Paris, where the medieval city persists virtually up to the Fifth Republic, it will not be difficult to correlate the materials of the *Arcades* with this sense of a slowly outmoding presence. So it is that even the 1920s Paris of the Surrealists carried the nineteenth century with it into a modernizing but not yet modernized twentieth-century world; the famous "now of recognizability" becomes a strangely fitful stereoscopic gaze. This is something that bears on theory and method as well. And if it is asked where Benjamin ever practiced a properly Marxist criticism (remembering his tactful complaint to his Soviet cultural hosts for importing everything tiresome and academic about the then-current Western bourgeois literary theories), we find ourselves obliged to revert to his Fuchs essay, that commission from his Frankfurt patrons that he found most onerous and that plunged him back into a social-democratic and, as it were, premodern nineteenth-century Marxist orthodoxy.

It is therefore all the more a matter of note to take account of this essay, which begins with the sentence: "The lifework of Eduard Fuchs belongs to the recent past" (III, 260; II, 465–505). Benjamin is exceedingly discreet in his treatment of these "predecessors," indeed his respect for Engel's famous interventions[4] is certainly not matched today by "dialectical historical materialists" (such as Althusser), who have savaged Engels's humanism and his construction of a whole Hegelian philosophy (what we now know as "dialectical materialism") out of Marx's discoveries. But Benjamin's apologists, such as Hannah Arendt (who left this crucial essay out of her pathbreaking collection), remind us that it was written on command for the Frankfurt School journal—a precious source of income for Walter Benjamin—and required a certain tact in its navigation of a Marxian tradition not particularly experimental or venturesome in the cultural area, where Arnold Hauser and Max Raphael might be thought to be the vanguard (Adorno's influence only kicking in much later, in the 1960s, and Brecht's theories heretical in the face of Lukács's seeming orthodoxy). The academic sobriety of Benjamin's presentation of Fuchs, rather disappointing for those expecting the usual fireworks, is perhaps itself a not-so-implicit commentary on the subject matter. Old stuff, it seems to say, the usual (save in the opening pages on history). Those of us reading the essay today from the vantage point of the academy will, however, certainly want to note his reflections on "the humanities," which the ruling class inveterately consigns to the sandbox (Benjamin's later thoughts on pedagogy always insisted on a class orientation, reminding us frequently that he always

---

4   In particular, Engels's attack on an ahistorical "history of ideas" in the late letters.

identified himself as a bourgeois intellectual and wrote and thought from that perspective).

Inasmuch, however, as in those early years the Social Democratic Party assumed the all-important task of forming and educating the working class—thereby directly raising the question of what to do with "the humanities"—Benjamin also takes the opportunity to criticize a wholesale adoption of bourgeois and positivistic positions (the same critique he had already offered to the Soviet comrades), and in particular of the Lukácsean concept of tradition, of the "*Erbe*" or cultural heritage, and of the scientism of bourgeois and non-dialectical epistemology. But in the light of his own life's work, Benjamin's discussion of technology is of particular interest, inasmuch as the left is in danger of adopting a middle-class glamorization of its wonder-working powers and the new comforts it offers, neglecting its "destructive energies," which the world has since experienced in war, an awareness of which any historian looking back at this golden age of the late nineteenth century will miss in the thinkers of that time, of whatever class. "The destructive element": this is the dimension which pervades Benjamin's lifework and which he insisted on fully, as much in literary and cultural criticism as in sheer machinery and material "progress."

The eulogy to Fuchs thereby becomes an elegy for the lost opportunities of the great age of social democracy, as well as a chance to set a new agenda for "cultural history," a field about which he must remind us, in a famous sentence, repeated dramatically in the "Theses on History," that "there is no document of culture that is not at the same time a document of barbarism" and that "the products of art and science owe their existence to the anonymous toil of their contemporaries"—a program for precisely that class-oriented pedagogy called for above, and fulfilled in Peter Weiss's *Aesthetics of Resistance*, which alternates its appreciation of the "masterpieces" of the past (as in its dramatic opening pages on the great friezes of Pergamon) with its vivid accounts of the anonymous labor of the slaves and craftsmen who had to bring them into material being.

But the problem runs deeper than this, for it becomes clear that if one approaches it from Benjamin's standpoint, with his conviction of the discontinuous nature of our access to the past, what is customarily termed cultural history becomes impossible. There are two fundamental reasons for this. First of all, any consideration of cultural objects independent of the production process—theirs specifically, but behind that, one assumes, the very structure of the mode of production itself—will reify the objects in question and "fetishize" them (the use of Marx's original term authorizes us to translate this language into the terms of commodity capitalism).

Meanwhile, as if the production of commodities were not itself essentially discontinuous, we may well want to conclude that the whole ideology of modernism, the telos that drives painting on from Manet to Cézanne, and thereafter to cubism, is out of question here: continuous history being itself repudiated by Benjamin's critique of historicism and of a contemplative view of the past. This will be discouraging to those of us—those "historical materialists"—who still work in the field of culture; but perhaps not as distressing as another "unassailable conclusion" quoted by Benjamin—namely, that "art cannot significantly intervene in the proletariat's struggle for emancipation." These twin obstacles must then pose Benjamin's cultural analysis a dilemma and a form-problem still unresolved today.

What, then, will he find to celebrate in the pioneering work of Eduard Fuchs? The portrait is itself inimitable and its pleasures free us from the doctrinal constraints of the earlier pages. They will center on the ambivalence—"the bipolar nature"—of the grotesque, its beauty and its more loathsome qualities (Benjamin refers back to the antinomies of the Baroque in passing).

But they require some preliminary qualifications. The more limited social-democratic features of Fuchs's work can be summarized as a persistence of bourgeois thinking in the two areas of an evolutionary view of history, along with an essentially ethical or moralizing, and individualizing, set of judgments on it; and of a reductive and simplistic view of psychoanalysis which is identified with the purely sexual. Both these limits signify a primacy of individual categories (including the Freudian concept of the Unconscious, as Benjamin saw it) over collective ones.

Yet once these limits are established, Fuchs's emancipatory views on sexuality are celebrated: he may not be Wedekind, but he avoids "as far as possible the theory of repression and of complexes," and "his brilliant defense of orgies" as a truly human ritual which separates us from animals is, for Benjamin, memorable and creative (perhaps anticipating the interests of that post-Surrealist "Collège de Sociologie," with which Benjamin sporadically associated).

This is the point at which Benjamin's appreciation of Fuchs as the quintessential collector emerges, along with the centrality of Daumier in his work. Indeed, our approach to Benjamin himself may well want to retain the revealing phrase: "the figure of Daumier accompanied him throughout his career, and one might almost say that this made Fuchs into a dialectical thinker." May we not take this as a reflection of the role of Baudelaire in Benjamin's own work, as the locus of contradictions that cannot otherwise be vividly confronted? Even Brecht is hinted at here, in Benjamin's characterization of the process of abstraction in Daumier's great caricatures: Daumier translated the public and private life of Parisians into "the language of the agon." The role of Daumier in Fuchs's achievement can then be made clear by a series of direct quotations. There is an analysis of the content-form reversal here worthy of Michael Fried: "A great many of Daumier's figures are engaged in the most concentrated looking," an observation which reverses the caricatures into the artist himself.

But above all, there are a series of visual analyses which deserve, in conclusion, to be noted in their fullness of detail. In such cases, the material world fills his writing even where explicit mention of it is avoided, as is evident in the masterful characterization of the graphic art of the revolutionary era:

> Everything is stiff, taut, military. Men do not lie down, since the drill square does not tolerate any "at ease." Even when people are sitting down, they look as if they want to jump up. Their bodies are full of tension, like an arrow on a bowstring . . . What is true of the lines is likewise true of the colors. The pictures give a cold and tinny impression . . . when compared to paintings of the Rococo . . . The coloring . . . had to be hard . . . and metallic if it was to go with the content of the pictures.

An informative remark on the historical equivalents of unconscious fetishism is more explicit. Fuchs says that "the increase of shoe and leg fetishism indicates that the priapic cult is being superseded by the vulva cult." The increase in breast fetishism, by contrast, is evidence of a regressive development. "The cult of the covered foot or leg reflects the dominance of woman over man, whereas the cult of breasts indicates the role of woman as an object of man's pleasure."

Fuchs gained his deepest insights into the symbolic realm through study of Daumier. What he says about Daumier's trees is one of the happiest discoveries of his entire career. In those trees he perceives:

> a totally unique symbolic form . . . which expresses Daumier's sense of social responsibility as well as his conviction that it is society's duty to protect the individual . . . His typical manner of depicting trees . . . always shows them with broadly outspread branches, particularly if a person is standing or resting underneath. In such trees, the branches extend like the arms of a giant, and actually look as though they would stretch to infinity. Thus, the branches form an impenetrable roof which keeps danger away from all those who seek refuge under them.

This beautiful reflection leads Fuchs to an insight into the dominance of the maternal in Daumier's work.

6

What is most durable in Fuchs is therefore to be discovered not merely in the visual but in the physiognomy; and when it is remembered that the Surrealists themselves were great amateurs of the visual, both oneiric and in painting, and also that much of what is original in Brecht, alongside the poetry of the city, is scenic and gestural; and when one recalls the relatively scarce analyses of literary texts in Benjamin (and his preference for an account of the writers' situation at this or that moment in time), then perhaps we may begin to feel that his own conception of the aesthetic transcends purely literary or linguistic limits.

But this is to reckon without two major statements. With "The Storyteller" and "On Some Motifs in Baudelaire," we are at the very heart of what is profound and original in Benjamin's work: the relationship between narrativity and the raw material of social life, the figurability and representabillty of history itself. Here he paradoxically takes his place with the most important literary and narrative theorists of the twentieth century, with Lukács and Bakhtin, the Formalists and Northrop Frye—the paradox being that he here gives us invaluable insights into the novel as a form while himself showing little or no real critical interest in any specific work in the history of the novel (the place

of Goethe's *Wahlverwandtschaften*, which had great personal significance for him, not only serves as a kind of crossroads for any number of
his theoretical interests, it also turns on a book which is surely one of the
white elephants of the canon if there ever was one). But about analysis of
the novel and its critical (and even philosophical) tradition, one must
note this strange fact: that the really innovative thinkers on this form
find themselves oriented not to the "novel itself" in its fullest moment of
development, but rather to the moments of its emergence or, on the
other hand, of its crisis and virtual disappearance ("the death of the
novel," and so on). The novel is, in other words, never really there, never
at the center of such attention; it is always lateral, coming into or going
out of being, and Benjamin is no exception to this particular "great
tradition" of speculation, which can be explained, as it is in Lukács's
central *Theory of the Novel,* by the fact that the novel is not a form at all,
not really a genre, but a stand-in for what cannot be said any longer,
what cannot be told or represented in traditional genres or forms, the
placeholder and disguise of an initial absence or impossibility.

It might be well at this point to clarify Benjamin's position on novels:
he reads them, certainly, that cannot be in doubt. But unlike poetry
(Hölderlin, George, Baudelaire, Brecht), unlike drama (Calderón,
Hebbel), he does not seem to find it useful to write about them as a
form. Here is a revealing comment entitled "Reading Novels," one of his
rare analytic statements on the genre:

> Not all books are to be read in the same way. Novels, for example, are
> there to be devoured. To read them is a pleasure of consumption
> [*Einverleibung*]. This is not empathy. The reader does not put himself
> in the place of the hero; he absorbs what befalls the hero into himself.
> The vivid report on those events, however, is the enticing form in
> which a nourishing meal is presented at the table. Now, there is of
> course a raw, healthy form of experience, just as there is raw, healthy
> food for the stomach—namely experiencing something for oneself.
> But the art of the novel, like the art of cooking, begins where the raw
> products end. There are many nourishing foodstuffs that are inedible
> when raw, just as there are any number of experiences that are better
> read about than personally undergone. They affect many people so
> strongly that individuals would not survive them if they were to expe-
> rience them in the flesh. In short, if there is a Muse of the novel—it

would be the tenth—it must bear the features of a kitchen fairy. She raises the world from its raw state in order to produce something edible, something tasty. Read a newspaper while eating, if you must. But never a novel. For that involves two sets of conflicting obligations. (II, 728–9; IV, 436)

The "*Denkbild*" turns on this comparison with food, and it may be said that it is eating, rather than reading, which is the tenor of this metaphor. Still, it seems to me that the key to Benjamin's thought lies in the relation to experience (which is, after all, along with history, his fundamental theme). Reading the words and verses of a poem and noting the interplay within it of meter and rhythm; watching a drama on the stage— these are the materials of an existential experience. No matter how numerous the collectivity around me in the theater, this last is also an element in my personal experience—it belongs to me, like Marcel's experience of Berma and of Racine. If it is a genuine experience (rather than an *Erlebnis*), it presents me with a unique task: that of finding the right words and sentences to capture it.

The novel, on the other hand, is someone else's experience. The protagonists, indeed, may have their individual experiences, which I can confront; the language of the novel may on occasion reach a poetic density which I can explore like an object. But the novel as a whole is not the same as the experience of its protagonist (this is the secret of the decadence of the form today, its increasing domination by point-of-view restrictions, its slippage into psychology and subjectivity); nor is this to say that it is the psychological experience of the author, either. But it is objectified experience, one which is offered to me from the outside. It is culinary and gastronomical, to use Brecht's language; I can devour it with pleasure and satisfaction (it can also be good or bad for me). But it is rarely mine. (There is a dialectic of the aura about experience as well: it can be "my own" or not.) Occasionally the experience of a novel is unique and marks me in some way, but mostly it is simply a pleasure. The question we then need to ask is whether the experience of a feature film (generically, the cousin of the novel) falls under the same strictures: the conventional reading of the reproducibility essay indicates that it does, but that the collective, mass-oriented nature of its experience (unlike that of the theater) marks a new stage, perhaps a qualitative leap, in that consumption, which transforms it into another, altogether different kind of experience. This remains to be seen; meanwhile, it also remains to be seen whether the same dialectical *Aufhebung* by the multitude can possibly hold for the novel, read in solitude. Perhaps it does for bestsellers today, in consumer society as it did for the nineteenth-century readers of serialized novels in the early newspapers. But that is, of course, not the kind of immanent aesthetic value our theoreticians are looking for.

Besides which novels, as we shall see, are not exactly examples of storytelling either. Why is "The Storyteller" Benjamin's most perfect essay? Not only because it tells a story about storytelling, or because it clarifies the much misrepresented Benjaminian concept of technology; not even because it turns on the central concern of his life's work, namely the idea of experience (*Erfahrung*) and what happened to it. Indeed, one would be hard out to find any of Benjamin's most crucial themes not touched on (and thereby redefined, reformulated) somewhere in this essay (III, 143–166; II, 438–65).

That it is about a Russian writer is, however, not this essay's most inconsequential feature (an occasional piece, solicited by the publisher of a collection of Leskov stories). For Russia was not only, for the West and, above all, for its leftists and revolutionaries, a symbolic space, redolent of the "Slavic soul" and religious mysticism, a place in which a peasantry still preserved the archaic folkways of some well-nigh original (Ur-)life on Earth, alongside a non-Western new literature and cities in which the most advanced musical, dramatic and pictorial cultures thrived. For the first enthusiasts of the Soviet revolution, like Max Weber or Rainer Maria Rilke, and even for Lukács himself, Lenin appeared to be a figure out of Dostoyevsky, and even Gramsci had access to his actual writings only a few years later. Moscow—the third Rome—remained a legendary city among cities, even when Benjamin himself was struggling from appointment to appointment in the midst of its overcrowded streets and trolleys. The Russian countryside retained its aura, even when Benjamin has failed to experience it directly, and after a collectivization whose catastrophic effects were then poorly known.

Indeed, it is from this immense countryside that Leskov's tales, and storytelling generally, emerge (just as, later on in the West, it will be from Vladimir Propp's analysis of the Russian tale that what we now call narrative analysis derives). Even today, it remains one of the crucial ambiguities of Sovietology whether the unique characteristics and destiny of the Soviet Union derived from Marxism or from its "Russian characteristics": Stalin, although a gangster and a non-Russian, seeming optionally to embody either.

A storyteller like Leskov seems increasingly distant from us, Benjamin tells us at the outset, and he does not seem to have the great Russian steppes and rivers in mind, the Gogol/Dostoyevsky provincial towns, the Chekhovian romantic snowstorms, the glamorous Tolstoyan officers, who conquer the Caucasus as Lincoln's veterans conquered the Cheyenne. "Distance" is the term we must evoke here, recalling the lone formulation of that mysterious thing he calls aura, which, as infrequently as it appears in his oeuvre (only three times, I believe), has known a prodigious theoretical afterlife: "a distance, however near it may be."

Leskov's stories have aura for us in this sense: they are distant in time. It is not their exotic content, however, which accounts for their fascination; it is, rather, the act of storytelling itself which is distant, and which the named author can still bring closer to us by his "presentation of the circumstances in which *he himself has* learned what is to follow." Benjamin forestalls misunderstanding here by distinguishing the form of what we call the "short story" (with its own prodigious, yet essentially modern tradition) from this age-old, premodern activity of the "*skaz*" or oral tale. Lukács did not quite grasp this difference, for whom the modern short story remained a kind of epic survival within the wasteland of modernity; indeed, his influential celebration and analysis of the novel as a uniquely modern form or non-genre (along with Bakhtin's analogous gesture), if it is in some sense the starting point for Benjamin's reflections here, utterly reverses the emphasis of "The Storyteller."

Distance, then, itself begins here to take on the appearance of a fabulous characteristic. It can only be transmitted by the traveler, of whom Benjamin was certainly one; it demands access, itself another strange and personally charged term in the Benjaminian private vocabulary. It can, finally, be brought near (as in aura) without losing its fundamental essence as distance in and of itself. Distance is, finally, a definitional property of storytelling as such, to which we now return. For if stories must be grasped by way of the physiognomy of the storyteller as a figure, then the traveler (or, better still, the sailor) has something to contribute to that construction of the personage, as does, on the other hand, his opposite number, the settled peasant with deep roots in place and soil.

Characteristically, Benjamin will complicate his own character scheme by imagining, not exactly a synthesis of these two polar opposites, the traveler and the hard-bitten dweller on the land, but rather something like a combination: it turns out to be the preindustrial labor system of master and apprentice, the latter going through a stage as journeymen and traveling apprentices before they reach maturity as masters in their own right. Stages but not progress: historical discontinuities, but shifting roles (as in Brecht's *Lehrstücke*).

But we have yet to say what it is the storyteller tells, and what the message may be, that must find its contradictory sources in distance and homeland, in the exotic and the familiar yet ancient and even in the legendary near-at-hand, itself a distance in deep time, just as in travel we carry that oh-so-well-known quantity, ourselves, always with us. This message, which is not a message at all, as we shall see, is called "experience," the German *Erfahrung*, and it seems to be, in Benjamin's mind, something defined by an assimilation which is, in his original version of it, so deeply physical that it is called *Einverleibung*, incorporation, a taking into the body, something deeper than habit, and no doubt a not-so-distant cousin of the Brechtian *Haltung* (bearing) or indeed of *gestus* itself. (But this, too, has no real opposite, and our later tendency, derived at least in part from Simmel on the city, to identify that opposite as *Erlebnis*—an experience which happens to us, a one-time event that makes its mark, a shock—should perhaps be resisted).

But first, and as long as we have the unique chance (Benjamin rarely expounds on what *Erfahrung* might be), we should seize the moment to describe this precious thing, about which he also wants to tell us that it is disappearing: so as, no doubt, "to find," as he astonishingly tells us, "a new beauty in what is vanishing" (let's retain these two features for future reference—the "new beauty" from the sores and pustules Baudelaire identifies for us in "*modernité*," the love of that just becoming outmoded which Benjamin learned from the Surrealists and their strolls in the *marché aux puces*).

Yet we must not imagine there is any immediacy about this approach to real experience: if it can be incarnated in characters, it must nonetheless always be mediated by its own transmission, by the telling of it, and its telling to other people (whereas its opposite number, the novel, deals, as we have seen, with "the incommensurable," what can barely be communicated, what is somehow unique to that individuality emerging in mutation, along with the form itself, from the collectivity of the village and its oral storytellers).

But this is not yet the full-blown McLuhanism with which so many of Benjamin's modern admirers have confused him. The essence of the story—from now on, I will call it the tale—is to be sure oral, inasmuch as it always implies a teller; the novel, on the other hand, is just as certainly an example of print culture, but not exactly for the technological reasons so often adduced. The secret of the novel, which holds the unknown key to its structural analysis, is the impossibility of its retelling. The poverty of the so-called plot summary is there to testify to the difficulties of passing the novel's events on to a friend in conversation, and these difficulties are not contingent but rather constitutive.

But the great storytellers have always known how to expand and contract their material according to the needs of the occasion: concentrating it in the form of a paradoxical *fait divers,* or spinning it out for a receptive public, an evening's central business, the proverbial campsite. The structural distinctiveness of this raw material is usefully dramatized by a term Benjamin does not use, one which itself only emerges in the forcefield of a wholly different narrative culture—I mean the word "anecdote," which might well have served as a bridge between André Jolles's "simple forms" (he also does not know the expression) and Propp's fairy stories, which constitute one of the still recognizable survivals of this older tale now falling, as Benjamin tells us, into disuse and social oblivion.

Experience is to be found at the juncture of orality and event and, above all, of memory. But this is not an ontology, and it serves little purpose to rehearse the Badolian question, whether the Event ever happens or only exists afterward, when it is already past: the essential lies in the fact that it can be repeated (in the telling of it), unlike the novel (which no one would want to repeat) or real life, either. This possibility of repetition might then, in another register, be rethought in terms of language, of a certain kind of abstraction (Benjamin will call it "nonsensuous similarity," his definition of mimesis) and, indeed, of the word, the name and the Platonic idea. And it is related, in the constellation of the literary genres, to the abstraction of the proverb. In yet another register—as everywhere in Benjamin, these key entities are rhizomatic, sending their relevance out in multiple directions—experience is related to practice as such, as a kind of habit to be radically distinguished from the instinctive, unconscious kind, as a learned skill is to be distinguished from a reflex; but more on that later on, too.

So one constitutive feature of experience is repetition, in some special temporal sense which remains to be defined. But it can negatively be circumscribed by its radical rejection of psychology in all its forms. Psychology is the domain of the novel; the word might well be here enlarged to include all manner of explanation, as when the novelist expounds the multiple motivations of a specific act. Explanation (shifting registers once again) may be grasped as a lower, fallen realm of language shortly to be redefined in terms of information. But here, in the tale, information is as useless as the directions on a package: if we need to have a spoon described for us, along with its manner of use, then we are no longer in the world of storytelling (but it is worth noting the unexpected appearance here of the Brechtian word "useful," which will become more relevant in a moment).

Finally, there is the context of the tale, a word one regrets having to resort to at this point. For context is here twofold: it is the world itself, which needs no explanations (psychological or otherwise) because it is that whole cosmos unified by its analogies (as in the opening episteme of Foucault's *Order of Things*), a world organized outside worldly categories either by God's plan or natural law (II, 153; II, 452). But more immediately, the tale is the practice of the tale teller, whose very body and unique temperament is inscribed on it ("the way the handprints of the potter cling to a clay vessel" [III, 149; II, 447]), just as it is in the body of the listener that the tale is assimilated (*einverleibt*) and becomes his "experience" as well.

This is the point at which Benjamin's account swings predictably into characterology, and a new physiognomy emerges. For the teller of tales, Leskov himself, the eponymous storyteller, is here reinscribed in his tale as a new kind of character, namely the wise man or sage. We come here perhaps the closest to that Judaic tradition which has constituted another temptation for Benjaminian fandom, for this figure, "the righteous man," "the man of counsel," is, to be sure, the classic protagonist of the Hasidic tale as such (in Benjamin's younger years systematically revived by Martin Buber). Oddly enough, this pedagogical figure not only prolongs Benjamin's earlier preoccupation with the youth movement, it also rejoins and draws new strength from Brecht and his artistic experiments, with the "learning play" and the insistence that art should dramatize proposals and open up new possibilities within a hitherto massively stable environment. Counsel then adds a revolutionary dimension to its rabbinical function, and art rediscovers an ancient forgotten didactic vocation (which proverbs and fairytales still demonstrate, but the novel has lost).

It is, incidentally, in this return of the story to pedagogy—but the pedagogy of the concrete examples, rather than the taboos and judgments, abstract and oppressive, of the law—that we discover the unique function of the fairy tale as such, which Benjamin never got to express, among his many unfinished projects. For recourse to the fairy tale is not to be understood as nostalgic, nor as that regression to the archaic promoted by Jung and by Klages. On the contrary, "the fairy tale tells us of the earliest arrangements that mankind made to shake off the nightmare which myth had placed on its chest . . . the fairy tale taught mankind in olden times, and teaches children to this day . . . to meet the forces of the mythical world with cunning and with high spirits" (III, 157; II, 458).[5] It is the chaos of myth that is the truly archaic and that constitutes the center of Benjamin's often confusing "philosophy of history" (reproduced by Adorno and Horkheimer in their *Dialectic of Enlightenment*, "with significant changes," as they say, in what is no longer I think a truly Benjaminian book).

In all of these aspects, "experience" is a temporal phenomenon, which Benjamin will here seek to correlate to historiography (we will return to this effort later on). In his pathbreaking *Theory of the Novel*, Lukács had defined this form in terms of a crisis in temporality; and much of Benjamin's theorization of the tale works with great originality within Lukács's new paradigm: the novel, for example, an essentially biographical form, must conclude, it must have a definitive ending, as in the desolate final scene of Flaubert's *Sentimental Education*. This allows Benjamin to counter thus: "Actually, there is no story for which the question 'How does it continue?' would not be legitimate. The novelist, on the other hand, cannot hope to take the smallest step beyond the limit at which he writes '*Finis*,' and in so doing invites the reader to a divinatory realization of the meaning of life" (III, 155; II, 455). I believe that Benjamin

---

5 In keeping with the proletarian virtues: "confidence, courage, humor, cunning, and fortitude" (IV, 390; I, 694).

means this to be a spurious invitation, and "the meaning of life" to be a purely metaphysical and useless question (part of the transcendentalism ruled out of rational thinking by the Kantian tradition).

It is "living happily ever after" which is the appropriate earthly question (as Auerbach might have put it) and death the illicit, meaningless answer to the novel's problem of totality. Narrative closure is for Benjamin another name for death (III, 156; II, 456), and I think we have every interest in depsychologizing this theme and in removing the appearance of melancholy and the death wish from pages Benjamin has designed to conclude with the image of practice itself and its pedagogy. The tale, he tells us, invents a different way of relating an "*entire* life"; the novel, however—even those most devoted to Enlightenment, such as Goethe's *Wahlverwandtschaften*—inevitably ends in death and destruction. Benjamin's lifework does not waste much time on such forms, in which doom is structurally inscribed.

7

This is why Benjamin will grasp both ends of this historiographic anatomy: the storytelling that preceded the elaboration of the novel and the symptoms of that crisis which made even its most seemingly prosperous development look in retrospect like signs of its end, the crisis of the form then in an unexpected way recapitulating Hegel's notorious "end of art." To which the second paradox is added, namely that Benjamin locates these signs and symptoms not in any of the great novelists themselves, but through a poet who lived and worked his very different craft contemporaneously with them, namely Baudelaire (1821–67).

It is therefore important, for all its Russian flavor (its pretext in Leskov), to grasp the almost immediate modulation of "The Storyteller" into the equally fundamental essay, "On Some Motifs in Baudelaire," a commissioned piece for Horkheimer's *Zeitschrift*, which it was the great merit of Adorno to have forced his mentor into writing, by refusing his earlier summaries of the *Arcades Project*: a profoundly culpable act with a happy outcome!

For both essays document together the existence and the disintegration of that supreme category which is the event (and with it, its memory, the concomitant notion of experience). It is a story Benjaminian commentary has told again and again, but which, like oral storytelling, always bears repeating and in which the crucial theme of the deterioration of experience in modern times is again rehearsed.

The idea seems first to have crystallized around the impact of World War I, a watershed in so many ways. John Berger, for example, credits the war with a complete reversal in our relationship to technology, Utopian before the war in collective fantasy as well as in movements like cubism, far more sinister after the experience of tanks and trench warfare, the first aerial dogfights and the unbelievable toll of lives lost.[6] Yet, in his crucial essay "Experience and Poverty" (1933), where, to be sure, the fateful word experience is already pronounced, Benjamin's emphasis is more on his old term "expressionless" and on the silences veterans brought back from the war: "Never has experience been contradicted more thoroughly: strategic experience has been contravened by positional warfare; economic experience, by the inflation; physical experience, by hunger; moral experiences, by the ruling powers. A generation that had gone to school in horse-drawn streetcars now stood in the open air . . . in a force-field of destructive torrents and explosions" (II, 732; II, 214)—an evocation repeated word-for-word in "The Storyteller" of 1936. Insofar as the war impacted German territory only after the 1918 surrender, the emphasis here lies on the generalized catastrophe of immediate postwar life (inflation); Benjamin was always careful to mark the "poetry" of the war (fireworks, aesthetic displays as in Marinetti and Apollinaire) as regressive and fascist; and to reserve for this destructive side of technology the terminology of an impoverishment, a diminution. It is a view more fully elaborated at the beginning of "The Storyteller" and quite different from the celebration of technology which has so often been taken to be the burden of the reproducibility essay.

Benjamin did not experience the war himself (he had fled the draft in Switzerland); the richer vein of this universal impoverishment he found elsewhere, in an essay by Georg Simmel which lived a virtually symbiotic life with his own essay "On Some Motifs in Baudelaire," and without which the latter (and its prolongation in the *Arcades Project*) can scarcely come into focus. It is probably not quite right to evoke Simmel as the master of this younger generation of writers and essayists, even though many of them followed his seminars (the somewhat older Lukács and

---

6   John Berger, "The Moment of Cubism," *New Left Review* 42, 1967.

Bloch, the younger Benjamin and his schoolmates). The character of Simmel's work set it apart from the then-emergent sociological establishment; even his book on *The Philosophy of Money* was too poetic for disciplinary purposes. His essays constituted, rather, probes into modernity in which an empirical or thematic particularity gathered theoretical interpretation around itself; it was the form of his essays that above all served as a model for those who were less disciples or intellectual followers than, rather, literary practitioners of the new theoretical genre Simmel pioneered.

The most famous of Simmel's essays, "The Metropolis and Mental Life" (1903) set the stage for Benjamin's reevaluation of Baudelaire's poetic modernism in terms of loss and deterioration rather than of plenitude and natural genius. Here, in the place of the exceptional events of the war, the new industrial city becomes the daily life of that impoverishment, which Simmel characterizes in terms of stress and nerves, the many forking paths of agonizing decisions to be made in its streets, and the abstractions of money to be somehow assimilated to an everyday life hitherto led among things (what Heidegger called *Zuhandenheit*). To be sure, sociology as a discipline was invented at the end of the previous century in order to furnish the materials, analyses and weapons that a threatened bourgeoisie will need to protect itself against this new "nation within a nation" which is the working class—for Benjamin the crowds and masses of the new industrial world. But Simmel's essays are also a geography of the enclaves, the lines of flight, within that modern existence (reminiscent somewhat of Lukács's notion of the survival of minor epic or traditional forms and genres within the properly modern formlessness of the novel): enclaves which, as in Benjamin, often project characters or physiognomies, such as the adventurer, the stranger or the lover.

What Benjamin will do with the "nervousness" of the city (an idea that became fashionable in the US around the same time) is to sharpen it into the language of a nascent experimental psychology, into the concept of stimuli which are also shocks. Baudelaire then became the treasure house of such new experiences, the living shoves and jolts of what assails the individual organism among the multitude of those *semblables,* the other city dwellers (unlike Benjamin, Baudelaire was no traveler!).

But with this modification, and the emergence of the concept of the

shock, it becomes necessary to construct an opposite, a radically different kind of life which can be set in dramatic opposition to this one (and
whose forms and genres will also betray that difference and stand as its
symptoms). This is why not only did Benjamin find himself obliged to
evoke a kind of landed or peasant, village life before the industrial city, a
different kind of temporality and metabolism; he also felt the need to
transcribe this opposition into a new terminology. So it is that experience, a kind of catch-all phenomenological term for whatever is lived in
general by the human being, finds itself increasingly specialized, and the
word *Erfahrung*—in which the pedagogical and the learned, the mean-
ingfully habitual, the practices of handicraft, also come to enrich its
sense—must now be radically differentiated from what is "experienced"
(in a different way) in the new world of stress, nerves, crowds and
money—in other words, the world of stimuli and shock. These last will
now be assigned to the domain of *Erlebnis,* or what happens in a one-
time event, a sudden sharpness, which is not only a punctual shock but
one constantly repeated under numerous forms throughout the urban
day and night. Unlike the older *Erfahrung,* which is stored in the body,
einverleibt in memory, the new barrage of stimuli incites its victims to
develop defense mechanisms and habits of resistance: so *Erlebnis* carries
habit with it, not as a wisdom learned and perfected from constant practice, but rather an outer armor, inner signals and warnings, a warding
off, even a deafness to a multitude of signals, as well as a wariness in
watching out for them. "Streetwise" is an Americanism that has arisen in
a particularly dangerous milieu of city life, but which Benjamin already
attributes to Baudelaire. It is offensive as well as defensive: this is the
relationship to Baudelaire's unique stylistic inventions and his slashing
language, as it cuts through the problems of representation and repre-
sentability associated with modernity as such.

    A number of philosophers are appealed to in both essays to account
for the temporality of these processes, and they have to do with memory
as much as with the present. Bergson is evoked to give an account of the
repression of lived time (in which he was associated with Proust: today
it is no longer fashionable to do so); Freud to establish the vital point
that "emerging consciousness takes the place of a memory trace" (IV,
317; I, 612). Yet in some peculiarly Benjaminian and notable way, drawing on his own characteristic bag of estrangement techniques or
V-effects, Benjamin's procedure is really the reverse of all this: not to

define the tale by way of memory, but rather to redefine memory in terms of the tale: memory is here little more than a sign of experience itself, it signals the presence of the object; memory can only be identified by the memorable—namely, what can be told, and told by the traditional storyteller.

Now to be sure, the moment of the oral storyteller is itself historical: the griot, the reciter of oral epic, the elder at the center of a nighttime or fireside circle, the uniquely gifted yarn-spinner as his voice still lived only yesterday on radios in China—these figures are preceded by a system as old as the immemorial struggle for power between Hegel's master and slave-to-be. This is the generic alternation, two sides of the situational coin, between the death-oriented, destiny-laden, bloody epic recital of the warrior, the samurai, the horseman (Marc Bloch tells us that in the earliest dark ages the emergent noble was simply anyone who had a horse) and, on the other hand, the life-giving world of wishes fulfilled, of restorative magic, the helpful animals and the adolescent exploits of the peasant fairy tale, the form to which Benjamin intended to devote his scholarly life after the completion of the *Arcades*.

At stake is, no doubt, the event itself; but it can be given no content in advance, for it is defined by the historical temporality that presides over the moment of its experience; even that of death is thereby modified. The "and they lived happily ever after" of the fairy tale marks, as we recall, "the earliest arrangements that mankind made to shake off the nightmare which myth had placed upon its chest" (III, 157; II, 458). The novel, however, betrays the coming into being of biography—that is, of a form profoundly mimetic of a life-and-death in time. Benjamin quotes with approval the remark of a contemporary critic, "A man who dies at the age of thirty-five is at every point in his life a man who dies at the age of thirty-five"; adding the proviso that it is "to remembrance" that he will so appear (III, 156; II, 456). In reality, Benjamin is here delineating the perspective of the tale and its mode of grappling with destiny; the novel preserves the destiny but strips it of any remembrance in such a way that its individual moments seem existential (that is, immediate and yet charged with an immanent *Sein-zum-Tode*, a "being-unto-death"). The tale, however, refers us back to "natural history" (III, 151; II, 450).

This essay, "The Storyteller," thereby glows uniquely with a "weak messianic power" from out of the length and breadth of the Benjaminian corpus. Virtually alone among his writings, it promises salvation. Its teller of tales, indeed, turns out to be the wise man, the man of counsel, the rabbi, who preserves *Erfahrung* in the midst of an otherwise ephemeral natural life. But, as in the Hasidic tales themselves, that man of wisdom is also the protagonist, present even where he least seems visible (in Kafka, for example). Yet in this very sense the glow his wisdom seems to revive in the world of things is easily appropriated by the false light of regression and the appropriation of myth by fascism: something like the confiscation of the fairy tale to serve as a sheep's clothing for myth, for the baleful prophets of guilt and destiny. Meanwhile, the form cunningly conceals within its structure that secret message of *apokatastasis*, which is for Benjamin the redemption of history and to which we will return in a final chapter.

As for Baudelaire, however, what is here hinted at is that other possibility, which the reproducibility essay rehearses in its turn—namely, that of the creation of a wholly new art based on *Erlebnis* rather than *Erfahrung*, an art of the instant, of the reduction of duration to sheer information, an art of the loss of historicity and imprisonment in the sheer present of time. It is a cultural (and political) dilemma which we, in the age of short-term memory and a well-nigh algorithmic present, of simulation and singularity, artificial memory and "the autism of addiction," are even more well-placed to appreciate than he was. "For someone who is past experiencing, there is no consolation" (IV, 335; I, 642). And yet there is still the last-minute hope of the gambler:

> *Souviens-toi que le Temps est un joueur avide*
> *Qui gagne sans tricher, à tout coup! c'est la loi.*

It is a misunderstanding of hope for the gambler: his is a no-win situation; it is time that (like the chess-playing automaton) can never lose, that "wins all the time" (IV, 389; I, 693).

Still, this is the moment to reflect on what is the deepest contradiction in Benjamin's thought and work: something McCole expresses rather mildly in a footnote: "the pathos of this work: there are no eras of decay, a reminder that must be balanced against the fact that he was entirely willing to speak of an atrophy of experience."[7] In fact, he spoke of nothing else, and what McCole calls pathos is, in reality, a fundamental historical contradiction, that crisis "which just goes on like this" and which is called capitalism. Benjamin tried to solve history by way of history.

---

7   John McCole, *Walter Benjamin and the Antinomies of Tradition*, Ithaca: Cornell University Press, 1993, 269n17.

8

The Hand and Eyes of the Masses

1

Benjamin's reputation, however, is inseparable from his great essay on the reproducibility of works of art, which dutifully ranges from ancient coinage through lithography, photography and the then state of motion pictures (the fullest version of this text being the second one, dating from 1936). There is a good deal of warranted uncertainty as to the basic subject of this essay. Is it not about film? Well, no: no single film is mentioned and only Chaplin and Mickey Mouse appear in person; not even Eisenstein gets a walk-on. But film is surely included within a broader topic—that of the media, a concept which did not exist at the time and in the course of which one would minimally expect a discussion of radio (Benjamin's own "medium") and a good deal more about publishing houses and newspapers (which were also an existential concern). Meanwhile, the most famous "idea" in the whole essay is the one called "aura," which seems to have more to do with aesthetics and with beauty than with that reproducibility which is supposedly rendering it extinct.

But we miss the point of Benjamin's project here if we take it to be the elaboration of a whole new aesthetics (for the "modern" or the "media" age, perhaps). He is very specific about its political function, which is to "set aside [*beiseitesetzen*] a number of traditional [aesthetic] concepts" (III, 101; VII, 350). The translator has, however, nudged this formulation forward in a useful direction by rendering the strategic verb as "neutralize," and this is precisely Benjamin's meaning. It is a matter of rendering such concepts inoperative, of disarming them, as one might disable a factory and sabotage its mass-produced weapons. The essay is, in that sense, designed to render older, now-obsolete critical values useless for aestheticization, which is to say, for fascism.

Nor is it necessary to grasp technology as the principal factor in this obsolescence of an older literary and artistic thinking: we tend to forget that it was only after World War I (not so terribly long ago!) that an effective mass politics came into being, with its parties and movements; in which virtually for the first time in history the demos took center stage in permanence rather than in rare and intermittent outbreaks. This is to say that number will now play a central part as a fundamental organizational category of Benjamin's thinking. The masses, for him, determine new categories, a new form of thinking, and not a sociological topic such as the study of new publics in the industrial era.

The third or most familiar version of this essay, on "The Work of Art in the Age of Its Technological Reproducibility" was, in effect, the product of censorship by his friends at the Frankfurt School's house journal, the *Zeitschrift für Sozialforschung* and thereby divested of its most visible political (or Brechtian) developments. The essay is, in any case, not a straightforward argument, but, like so many of Benjamin's longer essays, whose true form was only visibly revealed in the final text on history, a set of theses, their center of gravity significantly displaced from section to section. I am tempted to compare this form—an episodization, to use our earlier terminology—with that contemporary photography which has no vanishing point and whose perspective shifts ceaselessly across its immense expanses. To give a simple example I have already touched on: despite its reputation, this is not at all an essay on film—only a few directors named in passing, Chaplin, Disney (not even Eisenstein), and no individual films mentioned. Film is, in effect, just one buoy thrown up here by the movement of Benjamin's thought through history, and in particular through historical change or transition.

My own feeling is that the "reproducibility" essay must be read as a sequel to the "Little History of Photography" (1931), in which a smaller-scale but comparable, and preparatory, historical sequence is interpreted; it thereby stands in what we will find to be the antagonistic relationship of analogy and causality at work in Benjamin's historical thought.

But this preliminary essay also usefully reveals an antinomy at the heart of every Benjaminian approach to technology, and it is the dilemma at the heart of every theory of photography, which is a temporal one. What distinguishes the photograph as an anomaly in the world of objects is, in other words, its simultaneous existence in the past as well as the present, even though the past does not exist. The most influential theories of photography (Sontag, Barthes, Benjamin himself) have made a virtue out of this necessity and have placed the ontological paradox at the center of their accounts, as a unique property not to be explained but rather to be described.

It is this paradox, endlessly rehearsed in all the reaches of this phenomenon, which accounts for the dual nature of photography as a technology and an art, as an image and an industrial product, as a historical event at the same time it is a potsherd or static marker; this antinomy can be pursued into the very heart of the concept of the image itself, where it has never been resolved. That a prolongation of human sensory experience should find its date in chronological history as a scientific discovery, is not the least of the dilemmas posed for its theorization. I believe that it is perpetuated in the problem of visuality itself (despite the echoing reproducibilities of sound and radio), for it is essentially in the realm of the visual that the original (if there is one) is reproduced, whether we have to do with coinage, printing or film itself. Indeed, we speak of acoustic images, as though visuality was the primary marker of a separation of meaning from sense data. The purely visual, without meaning or theoretical content, is the purely contingent; even its concept is idealistic, at once bringing with it all the problems of philosophical idealism and in particular that of the abstract and the universal. This is the seam between mind and body which, however sutured in a variety of modern philosophies, must still necessarily leave the faintest scar behind it (and must then, inevitably, send us back to that undesirable philosophical place of origins in which the human emerges from the blooming, buzzing confusion of the telluric).

In the stylistic realm, however, it is with Goethe's famous "tender empiricism" that we find that compromise between abstract classification and visual observation in which some kind of Ur-form can be hypothesized. It will have become clear by now that Benjamin's *Denkbilder* are precisely compromises of this sort, images with a theoretical charge, which mediate (it was Goethe's word!) between figures and theories, never fully surrendering to either category. But if the so-called *Denkbild* or "thought-picture" finds its objective realization in language, then we can at least see how the photograph, for Benjamin, might offer some distant and reciprocal formal equivalent on the side of vision. The painting is a fully visual object; only in its reproduction does it begin to take on a theoretical and abstracting function as illustration or example (Malraux's *Voices of Silence* underscored this process of abstraction by reproduction from the very outset). But the photograph, somehow, always thinks. It may think sentimental thoughts, as in the much-maligned family photo (the nadir of all photographic aesthetics) or even in the portrait. It may think the thoughts of the tourist—but then Atget is there to demonstrate how those vulgar cityscapes can be sublimated into "great art" (the scene of the crime, as Benjamin calls them). But human intelligence and attention (in its psychological and philosophical senses) necessarily intervene between the sense-datum and the finished product: selection is already the fleeting sketch of a thought, and the *flâneur* is a precursor of the photographer (Baudelaire's own example of the modern, the "painter of modern life," Constantin Guys, already takes snapshots avant la lettre).

Benjamin's essay on photography (II, 507–30; II, 368–85) can thus be seen to track the steps of the reproducibility essay in advance and thereby to illuminate its more obscure intentions. Its first pages at once spell the lineage from invention to commodity and cast a harsh artificial studio light on the destiny of film in the process.

Its two outer limits then enunciate the following. First of all, the invention of photography, Nadar, Daguerre, the first photograph, are to be chalked up to handicraft. Labor, but the work of the hand, is present in storytelling as well; the novel is suspiciously far from it, and history, as we shall see, cannot be narrated. Production as such is the Marxian core of this theory, and against it will be measured all of those aesthetic terms, such as aura, which seem to appear independently, as aesthetic values or theories.

At the other end of the historical development, the industrial commercialization of the photograph must be grasped (although he does not use the word) as commodification. But Benjamin has something to add to our conventional theories of the commodity as well, and this will illuminate his account of aesthetization in the concluding (political) pages of the reproducibility essay. For here it becomes clear that the aesthetic is the compensatory regression which is required in order to restore the appearance of the original. Pierre Bourdieu and his collaborators, in a remarkable little book on amateur photography (*Un art mineur*), documented features of amateur photography which confirm Benjamin's theorization here. The first is the absolute contempt shown by these amateur photographers, who want to think of themselves as artists, for the family photo: their primary motivation, indeed— or such is Bourdieu's diagnosis—was to escape the home and the family in the first place, to invent an independent life outside the bourgeois foyer. Amateur photography is thus revealed to be itself a "line of flight," a form of resistance to bourgeois society (albeit a "minor" one).

A second feature, however, accompanies this first one, which can in this sense be seen as a form of political disavowal: the amateur photographers of this period, in full flight before industrial or commercial photography as well, all tend to rationalize their hobby by borrowing from the aesthetics of painting. This is thus a secondhand aesthetics; it clearly enough omits all the problems of reproduction and technology (not even acknowledging it as a dilemma, as do the contemporary or postmodern theories of photography already mentioned). The borrowed apologia is precisely what Benjamin means by "regression" throughout his work (and on a variety of topics) and what he will ultimately diagnose both as a symptom of fascism and, in another sense, its very structure. In the crisis of its wholesale commercialization and commodification, then, "the creative" (Benjamin is using the word in a heavily ironic emphasis) "becomes a fetish, whose lineaments live only in the fitful illumination of changing fashion. The creative in photography is its capitulation to fashion. The world is beautiful—that is its watchword." Leave aside his nod to the "tiger's leap" of fashion in the final *Theses on the Philosophy of History*, but retain the word "fetish," already used by Marx in his "definition" of the commodity; and observe the persistence of Benjamin's attack on "the artistic," on "beauty" (*schöner Schein*) and on aesthetics as such. Aesthetization thus emerges as aesthetics, as compensation and regression, as the symptom-formation of a world better reproduced by stripping away, by the violence of Atget (who removes the people and thereby destroys the ideological category of humanism), by demystifying "the dream-laden subjects . . . a forerunner more of its salability than of any knowledge it might produce." Benjamin also thereby restores everything negative and destructive in his own recourse to concepts like phantasmagoria (in the *Arcades*) and implicitly endorses Freud's method, which remorselessly strips every bit of charm and aesthetic fascination from the dream in the process of its interpretation.

What is useful and instructive here for our reading of the reproducibility essay is the way in which, paradoxically, the more direct consideration of photography, by introducing time into the analysis, dispels the multiple temptations of aestheticism from visuality. As a quote from Tristan Tzara puts it, turning his power lamp on light-sensitive paper, the photographer "discovered what could be done by a pure and sensitive flash of light—a light that was more important than all the constellations arranged for the eye's pleasure." Here the machine outstrips the body and its perceptions, not so much for reproduction in the sense of the famous essay (that is, the multiplication of the image for millions of other people), but rather in the dual sense of Benjamin's peculiar notion of mimesis or "similarity." It is an outstripping and a transcendence which takes us potentially a good deal beyond what is envisioned for film, and projects itself into those future powers of the computer that will give rise to theories of the specifically "posthuman."

Here, however, what we need to retain are the twofold effects of time on the auratic image itself. Indeed, as we shall see, Benjamin's little essay will take his notion of the auratic well beyond technical definitions and return it to the area of aesthetic value (which was surely its initial starting point). Value emerges in the reproducibility essay only in political form, when in the famous peroration that concludes it, the writer foresees the portentous alternative of an appropriation of the new medium for either fascist or communist purposes.

In the essay on photography, we are given a rather different history of this new technical form, one perhaps framed more purely in terms of aesthetic taste: its earliest specimens (above all, the daguerreotype) have a value which is at least in part that of craftsmanship—an activity inseparable from the immediacy of the body itself and its manipulations. But, predictably, the generation of photography's first artists/craftsmen is overtaken by capital: "businessmen invaded professional photography from every side; and when, later on, the retouched negative . . . became ubiquitous, a sharp decline in taste set in."

He follows this development up with what is a stunning performance of the Marxist-Hegelian, the truly dialectical, method: the affirmation of an evolution (for the worse) of the technique or form is matched by a concomitant development of its object or content: "In this early period subject and technique were as exactly congruent as they became incongruent in the period of decline that immediately followed." Lukács himself could not have more elegantly wedded historical subject and object together in all their parallel autonomies. The moment of aura in the photograph (which we will examine in a moment) is matched by its appearance in real life, as it were—for just like the photographers, the businessmen were also evolving, and with them bourgeois society as such. We are given a few illustrations in this text: the elderly Schelling, but above all, some burghers, a transitional species who fill in the evolutionary gap between the great merchants of the eighteenth century and the slick moneymakers of the mid-nineteenth century: Keller's *Martin Salander*, Mann's *Buddenbrooks*, but above all, a little beyond Balzac's eye range, the emergence of Zola's great department store, across the street from a traditional clothier, down whose steps you select your material from bolts of cloth. That older world still produced clothes *built to last* (an expression Benjamin intends to apply not only to the subject of the photograph but to the daguerreotype itself): "the very creases in people's clothes have an air of permanence. Just consider Schelling's coat. It will surely pass into immortality along with him: the shape it has borrowed from its wearer is not unworthy of the creases in his face . . . the photographer [of this first period] was confronted, in the person of every client, with a member of a rising class equipped with an aura that had seeped into the very folds of the man's frock coat or floppy cravat." We should not make too much of the incongruence of the term "rising class" with these sad images of a classical burghertum in decline, for, as Lukács or the Sartre of *L'Idiot de la famille* tell the story, this class ceased to "rise" in 1848; its replacement, documented by Zola and Maupassant, "corresponded" (to use the shorthand of that Marx-Hegelian method we are illustrating) to the evolution of photographic technique that Benjamin wishes us to grasp—that is, to the advances in technological reproduction and, in particular, to the shortening of the time required to fix light on the negative. That seeming immortality of the subject to which we have seen Benjamin refer in an earlier passage—the length of time to which the subject is subjected in order for the inscription or registration to take place—that *durée* is itself the aura. What we feel in gazing at a daguerreotype is the time of the process itself: aura and authenticity have now been revealed to be the eye-witness evidence of sheer temporality as production. The emergence of the studio and its "artistic" poses thus turns out to be the attempt of this nascent industry to artificially restore its initial aura [now lost]; there is a Lukácsean motif here somewhere, perhaps his denunciation of naturalist description in the name of the immediacy of true Balzacian realism. I have just read the review of a book which purports to draw our attention to the role of time itself in gastronomy, not only in the minutes of cooking required by the notation of the recipe, but also in the very taste of the dish itself; this evocation of a temporality *einverleibt* in the auratic object has its equivalent in the age of the rare book, and somehow in the *Erfahrung* into which the various *Erlebnisse* of the novel have been transformed. Perhaps it also has some relationship to the child's appropriation of a favorite film, which, in the old days, one could see over and over again without buying another ticket. Is it fair, then, to add, with Michelet, "*l'histoire, c'est le temps!*"? He must at least have thought so himself, when, arriving at the climactic night of August 4, 1789, he cried out:

> *Que vous avez tardé, grand jour! combien de temps nos pères vous ont attendu et rêvé! . . . L'espoir que leurs fils vous verraient enfin a pu seul les soutenir; autrement ils n'auraient pas voulu vivre, ils seraient morts à la peine . . . Moi-même, leur compagnon, labourant à côtés d'eux dans le sillon de l'histoire, buvant à leur coupe amère, qui m'a permis de revivre le douloureux moyen âge, et pourtant de n'en pas mourir, n'est-ce pas vous, ô beau jour, premier jour de la délivrance? . . . J'ai vécu pour vous raconter!*[1]

How long you've made us wait, great day! How long our forefathers have waited for you and dreamed about you! . . . only the hope their sons would see you sustained them, otherwise they would have been unable to live, they would have died in harness . . . And I myself, their companion, laboring beside them in the fields of history, drinking their bitter cup, who else would have allowed me to relive the painful middle ages and not to have died from it, but You, O splendid day, the first day of freedom? . . . I have lived to tell your story!

---

1   Jules Michelet, *Histoire de la revolution française*, Vol. 1, Paris: Gallimard, 1952, 203.

Indeed, this was the cry of relief of the writer, when, after the composition of sentence after sentence of his multivolume history of France, pen in hand, before all dictation or typewriters, he finally reached the revolution itself. The dried ink on these ancient hallowed pages surely still gives off an aura in its own right.

The advantage, then, of superimposing the "Little History of Photography" on the reproducibility essay is that the former, in its demonstration of the dialectic of subject and object, of the apparatus as well as of its subject matter, reminds us that history continues on both sides and that there is a history of the object which must somehow accompany the history of the subject (and vice versa). The weakness of histories that limit themselves to technological development—such as that of photography or film as media—is that they omit those parallel developments in the social history, in the raw material that the new medium must also "register." This is, then, where we confront again, and more adequately, the problem of "aura" (and also, quite unexpectedly, that of the storyteller and storytelling as well).

2

Aura is in Benjamin a peculiarly marked and central concept, problematic not least on account of the multiple theoretical contexts in which it functions. The selection of the term (which keeps its identity across the Western European languages) demonstrates a tactical use of sensory ambiguities: for this painterly term, often used to convey the nimbus of painted saints, derives in fact from a classical word for breeze that itself also includes a breath of fragrance. Fringes of the sensory, then, convey something of an accessible immateriality and retain a bodily immediacy winnowed to its most transcendental. The message is conveyed by way of the quality of the figuration and not its terms. It can be reckoned as a name for a certain kind of experience, the latter always being a thematics central for Benjamin's thinking (provided it is grasped in a Platonic and philosophical way as lasting experience—*Erfahrung*—and not just as something random that happens to us). In this form, what becomes significant, and worthy of attention, is the historical waning or disappearance of this "experience."

It is, to be sure, subject to phenomenological analysis: here, the subtlety of Benjamin's formulation—only reiterated a few times throughout his work—must be emphasized: "the unique apparition of a distance, however near it may be—'*einmalige Erscheinung einer Ferne, so nah sie sein mag*'" (III, 104–5; VII, 355). I believe it is best initially to approach this "definition" biologically, as the evocation of that membrane which separates the living organism from the outside world, from what it is not. That organic separation is the "*Ferne*," the distance between inside and outside, between the self (my body) and the non-self: it is this distance which makes the source of the auratic into an object as such, an object for consciousness or, as it will be called later on, the "autonomous" work of art.

But this feature of the description must not simply be understood as one characteristic to be lined up in the inventory alongside that other characteristic, which is proximity or nearness. The relationship of near and far here is absolutely and strictly dialectical: they define each other, neither can be grasped without the other, their separation as two distinct words is the mark or scar of their necessary passage through language itself. Their combination must be understood as paradoxical and dissonant—we are to grasp the unique peculiarity of a distant nearness, an intimate and infinitely close remoteness; the external "object" must be something at one and the same time very close and unreachable, and this difficult combination means that such objects will be extremely rare and indeed of a unique type. That requirement defines these objects as "aesthetic"; and with this specification, the description of the experience of aura passes over into that exclusive philosophical field we call aesthetics (and which, since Kant, makes up the three great domains of human thinking alongside the epistemological and the ethical, inasmuch as Kant essentially ruled out metaphysics as such—the transcendent—as a rational field of thought).

"Aura" here becomes a rough equivalent of what remains the central and constitutive concept of academic aesthetic, namely beauty. Beauty, in fact, remains central to Adorno's aesthetic, as sophisticated as that may be. Even if—especially if—with the Romantics and Victor Hugo, you wish to introduce ugliness into the experience of art, it is still within the forcefield of beauty that ugliness is identified. *Schein* or appearance, a wider and perhaps more usable philosophical concept (especially for the German philosophical tradition in general and Benjamin in particular), remains closely affiliated with beauty and thereby, however secretly, with aura. Only the aesthetic notions of play (first associated with

Schiller) and, later on, of construction have historically managed to make a place for themselves independently of appearance or beauty—but neither can be grasped as the opposite of aura; indeed, one of the dilemmas confronting us in our dealings with this uniquely Benjaminian term is that it has no opposite: the non-auratic cannot be considered a dialectical opposite to the auratic, but merely its privative state, whence the difficulty of attributing to Benjamin anything like an aesthetics of film (let alone of media or new media). The loss of aura (and with it, the very concept of beauty) spells the extinction of aesthetics as a philosophical discipline.

At this point, then, the function of this unusual concept is modified: from an experiential, and then an aesthetic, one, it becomes, by way of its waning or disappearance, a historical marker. Thus the obsolescence of aura in the arts—and, no doubt, in human experience and perception generally—can be a sign and potential definition of what we call modernity. If the auratic is no longer available, then we find ourselves in what can recognizably be identified as modern; in that case, other features of modernity can be turned back on "aura" in order to refine the concept further. The association of modernity with industry and the machine, for example, then alerts us to the possibility that aura was something associated with handicraft and the tool (indeed, we have seen this association confirmed by Benjamin's elaboration of the unique nature of storytelling, not exactly at first glance an auratic phenomenon, but whose deeper interrelations begin to emerge as his great essay on the subject develops).

But several other philosophical consequences also begin to emerge when we consider aura in the context of modernity. I passed over, in my initial account, a secondary association that always seems to accompany Benjamin's rare attempts to pin aura down: it is the "mountain range on the horizon or the branch that casts its shadow on the beholder"—in other words, nature itself, or the problem of "natural beauty" as Adorno identifies it in *Aesthetic Theory*. The association suggests that an outworn aesthetics often (if not always) will seek to justify its existence by way of an evocation of Nature as such; and also, more ominously, that when aura wanes, then nature is itself in the process of approaching extinction (something our own time is better placed to understand than Benjamin's generation, which only had the benefit of the wasteland left by World War I—see "Experience and Poverty" [II, 732; II, 214]). This threat to nature is then logically accompanied by a diminution in the physical and perceptual capacities of the subject or, in other words, an impoverishment of experience as such, which furnishes yet another definition, by negation, of modernity.

But the fragility and eventual loss of aura in the historical lifeworld sets another train of thought in motion, generating not only yet another function of this protean concept, but also a wholly original line of cultural and eventually political interpretation. For what is more inevitable, in the wholesale abolition of aura in modernity, than the attempts of artists and other apologists to reinstate it, or at least to reproduce it artificially? This attempt will ground Benjamin's critical use of the notion of the "regressive" and it will furnish a whole new strategy for those wishing to avoid a modernism that acknowledges its dilemmas— Baudelaire, in the warding off of the shocks of the various urban *Erlebnisse*, or Le Corbusier, in the stripping away of ornament and excess in his steel-and-glass constructions. This new strategy will aim at restoring an illusion of social and aesthetic plenitude. It will be identified as aesthetization and called upon to mask the poverty of capitalist existence and will gradually be associated with the latter's fundamental logic, that of commodification. Indeed, it is by way of the commodity that aesthetization celebrates its triumphs, which include the beautification of warfare (and its availability for celebration as an aesthetic experience) and culminate in fascism.

Aura, therefore, or at least in its historical absence, will have become a diagnostic tool; but the structural absence from the concept of any genuinely opposite term means that it cannot itself furnish the means to construct a new aesthetic for the modern era (Benjamin recommends politicalization, the historicizing of experience, as the only corrective to fascist aestheticization). An advanced art, one which escapes regression and offers a genuine alternative to it in the difficult situation of the modern capitalist world, will eschew this henceforth outmoded and aestheticizing concept for something else. Implicitly, what is offered is not art at all—see the questions at the end of the essay on Surrealism; depressing questions for the artist, such as "mightn't the interruption [*Unterbrechung*, abandonment] of his 'artistic career' perhaps be an essential part of his new function?" (II, 217; II, 309). In other words, give up art altogether; take up an intellectual life of another, political kind.

In a sense, Benjamin himself has already done so, although he is certainly vividly aware of the contradictions inherent in a cultural-journalistic life under capitalism as well, and frequently spells them out. But I suggest a deeper theoretical solution: it involves the abandonment of categories which, like those of ethics or aesthetics, presuppose the domain of the individual and its limits and limited function, and aims to substitute the wholly new categories of number, masses, multiplicities, in which an experience like aura has no place, but in which, perhaps, a different kind of Experience might be available.

And it is there that we find a far more precise and complex account of aura than in the summary references in the reproducibility essay. Aura, as we witness its fate in photography, has its positive and negative faces: a seemingly dialectical opposition which is rapidly dispelled into a sense of mixed feelings and a kind of double bind, inasmuch as Benjamin is deeply invested in both versions. A positive form of aura attracts accounts of authenticity and the unique value of this or that one-time experience. Yet the negative form—in which aura is part and parcel of that immense cultural swindle that compensates the commodified poverty of industrial "ever-sameness" and stamped-out copies for the masses—that simulated aura arouses a no less passionate denunciation on Benjamin's part. These seemingly contradictory versions of aura will then, in his work, be reconciled by a historical narrative of the passage from the earliest moment of invention to the final stake of commercial exploitation (II, 507–30; II, 368–85).

"The Little History of Photography," however, gives us a good deal more material to work with than the simple formulation of aura he will quote and reuse in the later essay ("the unique appearance or semblance of distance no matter how close it may be"). Reproducibility will reduce the one pole of this dialectical relationship and, at their own demand, bring phenomena ever closer to the masses, with their "need to possess the object in close-up in the form of a picture, or rather a copy." The German original, however, eschews the charged term "possess" for "*habhaft*," a far more tactile and handicraftsman-like word, one closer to the body than the web of legalities summoned up by the question of possession. Still, what the masses get to "possess" here is something as fundamentally different from the original as time from eternity: "uniqueness and duration are as intimately intertwined in the latter as are transience and reproducibility in the former." There a sense that the

Brechtian/Heraclitean metaphysic of ephemerality is awakened here, but it turns quickly into a method—less one of estrangement than of the unmasking of aura as the deceptive outer appearance of a far more unpleasant reality:

> The peeling away of the object's shell, the destruction of the aura, is the signature of a perception whose sense for the sameness of things has grown to the point where even the singular, the unique, is divested of its uniqueness—by means of its reproduction.

We are very far here from the phantasmagoria, the world of simulacra, of commodification; and thereby approach the political asceticism of a truth of ever-sameness. Benjamin once again summons Atget to his witness stand and celebrates the novelty of his empty streets, their "salutary estrangement between man and his surroundings." There then follows a momentous sentence whose promise will not begin to be fulfilled until the later reproducibility essay. Evoking this new, disabused vision of a world stripped of its aura, he declares that "it gives free play to the politically educated eye, under whose gaze all intimacies are sacrificed to the illumination of detail." It is a peculiar way of celebrating our new political insights; and perhaps it is worthwhile returning to the intimacies evoked earlier in this essay, which uncannily anticipate all kinds of modern visual analyses (Michael Fried's absorption, Roland Barthes's punctum, Rosalind Kraus's version of the "optical unconscious"). "In Hill's [photograph of a] Newhaven fishwife," for example, "her eyes cast down in such indolent, seductive modesty, there remains something that goes beyond testimony to the photographer's art, something that cannot be silenced, that fills you with an unruly desire to know . . . the woman who was alive there; who even now is still real and will never consent to be wholly absorbed in 'art.'" This strange transcendent immanence perhaps goes beyond what Fried wishes to capture by the notion of absorption and begins to approach the Barthesian punctum, here, however, evoked not as some mere contingent visual detail but rather as the inassimilable radical otherness of the gaze of the subject—in this case, a fiancée whose husband-to-be "seems to be holding her, but her gaze passes him by, absorbed in an ominous distance . . . [This] is another nature which speaks to the camera rather than to the eye: 'other' above all in the sense that a space informed by human consciousness gives way to a space informed by the unconscious." One is tempted to speculate on that distinction between the look and the gaze-object which Lacan deduced from Sartre[2]; all the more in light of Benjamin's observation that some of the earliest beholders of these industrial images felt a kind of dread at the prospect that "these little tiny faces in the picture could see *us*."

It was not only tribal peoples, we recall, but Balzac himself, who believed that the photograph could steal something of his own soul. Meanwhile, it might well be conjectured (Benjamin never goes so far) that from the reproducible work there also gazes back an Other, but in this case the otherness of the multitude itself, the masses; the crowds, whose long-lost unseen gazes return to us from what was once seen by so many, now as dead as the subjects of these still living daguerreotypes.

Aura is also material, in the sense in which it captures for all eternity the warp and weave of Schelling's coat in the philosopher's 1850 photo portrait; it is a materiality of time and not of spatial objects. Benjamin entertains the speculations of the contemporaries of these first photographic images: that time is somehow inscribed in them by virtue of the patience with which the poses had to be held, the very grain of time slowly imprinting itself on the plate. But surely, when we look back at the great silent films suggested by Benjamin's reproducibility essay—at those of Chaplin or Eisenstein—and even when we once again rescreen the studio classics of Hollywood's golden age, or film noir, or even the French New Wave, the outmoded photography and the black-and-white medium itself express a time which is more than merely historical; the outmoded has become a kind of aura in its own right.

I will not dwell on the painful, delicious pages in which, via Kafka's portraits as a child, Benjamin evokes his own dreaded sessions among the potted plants of the photographer's studio; I will only juxtapose them with that great discovery on which all modern cinema is grounded, namely Griffith's accidental invention of the close-up, comparable as a technological miracle in its own right to Madame Curie's discovery of radium. Here we may evoke Deleuze and "faceness" (*visagéité*) and observe the same inexorable transformation of a primal dimension of humanity (animals have no faces) into a commodity which can be

2   See Jacques Lacan, *Seminar XI*, Paris: Seuil, 1973.

bought and sold and on which the star system itself is founded. We do not have to prolong the meditation into contemporary facial recognition technology to experience the inescapable duality from which Benjamin's mixed feelings spring as he attempted, impossibly, to fashion "aura" into a coherent abstract concept.

3

With these preparatory qualifications—the emphasis on temporality and its dilemmas as well as the peculiar adaptability of the "concept" of aura to new contexts and arguments—we may return to the central reproducibility essay (in its fundamental, second version) and follow its theses to what is not exactly a conclusion. For theses are not discursive, as the philosophers like to put it; they are not steps in a logical argument or demonstration, but rather moments of historical consequence that fan out in some well-nigh synchronic or structural fashion. Perhaps it might be better, given its intent to neutralize inherited concepts, to read the essay negatively, as arguments against more established positions rather than as affirmative statements.

Still, the text (III, 101–21; VII, 350–84) begins dutifully enough, with a historical review of reproductive technologies which reaches its climax in lithography, reminding us of Fuchs's essay and situating us in the decisive moment of the mass press and the popular newspaper (the 1840s, the moment of photography as well as of "socialism" as a word and a nascent reality). Chronology is, however, not really the point of this discussion, which is to swerve, however fleetingly, to a dialectical modification of the very latest of these technologies, namely film. In film alone does "technological reproduction . . . capture a place of its own among the artistic processes."

This is only one of the ways Benjamin begins on what is a series of problems. Other beginnings will be tried—an analysis of the here-and-now of the older artwork; an evocation of the history of perception. This first beginning, however, plunges us at once into a discussion of authenticity as such, of that unique *Echtheit* which not only authorizes practices of "authentication" in the historical study of the visual arts but seems to define the very nature and essentials of art as such. To be sure, this will not only lead us to aura, but will turn out to form the basis of all those outworn aesthetic values the essay wishes to "neutralize." Just as Bourdieu and his collaborators showed us the anxious attempts of their amateur photographers to justify their hobby in terms of the apologias for painting current in their period, so also the new apologists for film (Abel Gance is quoted) appeal to "Shakespeare, Rembrandt, Beethoven" to make a tradition for themselves, not realizing, says Benjamin, that they were "inviting the reader, no doubt unawares, to witness a comprehensive liquidation." If it is truly authenticity which constitutes the nature of genuine art, then the new techniques of reproduction invite us to an enormous fire sale of tradition, and works like Malraux's *Voices of Silence* become something like its Sears-Roebuck catalogue.

But if Marx is right in observing that there exists something like a "history of the senses," then we must not only question the modifications reproduction brings to the sensorium and human subjectivity; we must examine such modifications in conjunction with changes in social life and the forms of society: "Just as the mode of existence of human collectives changes over long historical periods, so too does their mode of perception." I believe that we must interpret Benjamin's thinking here in terms of number and population, at least insofar as the present of both society and art is concerned.

But speculation is now in order as to what that new and modified type of perception, that new structure of subjectivity, could be, and what satisfactions it might offer to replace those of the uniqueness of work and its experience. Here, it is as though sheer number, the masses, is willing to give up one pole of aura—to sacrifice the distance that makes the object into a work for the individual subject—in order to achieve nearness alone: "the desire of the present-day masses to 'get closer' to things," indeed, "their equally passionate concern for overcoming each thing's uniqueness." One imagines the sacking of the Tuileries in 1848 (via Flaubert) or the invasion of the Winter Palace (via Eisenstein): can it be that the hitherto jealous preservation of "each thing's uniqueness" (the "*Einmaligkeit jeder Gegebenheit*") is the object of class resentment and violence? And that the individual "work," in its here-and-now authenticity, is somehow also a class signal, a mark of privilege and hierarchy to be destroyed? (In the next section, he will associate the older art with ritual, with cult value—which is to say, with that church and religious hierarchy which also forms so essential a part of class power and hierarchy in the various anciens régimes, where it was always explicitly the target of Enlightenment revolutions.)

In fact, however, Benjamin here introduces a wholly new theme: it turns out that authenticity (genuineness and the here-and-now, the older work of art, the not-yet-baptized aura) acquires a new and unexpected opposite number with consequences for time as well as for space—this is that *"Gleichartige in der Welt"* (a phrase of Johannes V. Jensen), which will appear in varying contexts later on as the "self-sameness," the universal identity, of the commodity world (and on which Adorno will ground his aesthetic—art's resistance to the commodity form). The sentence is worth quoting in its entirety: "The stripping of the veil from the object, the destruction of the aura, is the signature of a perception whose 'sense for sameness in the world' has so increased that, by means of reproduction, it extracts sameness even from what is unique." The political signals of this sentence are surprisingly contradictory: one would have expected the masses' activity—stripping away, destruction, demystification, critique—to be a positive development, yet in the second part of the sentence those same masses seem to be on the point of changing into the low-brow philistine publics of a more bourgeois extraction denounced by the left-wing (Frankfurt School) critics as a debased mass culture in the 1930s and '40s. Benjamin himself seems aware of this ambiguity and, in a crucial footnote on the "double meaning" of popular works, testifies that it could also be argued that judgment of this kind is always ethical and thereby ideological, even when it seems to bear on political positions, and that "the dialectical materialist" must always find a position above mere judgment in history itself and in the historical necessity of changes of this kind. The occasional confusion arising from this essay, in particular, would then most often be the result of our desire to find judgments by Benjamin in what he stubbornly means to be a historical account of transition and change. The disappearance of aura, for example, which so many readers might well expect him to deplore (as Adorno does), is observed by Benjamin dispassionately and without any overt regret, just as one might have expected from a "historical materialist" (not to speak of some Hegelian evocation of "the end of art").

The next sections of the essay chart the historical relations of art with a cult value it is obliged to abandon, leaving the secular consumer without any stable criterion for aesthetic judgment—or even, as in the duel between photography and painting, without any clear sense of what art actually is in the first place. This uncertainty, as we have already indicated, also spells the end of aesthetics, a philosophical system inevitably organized around beauty or aura as a permanent norm.

This is, then, the moment in which Benjamin's essay launches itself into the void, in a series of discussions heavily censored by his Frankfurt School examiners. For now a new proposal about what a new art can be, or at least about what should take the place of traditional art as such, is massively informed by Brechtian practice. The new art, now definitively identified as film, will be an experiment, analogous to a set of tests: "Film makes test performances capable of being exhibited, by turning exhibition itself into a test." Here the Brechtian language of a public of experts returns with a vengeance, the cigar-smoking judges of the boxing match or the horse race, in short "of all test performances" [*Testleistungen*]. The argument is clearly part of that operation of neutralization referred to above, reducing the value of "artistic production" to that secular pragmatism of tests and job interviews which increasingly absorb the activities of our modern populations.

Here, however, the alienation of the actor becomes the central figure for the dismantling and deconstruction of the individual subject in general under capitalism. The close-up was only one aspect of that more general "alienation" or dissolution into a multiplicity of parts and aspects (phenomenological *Abschattungen*). Now, aura is shown to have been the accompaniment of personal identity and bodily unity: film destroys both, as a magnificent passage from Pirandello's film novel *Shoot!* triumphantly demonstrates (no wonder he was also the author of *Six Characters in Search of an Author!*): "The film actor feels as if exiled. Exiled not only from the stage but from his own person . . . his body has lost its substance . . . he has been volatilized, stripped of his reality, his life, his voice, the noises he makes when moving about, [he] has been turned into a mute image that flickers for a moment on the screen." This is no longer *Schein*, Benjamin concludes, and in two of his richest philosophical footnotes he sets about demonstrating the proposition that "film is thus the first artistic medium which is able to show how matter plays havoc with human beings" (a nice but slanted translation of "*wie die Materie dem Menschen mitspielt*").

What is thereby alienated, however, is not necessarily the reality of some earlier, more purely human state (or the expression of some nostalgic belief in an earlier non-alienated condition). Rather, it is a critique of the aesthetics of aura, of the philosophical defects of the concept of beautiful appearance as such. This whole essay is, as we have already insisted in several places, *Ideologiekritik*: the neutralization of aesthetic theory rather than the attempt to mount a more satisfactory analysis and description of film as such. But here, exceptionally, we work our way back to something more fundamental, namely the concept of mimesis.

"The disciple," Adorno, as Benjamin himself called him (with whatever amusement), and the so-called Frankfurt School in general operate with a terminology of mimesis and the "mimetic impulse," which (like their notion of "myth") has often seemed foundational for their thought while remaining as mysterious as any axiom (it has nothing to do with Auerbach's eponymous book, I hasten to say). The derivation always seemed to lie in several crucial fragments of Benjamin's work, which are equally enigmatic, if seeming to point in a rather different direction. Here, finally, we touch on one of the latter's more solid formulations: "the polarity informing mimesis."

But to grasp what is at stake in this peculiarly Benjaminian notion of mimesis, whose origins are probably to be found in Rosenzweig, we must remember that it is, for Benjamin, first and foremost a linguistic concept. What "imitates" a given object or reality is a verbal construct, or, at least minimally, a name. I take the liberty of assuming that for most of us, the instinctive (or pre-philosophical) grasp of the idea of mimesis will involve the drawing or modeling of a physical object—a child's effort or the cave painting. For Benjamin it is language which is first and foremost mimetic, and whose first "reproduction" or "imitation" of the world underpins all the later, more artistic ones. Indeed, we have earlier identified the fundamental formulation of mimesis in Benjamin as "non-sensuous similarity" (II, 270; II, 211: *"unsinnliche Ähnlichkeit"*), a formulation which is meant to exclude any overtones of the visual or of resemblance in the ordinary sense. The dilemma which then results is this: the child or the caveman (mimesis always seeming to involve primitivist overtones) reproduces a visual object in visual media; Benjaminian mimesis, however, posits two kinds of media (if that is the right word to use)—the solid visual world around us and "language as such," which is neither visual nor solid, nor even auditory or sonorous, but which has the advantage of being mimetic by virtue of its nature as a name. Both word and name are for Benjamin profoundly mimetic in nature, by way of creation itself. The world is, in that sense, already named, even before Adam; things are their names in advance, and this is why one can say that the world is already a language, if not "the language of man as such." Once again, a relevant contemporary analogy can be found in Lévi-Strauss's "*pensée sauvage*," even though the latter is couched in anthropological—rather than in a Benjaminian-theological—terminology.

But this means that both the world and language are already mimetic, and the various arts and their languages are but secondary manifestations of that primary mimetic reality (which is thus quite different from the Adorno/Horkheimer thesis of a "mimetic impulse"). This is where the "polarity" mentioned above comes in: artistic mimesis simultaneously mobilizes two distinct operations or dimensions: semblance and play, "interfolded like cotyledons." This weird biological or even evolutionary reference—the first leaves emerging from a seed—introduces history into the process and determines the relative quotient of each of these entities in the structure and emergence of the artistic medium as such. Our terminological uncertainty, indeed, reveals a dissymmetry of these two terms, which is in fact their source of productivity: activity or attribute? Semblance would seem to be an attribute, play an activity: there can be no question of assimilating both to a single field of conceptuality in which they might be united in a philosophical aesthetic (like that of R. G. Collingwood with his interplay between structure and expression). For aesthetics is always, however secretly, normative; here, however, we have a historical interaction constantly modified by advances on either side. Semblance becomes a situation in which a certain kind of play finds its possibilities but also its restrictions; play becomes an activity in which certain forms of semblance become available for perception as well as for performance, and others are ruled out. Such variabilities are "determined by the world-historical conflict between the first and second technologies," the age of the tool and the industrial age, at which point we return to the more immediate concerns or the reproducibility essay and the form art takes in the present. The "aesthetics" of the first age, the age of the tool, was one of individual handicraft and of the aura of the unique work, the indivisible whole without parts (a sculptural "body without organs"?); that of industrial reproduction a collective and episodic production, mediated by an apparatus (here, the camera) in the alienation of the subject to its various faculties. But, to echo Mao on the splitting of the atom, this second machinic fragmentation of the collective produces an immense release of new energies. Benjamin being essentially a modernist, his aesthetic reflections naturally enough celebrate, along with Brecht, the new and the advanced, the more "highly productive use of the human being's self-alienation."

But we must here anticipate the later sections of the essay to point out that the new reproductive aesthetic is also more advanced in the sense in which it produces a new kind of content for the work as such, namely the very process of production that becomes visible with reproduction. We must not reduce this observation to the standard descriptions of modernity as self-consciousness and reflexivity, although this is, no doubt, one extreme form of that idea. Here, however, there emerges a reality which is itself a process of construction and which one cannot observe from the outside.

This—the standard poststructuralist theme of the "death of the subject"—is the burden of a new and much briefer thesis. The alienation of the subject is no longer the individual experience described by Pirandello (and the young Marx, as well): it takes place at some new level in which the individual actor is alienated by a whole multiplicity of absent collective subjects and observers everywhere in the world. But at this point, we must be vigilant about the ambivalence of the process, whose loss of aura (here, individuality) inevitably calls out for its spurious restoration on the higher level of "the cult of the movie star" and offers an equally spurious counterpart in some "cult of the audience" preeminently available to fascist appropriation.

Here, in a rare combination of characteristic Marxian terminology and polemics, Benjamin will refer to "the putrid magic of its own commodity character"—a characterization of Hollywood a good deal stronger than anything Adorno and Horkheimer cared to articulate in *Dialectic of Enlightenment*. It seems possible, however, that this outburst, rare in Benjamin save for some powerful polemic interventions, expresses his impatience with the limits of the essay form, in a situation in which we find a variety of rich and original footnotes whose conclusions one wishes he had been able to incorporate. Thus, for example, one of these, on class and class consciousness (III, 129n24; VII, 370–1), a passage suppressed from the third and final, published version, sketches in a theory of mass consciousness which overcomes the antinomy of activity and passivity ordinarily attributed to problems of collective culture. In it he repudiates the traditional "mass psychology" analysis invented by Le Bon and even followed by Freud himself, displacing it to the analysis of the petty-bourgeoisie, which does form just such an objectified mass public (on the order of Sartrean seriality). On the contrary, Benjamin claims, the revolutionary (or proletarian) collectivity in fact individualizes itself in its uprising, the leader being himself received back into it as yet another individual. It is an analysis of great originality which might have led, if developed further, to a solution for some of the aesthetic antinomies of the reproducibility essay, if not to a wholly new theorization of political action.

Characteristically, however, Benjamin here turns away from psychology to the more objective question of the content of the new art, whose originality lies in its democratization: "any person today can lay claim to being filmed." As we know, in the era of selfies and facial recognition technology, this is no guarantee of political productivity. He himself was always struck by the way in which, in Soviet culture, "work itself is given a voice," workers are encouraged to describe their own experiences, and the mass public itself thereby becomes its own producer. Here, then, the new fact of reproductive multiplicity alters the traditional relationship between form and content, furthering "an interest in understanding themselves and therefore their class" in a way which the property-owning classes have every interest in blocking.

But these observations also tend toward the elaboration of a new aesthetic, which, as we have seen, is not the purpose of the present essay and which Benjamin no doubt (unlike Brecht) has personal as well as political reasons for abridging. What he will now pursue is, rather, that new content of film production which distinguishes this art or medium from traditional forms and, which we have already anticipated. First of all (it is the very burden of this thesis), film has no place for an individual point of view; the interposition of the apparatus means that there exists no privileged standpoint for the viewing (and, indeed, for the theorization) of the process, inasmuch as all such standpoints are necessarily mediated by an apparatus, and there exist, in any case, a multiplicity of standpoints from which to view it ("the camera, the lighting units, the technical crew" and so on).

Thus, the individual point of view on all this—the view from the orchestra seat in the theater, the reflexivity of the narrator or omniscient author in literature, the coherence of a spectacle secretly organized by an invisible director or a visible conductor and unified out of a great multiplicity of actors and elements—this unified standpoint is an illusion, and one which can only be "the result of a special procedure . . . and the height of artifice." It is an illusion produced by the very technological complexity and multiplicity it wishes to register; and Benjamin expresses this thought ("there is no metalanguage") in an unusually tortured and desperate sentence: "In the film studio the apparatus has penetrated so deeply into reality that a pure view of that reality, free of the foreign body of equipment, is the result of a special procedure"—in other words, there can be no such thing as naïve realism.

But this intricate thought at once gives way to the most luminous (and celebrated) of Benjaminian pedagogical images, the one that compares the magician to the surgeon: "The attitude of the magician, who heals a sick person by the laying on of hands, differs from that of the surgeon, who makes an intervention in the patient." In another moment, this distinction will give rise to the famous doctrine of the "optical unconscious," in which the camera opens up aspects of reality either too vast or too minute for us to see in daily life, just as the surgeon affords a glimpse of inner organs (or, perhaps, of cells under a microscope).

For the moment, however, Benjamin returns to a more conventional comparison, that of painter with filmmaker, which draws out another, equally familiar consequence, namely that the painter still paints a whole, an individual work, whereas editing or montage in film necessarily works with multiplicities—an opposition reproduced in our time by that between the analog and digital.

The reader's predictable reaction to this new proposition—does not cubism do the same thing in painting?—is now the starting point for the next thesis, a new one, which rethinks the relationship of the new art to its public: a public, you will remember, which it was supposed to train in new realities. The answering question—why is Picasso not as popular with the masses as Chaplin?—will bear on the priority of the new arts and begin to outline a theory of historical evolution. The answer, of course, lies in the dialectic of the individual and the masses. Perception itself is modified by its massification, and what is not acceptable to individual taste undergoes a profound change when "determined by the imminent concentration of reactions into a mass." Architecture, above all—but also epic at a certain moment in its history (especially when still recited before a group), and, of course, film today—preselect distinctive mass publics, "while efforts ... to present paintings to the masses in galleries and salons ... give the masses no means of organizing and regulating their response." It is a suggestive proposition which exceeds the matter of mere individuality and finds a political nerve somehow "innervated" by all collective reception (a proposition Benjamin does not pursue). In our time, however, what Baudrillard called the "implosion" of the museum suggests a fresh development in the social structure of such aesthetic institutions (a development simultaneous with the disappearance of individual artworks and their replacement, in the new primacy of the curator, by various kinds of assemblage). Meanwhile, there are also historical events—the triumphant bearing of Duccio's Madonna aloft through the streets of Siena—which suggest a possible reconsideration of the political role of the "cultic" at newer moments of aesthetic reception as well.

But this assertion of the political logic of collective response must, in the current situation, be accompanied by some specification of the relationship of that response (today) to the new *Apparatur*, of which it is never clear whether Benjamin is proposing a Lukácsian notion of the new "second nature" constructed around us by industrial or machine culture (a non-Marxian theory of "industrial revolution") or merely designating the technical bases of this new art in and for its own sake. In fact, he offers instead a picture of the new forms of gratification provided by the perceptual expansion of film: this is, then, the moment in which the notion of an "optical unconscious"—already suggested by the figure of the surgeon—is fully developed (by way of a rather unconvincing and superficial use of psychoanalytic concepts). But the new spaces revealed by the camera are somehow less significant than the Brechtian magnification of human activity, or *gestus,* where instinctive habit is analytically dissected into the moments of a not-yet-conscious awareness (to use Bloch's term, by which he meant precisely to expand and supplement traditional psychoanalytic concepts).

Here, however, the ambivalence of the new processes, which has only slightly been touched on, comes into play, for the enlargement of consciousness also includes the possibility of the irrational, of dreams and psychoses, and of "the forced development of sadistic fantasies or masochistic delusions" susceptible of a "natural and dangerous maturation into mass psychosis," which is to say, into fascism. Thus, just as the traditional arts are subject to an artificial revival of aura in their moment of degeneration, the new "optical unconscious" of the industrial arts is also threatened, but by an appropriation for irrational experience. This is, then, also the moment in which the powerful new critical concept of regression and the regressive comes into play: it diagnoses the place of a dual weakness in the situation—a waning of traditional artistic experience which leaves a gap, the organization of new techniques which are available for appropriation. Regression will be the name for a fascist seizure of that cultural and social opportunity.

Yet, as the surrealists discovered, collective laughter also affords a powerful therapy for such impulses; and its release is epitomized by one of those characters (like the tyrant, or in other contexts, the *flâneur*) narrativized by Benjamin's dramatistic method, in this case "the eccentric"—preeminently embodied by Chaplin, but whose impulses are also, for Benjamin, fulfilled by American slapstick comedies and Disney films (we are still in the 1930s). In the same way, later on, despite their repudiation of the Hollywood culture industry, the Frankfurt School will still be willing to endorse the "zaniness" of the Marx Brothers.

With this thesis, we turn to a different historical aspect of this overlap of two kinds of forms: the older auratic tradition and the newer reproducible arts. At issue now is the theoretical problem of a transition from one to the other (a problem already richly debated in the Marxian discussions of "transitional modes of production"). Benjamin draws here on Marx's own, as it were, parturitional, figure—the new mode of production maturing within the womb of the old; in other words, the gradual monopolization of capital fulfilling without knowing it the requirements of a new collective system.

Benjamin will here demonstrate the way in which Dadaism subverts an auratic literary tradition from within. Dadaist nonsense poems demonstrate the new "uselessness of [traditional artworks] as objects of contemplative immersion," enacting "a ruthless annihilation of aura in every object they produce." But this has its social equivalent, which Brecht himself had evoked in speaking of his own early anarchist period (in plays like *Baal*): the distinction between the asocial and the antisocial, a distinction here coupled with Benjamin's fruitful new concept of diversion *(Ablenkung,* and later on *Zerstreuung,* as we shall see below): "Contemplative immersion—which as the bourgeoisie degenerated became a breeding ground for asocial behavior—is here opposed by distraction as a variant of social behavior." Dadaist scandal is designed to undermine the degenerate form of the older arts and the older aestheticism ("asocial behavior"), and thereby to prepare the path for the reception of a new kind of collective art altogether—in which the individually asocial will become collectively antisocial, that is, revolutionary and political. "Film has freed the physical shock effect—which Dadaism had kept wrapped, as it were, inside the moral shock effect—from this wrapping"—namely the older aestheticism. Dadaism thus "turns the artwork into a missile."

A final thesis (technically the last) will then elaborate the important new concept of distraction, which Benjamin has disengaged from his analysis of film, and the effects of multiplicity in the new collective of the filmic audience and, implicitly, the mass party. The word—*Ablenkung* merely means to attract your attention away from something, *Zerstreuung* also designates mass culture as such and its diversions or entertainments—will attempt to describe and analyze a new kind of perception, as it were, a lateral one, which happens when we are primarily concentrating on something else. We must try to couple this new and problematic psychological category with a more philosophical notion of dialectical attention and heightened consciousness to be found everywhere in the late writings for which Benjamin could only find the blurred expression *Geistesgegenwart* or "presence of mind."[3] This is to be juxtaposed with any number of historical theories of a kind of third consciousness, which is neither that of immediate "intention" (in Husserl's sense), nor that of personal and ideological reflection, but which attempts to transcend both in some perceptual but also historical and dialectical fashion. One could or should write a history of these attempts, which in the West began with patristic theology and forms of mysticism (Böhme), and were refined in different ways by Spinoza and Hegel and then appropriated by Marx's notions of ideology (which necessarily presuppose a place outside ideology, as does Lukács's "standpoint theory"). We must

---

3   The historical significance of the substitution of the problem of "attention" for that of consciousness is the subject of Jonathan Crary, *Suspensions of Perception*, Cambridge: MIT, 2001.

always try to read *Geistesgegenwart* in this heightened dialectical sense, by contrasting it with the kind of thinking or perception it tries to rise above.

But in the focus of a more narrowly aesthetic attempt to explore the new collective and political possibilities of film, it is the notion of distraction that can be seen as a preparatory sketch which attempts to transform perception into "participation." The opposite of such distraction, then, becomes *Sammlung*—not quite the "concentration" as which it is translated, in other words—what is "calm" and literally "collected": *Sammlung* is, rather, a kind of preparedness in waiting, a selfless openness to what comes, to which we bring no prejudices or preconditions, but which we approach with full attention as well.

None of this, however, quite fits the little fable Benjamin offers as a clarification (one elaborated more fully in *Berlin Childhood* [III, 393; IV, 262–3]). A Chinese painter exhibits his new landscape to some friends, who, having examined it with interest, turn to him with their comments and appreciations. He is, however, no longer there, and turning back to the scroll they find that he has himself become part of the painting. The immediate association will be the remark about never using the first person, in order, when you are done, to disappear into your own essay, your own writing. Still, it is not clear what this has to do with distraction, unless it is the distraction of the painter's companions, who do not see him disappear. The story can more easily be understood as a parable of the autonomy of the work, into which the external (save for its beholders and consumers) is ultimately reabsorbed into the work itself, as perhaps they also risk being?

But then this concept of *Sammlung*, with its fable of the disappearing painter, needs itself to be absorbed into the example that follows, which no longer has to do with the medium of film but rather with architecture. Benjamin's conception of architecture reminds one of Proustian experience, which you can never live directly, by an effort of the will, but must always laterally surprise, living it "for the first time" only later on, in a seeming repetition which is in fact a kind of accident. So the willful effort to grasp the great building head-on, by way of some properly "concentrated" attention, gives us only the facade, the storefront of what Venturi called "the decorated shed," a flat screen full of detail that cannot be summed up in any unified impression. On the contrary, it is recommended that we stroll through the cathedral, absorbing it laterally as we observe this and that on our way: allowing the immense but shaped space (which cannot itself be the object of any perception) gradually to make its mark on us and by taking us into itself to absorb us (like the painter) and reshape our consciousness of it.

Benjamin then, in another attempt, produces an opposition between the two approaches of the optical and the tactile, where the failure of the optical—associated with contemplative knowledge (that bad method of science and positivism, in which the object stands before us independently—literally, a *Vorstellung*—and offers itself for "disinterested" inspection)—now gives way to a tactile reception whose function is not to disengage an external picture or idea of the thing but rather to *form habits.*

The evocation of habit is then the most decisive moment in Benjamin's projection of what he cannot yet call "cultural revolution" (although it was an expression already invented by Lenin himself). That it involves a reconstruction of perception is, however, decisive: "For the tasks which face the human apparatus of perception at historical turning points cannot be performed solely by optical means—that is, by way of contemplation. They are mastered gradually, taking their cue from tactile reception, through habit." So it is that the dramatistic surgeon's scalpel intervenes in the habitual *gestus* and makes us conscious of its individual components, the segments of the walking leg's gait, the episodic moments of an expression, a desire, a will or intent. The new habit of cathedral space will then be something like the absent presence of language as such, a transcendent unity which can only be sensed beyond all individual texts and utterances, all speech acts delivered in a particular idiom. It is this unity of the masses, beyond any individual perceptions or personal feelings, which reveals its enormous power—that of the General Will—beyond all particularities or singularities. The new media are its "training ground."

With this, we come to the end of Benjamin's effort to convey what we will call his version of a cultural revolution, and to which he adds an activist imperative if not an aesthetic: politicalization rather than aesthetization. The essay was neither a statement on technology nor a theory of film (both of them now, almost a century later, completely outmoded). Yet, oddly, what might have seemed the most obsolete for those first postwar readers, whose enthusiasm reached its paroxysm in 1968—the political diagnosis, the warnings of fascist appropriation—are now once again the most relevant.

To revel in the technological advance of the new reproducible arts turns out to be sheer aesthetics (the *Wehrmacht* filmed more hours of the war than any cinematographic project before or since—whence Syberberg's characterization of Hitler as the "greatest filmmaker of the twentieth century"). Benjamin rightly cites Marinetti's delirious evocations of the beauty of war, adding his own subtle diagnostic that its extraordinary aura is the result of the repression of genuine technological productivity by capitalism, the return of the repressed of an advance that has not been used, of a wasted energy that "will press forward toward an unnatural use." The aesthetics of war "furnish proof that society was not mature enough to make technology its organ, that the technology was not sufficiently developed to master the elemental forces of society." Socialism is thus a theory and a politics of the productive uses of the ever-heightening power of the forces of production.

This is why Benjamin is not a theorist of class struggle: his immensely reactive intelligence is directed at an angle to that kind of Marxism; it aims at theorizing the consequences of the emergence of mass society and mass politics. We have forgotten that historical emergence—the postwar generation scarcely noticed the new world into which it emerged, while the twenty-first-century generation could no longer imagine such changes, and no one even asked it to.[4] Even the historians neglected to remind us that it was only in the twentieth century itself that something like the new mass politics—for which we now use the misleading word "democratic"—never existed before in the history of the world. After the victory of World War II, it was no longer necessary to mention fascism; after 1989, communism could itself be forgotten, along with the Cold War. The antitheses Benjamin evokes at the end of his great essay seem no longer to exist, or if at all, to have been replaced by some kind of struggle between representative democracy and its enemies, as though the former existed anywhere or even functioned in the first place! We have regressed, in other words, from a world of class struggle to a world of virtue and corruption, an eighteenth-century world, in which, as in all the millennia that preceded it, the suffrage and

---

4   See Eric Hobsbawm's remarkable chapter in *The Age of Extremes* about the post-war changes that make older historical periods inaccessible to younger generations.

the control of money and riches is the rationale of government and the reality of history. The modernist belief in a progressive increase in productive forces and energies has congealed into a static view of the future as dystopia and the present as a struggle for the value of the technological spoils.

So the three-way rivalry which Benjamin observed in the 1920s and '30s, the years of his mature lifetime, a rivalry between communism, fascism and capitalism, seems to have been a historical aberration, whose lessons are scarcely of any use to us today. One is tempted to borrow Benjamin's own conceptuality and to suggest that all of the advances in theoretical productivity he himself achieved have, in the absence of any possibilities of positive investment and development, been sidetracked and reappropriated by purely aesthetic speculation of an often mystical and hypertheoretical sort—"the artistic gratification of a sense perception altered by technology," as he puts it himself. Theory, which once eagerly fed on these new sources of thought, has itself become a purely aesthetic and consumerist process.

But without the danger of fascism and its idiosyncratic sibling Nazism, Benjamin's work lays before us as so many gratuitous exercises. In the decades following World War II, it became obvious that to use these words as epithets was not only imprecise but bad politics. Socialism, meanwhile, made its way under the surface, as it always does, producing local flurries and isolated spokespeople, but drawing its life from the contradictions without which capitalism itself cannot live; it has perhaps today reached another of those moments of crisis in which it threatens to reappear as the only solution to otherwise insuperable economic problems, those, finally, of the world market which Marx saw as the end of the current system.

Mass politics, however—for which the whole issue of representative democracy has by now become a rhetorical convention, less a cause than a form of corruption in its own right—now once again seems on the point of reinventing a fascism whose name it had forgotten. Perhaps, if we want to learn to read Benjamin correctly and to draw new energies from his prophecies—"weakly messianic" as they may have been—we should once again begin to distinguish the forces of communism and fascism at work beneath the surface of world politics and self-consciously rearticulate a struggle in which he had his word to say. Mass politics lies at the very center of Benjamin's thought: in Max Horkheimer's memorable formula, "He has nothing useful to say about fascism who is unwilling to mention capitalism."[5]

4

These texts carry along in their flow a number of concepts about which one would like to say, with the logicians, that they are not "on all fours" with each other: aura and reproducibility, for example, surely do not belong to the same conceptual worlds; a political and demographic concept like "the masses" does not at first glance seem to rub shoulders with the problem of the distance of the camera from actors' bodies. Nor is it clear what the doctrine of "experience" has to do with the invention of the iodized silver plate (unless the latter be taken as the place in which an "*Erlebnis*" can best be seized and immortalized, which is not the position of either Benjamin or Baudelaire). Nor is this grab bag of concepts and problems in any way assimilable to a toolbox, let alone the constellations of themes whose infrastructure we detected in Benjamin's various and unrelated groups of friends and interlocutors. Discontinuity is not a good explanation for the semiautonomy of thematic or allegorical levels (whose discontinuities are presupposed, in any case, in advance); the chaos of random interests and attention deficiency disorder can scarcely function as a principled stand taken against systematic philosophy.

Still, I believe that there exists a thread capable of guiding us through this thicket and it is the value Benjamin attaches in various places to what is "advanced" (as opposed to what counts as "regressive"). For this to work, however, we must exercise extreme caution in separating this qualification from anything resembling the detested notion of "progress" and even more sensitivity in peeling away from it the inevitable suggestions and overtones of the technological and the economic with which we are accustomed to associating this idea of change and qualitative improvement-cum-invention. The new is certainly part of it, but it must not be the new of the generalized modernist telos; productivity is also there and may be admitted through the strait gate of Marxist theory, but only as something philosophically more all-embracing than the

---

5   Max Horkheimer, "The Jews in Europe" (December 1939).

empiricist "science-and-technology" to which it is so often reduced (and then used as a weapon against the allegedly reductive Marxist productivism).

These are a good many warnings to accompany the handbook on the proper use of the term "advanced"; and they might well be accompanied by a final imperative, namely to identify the opposite of this value without falling into the pejorative sink of its degeneration into the regressive. When we remember that for Benjamin, the archaic comes in two forms—the bad chaos of myth and the good harmony of the cosmos and its similitudes—we may well want to refine the terms of our judgment or transcend it altogether.

Fortunately, there is one place in which we may hope to find a more developed answer to these questions, and that is the program-essay called "The Author as Producer" (II, 768–82; II, 683–701), composed for a conference of antifascist intellectuals in the early 1930s but never delivered; unpublished in Benjamin's lifetime and perhaps uncirculated (it would be interesting to know whether it came to Brecht's attention), but knowing a brief and glorious afterlife in the 1960s, where it confirmed the work of Enzensberger and Negt and Kluge on the media and inspired a whole aesthetic in the Parisian *Tel Quel* group, after which its proposals seem to have lapsed again into archival oblivion (along with the '60s themselves).

Yet its theoretical speculations are among the few practical suggestions Benjamin ventured for intellectuals and might equally, although more awkwardly, be enlisted in the construction of some hypothetical Benjaminian aesthetic (which, as we have seen, the reproducibility essay excludes).

The text begins with a powerful polemic on current left literary and cultural positions (the attack on social-democratic intellectuals or so-called "left-wing melancholy") but omits its true starting point in Marx's nonproductivist conception of a mode of production in which the duality of base and superstructure is echoed by an even more significant, but fainter, duality within the base itself: that between the forces of production and the relations of production. This duality is what led Korsch to speculate that Marxism in fact possessed two distinct languages or idiolects, which could be translated back and forth depending on the situation. On the one hand, there is the "economic" language of machinery and productivity; on the other, that of the labor process and exploitation and surplus value. The first is clearly more quantifiable than the second, just as production in general is a more tractable raw material than vaguely superstructural developments, which can only seem idealistic because they are ideas in the first place.

In literary history we face the same duality: on the one hand, there is a language of publishing and of distribution—as it were, the materialist underside of literature, which seems to have as little to do with the texts themselves as Marx's boils with his grasp of the workings of capitalism; on the other hand, there is the content as well as the form of these discursive objects, both of which ought ideally to be the domain of ideological analysis. Ideology is no doubt itself a kind of production, as is "écriture" as such. But if we try to assimilate these "relations of production" back into the material ones, we tend to come off with feeble allegories.

Benjamin proposed another line of approach, in which it is the status of the producer which suggests a promising entry point. This was clearly a sensitive matter for him, as a "free-floating intellectual" in the grimmest sense of the expression: radical unemployment; no job, either academic or journalistic; a hand-to-mouth peddling of book reviews; a meager allowance from the patrons in Frankfurt (and later on in New York). There is a moment in which he was willing to disclose the constitutive relationship between this perilous situation and his political commitment: the Soviet Union had a writer's union and included an official status for intellectuals; it would thus provide him with a secure position. To be sure, years of Cold War training immediately conjure all the sacrifices—*sacrifizio dell' intelleto*, Adorno calls it in his essay on Lukács, the censorship, the propaganda production—such a status would have entailed in Stalin's Russia, not excluding the more obviously physical dangers as well. Benjamin, however, seems to have had enough confidence in his cunning as a writer to discount this cost. But he was clearly materialist enough to be conscious of the relationship, and it is this consciousness that is not only at work in the essay but also lends it its content as a program.

Meanwhile, he was willing enough to criticize Soviet cultural policy (in the Moscow essay) on the basis of what he considered their import strategy. Why translate the stodgiest academic cultural and intellectual materials from the West, when you are so keenly aware that in the relations of production you are already pioneering revolutionary advances on Western economic production? This is yet another (perhaps minor or overlooked) intervention in what will later on be misnamed the "Expressionism debate" or, even worse, the "Brecht–Lukács debate"— the struggle over a socialist cultural policy, misunderstood if we simply interpret it in terms of form versus content. Anyone who takes the quasi-manifesto which is "The Author as Producer" as hostility to some future socialist realism needs to reread his review of a socialist-realist classic: "Gladkov's *Cement* is one of the crucial works of modern Russian literature" (II, 49; III, 61). Still, he was openly willing to promulgate a double standard insofar as it is a question of the production of some new socialist culture: "There are times when things and thoughts should be weighed and not counted. But also—though this often escapes notice— there are times when things are counted and not weighed" (II, 9; II, 747). Benjamin lived in a world running on multiple times, in multiple time zones, which are also potential homelands, or at least places of refuge and exile. France was a future modernity, for which he had only a temporary visa (but Paris was also a very old city); the distant Soviet Union was another kind of future, now sunk beneath the eyeline. The Mediterranean was a place of inexpensive living and dwelling, and also of ports of escape; America and Jerusalem were unimaginable words and names from which news still came, in the form of letters; Germany a terrifying present, best repressed, surrounded by neutral countries whose very present of time was illusory. How to tell time, to feel the direction of the winds of history, in such a multiverse?

It is interesting that in the planned "intervention" in the Paris Writers' Conference of 1934 (which is what "The Author as Producer" was meant to be), Benjamin does not once pronounce the charged and personal word "experience"; he also very specifically sets out to undermine the status of the old form–content distinction, with its inevitable political undertones (the left is supposed to be naively wedded to a realism of content, of the unmediated testimony of social realities; aesthetes are whether they know it or not, supposed to harbor right-wing idealist and antipolitical tendencies and pure formalisms). Benjamin does not here posit some progressive synthesis between the two mentalities (as Lukács might later be supposed to do); nor does he (also following Lukács) propose some new and radical aesthetic (we have seen him specifically recommend against doing so at the outset of the reproducibility essay). What he does observe here is that a country in the process of constructing socialism will face very different artistic and critical tasks than those still deeply immersed in the ideological fabric of a capitalist system and its various bourgeois cultures.

Indeed, his indictment of a left-leaning or social-democratic intelligentsia recapitulates much of the spirit of a well-known essay on "left-wing melancholy," whose title has often been misread as an attribution of this affective attribute to the political left in general (it is in fact a denunciation of Erich Kästner, a disillusioned wit whose sweet-and-sour verses lie somewhere between Larkin and Auden.) This is to evoke with Brecht a gastronomical literature with all the tartness of a literary cocktail; it is the after-hours of the left-wing intellectuals whose native wit relishes the disillusions they enjoy sharing with one another, the pessimism of sharply formulated intimations of doom, the gusto with which they remind each other of the stupidities of the age, its incorrigibility, human all-too-human, the flaws in the national character which only disaster can chastise.

In much the same spirit as Sartre denounced the idealism of much Marxist "materialism," Benjamin reminds us that form has its own specific ideologies which potentially defuse the most radical kinds of content: "the bourgeois apparatus of production and publication can assimilate astonishing quantities of revolutionary themes—indeed, can propagate them without calling its own existence, and the existence of the class that owns it, seriously into question." How much timelier is this reminder in a situation like our own, where an absolute monopoly reigns over cultural and intellectual production? But this very competition offers even more substantial grounds for "left-wing melancholy" when we ponder his solution, namely for the producers of culture to become conscious of their own position in the apparatus of cultural production and to work on that: "Rather than asking, 'What is the attitude of the work *to* the relations of production of its time?' I would like to ask, 'What is its position *in* them?'"

The word he offers as a way of transcending the sterile opposition of form and content—the word *technique*—is not a recommendation for modernist experimentation. Here, indeed, is the fateful placement in his scheme of things of that fateful word, the modern: bourgeois art today (he is thinking of photography) "becomes ever more *nuancé*, ever more modern; and the result to that it can no longer record a tenement block or a refuse heap without transfiguring it . . . it has succeeded in transforming even abject poverty—by apprehending it in a fashionably perfected manner—into an object of enjoyment." In short, the political sin of what we call modernism is not technical innovation and experimentation, as in the realism debates; it is aestheticism as such, the consumption of beauty, the Brechtian gastronomical. This does not bode well for the practice of traditional forms, such as the novel; to be sure, Benjamin will go on to follow Tretiakov's experiments with reportage, the newspaper and other media with a recommendation of a different kind of experimentation, namely one with the very media themselves. He calls for hybrid forms, like the "caption that wrenches" a picture "from modish commerce and gives it a revolutionary use value." These unnatural conjunctions of word-and-image—so scandalously explored in our time by Jean-Luc Godard, or the Brecht-Weill words-and-music—are examples of the production of new and "advanced" forms: "the barriers imposed by specialization must be breached jointly by the productive forces they were set up to divide." Still, for us today, these recommendations seem as postmodern as they once were revolutionary. Even the recommendation to transform a "struggle against poverty" into an aesthetic doctrine of *arte povera* is less dramatic in the light of recent history; and in the world of the Internet and contemporary new media, we may continue to wonder how to convert "work on production . . . always, at the same time, [into] work on the means of production." Predictably, the ultimate example furnished is that of the epic theater of Brecht, on which this essay contains luminous pages. This "advanced" theater "portrays situations rather than developing plots." It interrupts narrative continuities and thereby establishes a montage whose "superimposed element disrupts the context in which it is inserted." "To the total dramatic artwork [the dramatist] opposes the dramatic laboratory." Instead of taking a position within debates, it exposes the debate itself. Above all, epic theater "replaces culture with training, distraction with group formation" (II, 585; II, 775): it is an extraordinary formulation, full of political promise on which this essay cannot really deliver.

The key to Benjamin's conception of the "advanced" in art and culture is thus his anti-aestheticism: in this sense, he coincides with Breton, who excommunicated those participants in the Surrealist project (Artaud, Bataille) who were felt to attach undue significance to aesthetic production as such. (Breton also excommunicated those who valued politics above Surrealism and joined the Communist Party, such as Aragon; presumably Benjamin would not have shared this prejudice, but it must be added that neither he nor Brecht joined either, although his brother and sister were both legendary party figures.)

What is advanced in art and culture is therefore not to be found in the products of artistic activity—in other words, in the works of art themselves; and it is a mistake to look for his aesthetics in works he admired, whether in Baroque plays, Keller's or Hebel's or Leskov's stories, Julien Green's novels, or Brecht's plays and poems. The phrase "process of production" puts us on the right track, but I feel that a word like experimentation, which assimilates aesthetic invention to scientific laboratory work, is less misleading. What he admired in Brecht, in other words, and above and beyond the plays themselves (he was never to know the later masterpieces), was "epic theater" as such, as a framework in which experimentation tirelessly took place, involving actors and publics alike, and endlessly modified texts and staging. Even though I have identified an underlying category of Benjamin's thought as that of number and the multiple, in his political insistence on mass parties and his aesthetic insistence on reproducibility and mass distribution (as well as on the production of art by the masses themselves), it would be well to avoid reifying this dimension of his thought into this or that simplified reception theory (or into pedagogy, either), but rather to retain an insistence on the kind of laboratory experiment Brecht himself dramatized within *Galileo* in the activities of its protagonist. This is why one cannot ascribe to Benjamin any specific aesthetic "solution" or generic or stylistic creed: his experimentalism moves in unpredictable leaps from medium to genre and from style and form to distribution, indeterminable in advance. His appropriation by new media theorists is perfectly acceptable, on the condition they consent to its abandonment for new and untried terrain in the next historical wave of aesthetic research.

The notion of "advanced production" will therefore be associated not so much with production for the broad masses and nonexperimental literary and cultural accessibility, as rather with what is political in a situation of massification and politically awakened popular publics. Experimentation is, in such a situation, not necessarily to be judged on the basis of popular reception: Brecht's *Lehrstücke* were not meant for a music-hall public (and possibly, indeed, not even meant for a public at all, but rather for the actors themselves), and even Mao Zedong himself made a place for artistic experimentation in the otherwise seemingly orthodox instructions of the Yenan Forum talks.

Still, we have not yet identified the qualification to be associated with what is no longer "advanced" but yet not to be characterized as regressive: we still search, in other words, for an "opposite" of advanced production which is somehow positive rather than degenerate in the historical sense. The most obvious place to look first would seem to be *Capital* itself, a theory of industrial production in which Marx is careful to distinguish an older kind of work in which the tool is the prosthesis of the human worker, from its modern kind, in which the worker has become the prosthesis of the machine. This is not yet, to be sure, a theory of capitalism as such, in which the production of commodities, and the theory of commodity fetishism and the commodity form, will be central. We may well suspect that commodification already plays a part in Benjamin's notion of aestheticism (as it does far more openly in the Frankfurt School theories that draw more explicitly on Lukács's *History and Class Consciousness*). We may likewise conjecture that a complete picture of Marx's theory of capitalism presupposes an intersection of these two lines—the theory of the machine and the theory of commodification—with a positive view of the subsumption of capitalist "advanced production" under socialism, a vision only sketched out in the fundamental chapter on cooperation, the Marxist theory of collectivity. (It was, it will be remembered, the remarkably prescient notion of "group formation" with which Benjamin's reproducibility essay broke off.)

The essay on "The Author as Producer" will then offer a new opening which Benjamin's insistence on "technique" provides to the seemingly unresolvable opposition between form and content, which both bourgeois and party-line critics take as their battle line. For as a remarkable note on radio instructs us, "the radio listener . . . welcomes the human voice into his house like a visitor [it is an observation that remains valid for television today]. And this is why programs that might seem totally irrelevant can hold the listener spellbound." But precisely this irrelevance of the content argues for a Benjaminian formalism, in which form and technique are identified: "it is the technical and formal aspects of radio that will enable the listener to train himself" (II, 544; II, 1507) and, in other words, in a Brechtian spirit, to reconstruct his subjectivity, lift it to the level of the new and more "advanced" medium. But it is along just such lines that we will be able to draw a path that runs from the similitudes of the Benjaminian cosmos to the advanced industrial and reproducible film as such (and perhaps even beyond it).

This path will, however, require us to be able to separate the detested idea of "progress" from the experience of the "new" which destroys it. The paradox lies, perhaps, in the existence of the idea of progress not as a concept but rather a belief, one that illicitly includes the future in itself (the famous *"lendemains qui chantent"*); the "new," on the contrary, is an experience of the present, one indeed so shattering that this vague conviction about a future as schematic as a soothsayer's prediction is at once dispelled. It is perhaps a dispersal of this same type which happens to bourgeois aestheticism, a bourgeois telos of the modern, when it is subjected to what it still considers the merely technical and technological "innovations" of media, like radio or film.

The immediate link, however, which transforms these disparate themes and insights of Benjamin into a genuinely monadic constellation is given to us in an unpublished fragment, dated by its editors to 1931 or 1932 in Ibiza, and apparently part of an uncompleted reflection on gambling. A single sentence from this seemingly insignificant fragment is enough, and it is luminous: "Experiences are lived similarities" (II, 553; VI, 88).

Now, all of a sudden, the whole doctrine of experience, and its fragility in the face of the modern city and, above all, of modern warfare—the shocks of *Erlebnisse* of technology as such—finds its origins in the great cosmos of similitudes that forms the Edenic landscape of which the mythic is little more than the toxic regression in a ravaged modernity. We remember that fairy tales are the anti-myth, their peasant optimism the antidote to the deathly aestheticizing rituals of a modern fascism, their storytelling a reminiscence and recovery of a non-alienated mode of being.

Storytelling is essentially handicraft: it is a bodily activity, like the potter's wheel; Benjamin's anecdotes, his physical activity as a raconteur, are his own personal attempts to recapture this non-alienated production, with which may also be coupled the letters handwritten by the German humanist writers of the *Goethezeit*, the dream transcriptions of the Surrealists, the fantastic images of Scheerbart's science fiction, the miniature tales of Hebel, perhaps even the radical simplifications of Le Corbusier—the glass and steel structures which stand as a kind of non-sensuous mimesis of this new "poverty of experience" and a lesson in how to use it productively (II, 734; II, 218). As for the postindustrial, may it not be conjectured that hackers' work is also a handicraft and that it is not necessarily a pipe dream to remind ourselves of the Utopianism of the first users of the Internet, now captured by vast cartels and business conglomerates and yet still artistically subverted in undiscoverable nooks and crannies of the known universe? If so, then here the "advanced" might recover the childlike fantasies of Fourier himself.

And as for some new and revised concept of aura for a post-technological age? Its disappearance was to have been the sign and symptom of the emergence of some new collective consciousness, which, if it exists today, leads but a shadow existence within our aestheticized commodity world. Still, one can conjecture three general areas in which Benjamin's idea might still have some relevance.

The first has to do with the collective *Erfahrung* produced by a new technology, for which the term "reproduction" no longer seems adequate. A universalized televisual reception has opened the way for collective events which are no longer simply news, but which involve popular participation of a quite different kind than the workers' writing that Benjamin (and Enzensberger after him) imagined to offer a "dialogical" alternative to the one-way broadcast. The Kennedy assassination, to take one classic example, transformed the nature of historical chronology, producing a new kind of date-event in which millions of people participated as a personal experience and which largely transcended the limits of the shock-type *Erlebnis*. The collective nature of television is thereby glimpsed as a new form of aura, whose political implications (as, for example, in flash mobs) have scarcely yet been explored, let alone exhausted.

Meanwhile, insofar as *Erfahrung* for Benjamin is a quasi-bodily phenomenon, and aura has its deeper family relationship with handicraft as such, it has not seemed too far-fetched to remind ourselves that Internet activity, such as programming and hacking, is also a physical matter and a kind of "labor" which can scarcely be adequately dismissed as immaterial.

Finally, even as viewing shifts from movie theaters to that home appliance called television, the new televisual forms themselves—drawing on global investments in production and representing the work of local actors, in foreign languages, all over the globe—become endowed with a kind of internationalist exoticism in which the here-and-now of mass contact surely has its own auratic quotient. But in that case, the film-festival moment, which recovers the multiplicities underlying world cinema and displays the unique products of minor cinemas and smaller countries and language areas, more exotic collectives—those unique specimens among the immense standard multiplicity of official film production today—might indeed once again qualify for an aura of a new type.

Meanwhile, as for the apparatus of reproducibility itself, Marx divided the infrastructure or economic base of what he theorized as a mode of production into "forces of production" and "relations of production," thereby anticipating his overall structural distinction between base and superstructure. The latter is too often read as the difference between idealistic and materialistic phenomena; in much the same way, Marxist theorists (Korsch was an important exception) have shied away from the analogous division in the base. This has meant that the stereotypical understanding of the base as economic has tended to collapse it into technology as such. "Relations of production" designate, however, labor and its structure (including proletarian consciousness); understood this way, the base–superstructure distinction itself becomes a good deal more complex, and the base can no longer be thought exclusively in terms of the economic or technological.

In an intellectual climate in which positions officially marked materialist are automatically promoted over the more suspiciously idealist kinds, relations of production are inevitably subject to deformation by the static materiality of what we most often identify as technology. In this situation, it is always safer to trust the position which acknowledges and theorizes history and change. I suggest that what is always confusing about Benjamin's reproducibility essay is that in its view of the media, it always takes sides, implicitly or explicitly, for relations of production over the purely machinic perspective. The resultant theoretical asymmetry is what makes for the essay's incorrigible lack of focus.

9
History and the Messianic

Two unforgettable images frame the famous theses on history ("On the Concept of History"; IV, 388–405; I, 693–704, 1230–46) and inevitably inflect our reading of them.

The Angel, Klee's famous *Angelus Novus* (which, entre nous, has very little in common with Benjamin's description of it), comes from a family of ephemeral angels, those created to praise the moment—the Now, the *Jetztzeit*—and then at once to vanish along with it. Is it that, surveying the immense garbage dump of history, today's mountains of nonbiodegradable plastic, this particular angel finds itself incapable of singing the praises of the present to which it has been assigned and, mute, is therefore unable to vanish?

What few of the commentators seem to have noticed, however, is that the wind immobilizing its open wings is blowing out of paradise and not towards it. The angel cannot turn its face toward the future, Utopian or otherwise. We have seen that Benjamin is only too willing to register innumerable signs of decline—the decline of skills, of handicraft, of storytelling, of the graceful and productive uses of the body, of experience itself—indeed, to scrutinize any number of contemporary techniques for what they can tell us about this decline and new ways of overcoming it. We have tried, however, to shake off the now-conventional image of a nostalgic Benjamin: there is, for him, a cosmos in which all the elements of the world echo each other, but it is not certain that he thinks we can return to it or that he even wants to do so. The most thoroughgoing geographer we have on these matters is Dante, who arrives at what is now called the Earthly Paradise (the Persian word for garden), situated on top of Mount Purgatory—but it turns out to be but a metro stop on the way to something very different, namely Paradise itself, in which all the Edenic festivals and *trionfi* would be quite out of place: the difference between a rowdy popular Volksfest, such as the one that greeted the aged Dr. Faustus on Easter morning at the beginning of his great adventure, and the great Busby Berkeley acrobatic lightshows of the Eternal Rose, rather totalitarian spectacles for the observation and delectation of the Leader, one would think. "Moscow" is about as far as Benjamin got in imagining the direction of this new social experiment; Brecht got a little farther, and "suggested some proposals" of his own. Marx himself had little interest in fantasizing about the nature of that genuine human history which would begin after the end of this one, which he called "prehistory" (and, like the Jews, Stalin forbade inquiry into it in the first place).

But in the end is our beginning: the angel's wings have very much the same problems as the boat's sails—they must be adjusted to catch the wind, to profit from the wind of history that is to propel them. This particular angel has been remarkably maladroit and has failed to reckon with the winds of a storm. Whose fault is that? The winds are still blowing somewhere. This angel is the awkward Benjamin himself, as is the shrunken dwarf "historical materialism" in the first image. We should simply note that he didn't have to fail; it became his fate only after it happened.

As for the dwarf, he finds his place in the famous chess-playing automaton, the image that magisterially opens this series of reflections, with its all-conquering Turkish warrior whose triumphant moves are plotted by that same shrunken dwarf, Theology, concealed within. Unsurprisingly, Benjamin here confronts us at the very outset with an allegory whose consequences are wide-ranging and unexpected. The sudden expansion of Islam in the years immediately following Mohammed's death is well known, as is the almost equally irresistible triumph of the Ottomans; both of them arrested at the twin opposite gates of Europe, much like the absence of a Soviet revolution in Europe in the 1920s or (what Benjamin was never to know) the boundaries of

Stalin's "empire" after World War II. Of an unstoppable force, an irresistible military expansion, what Benjamin knew at the end of his life was, on the contrary, the blitzkrieg and the Hitlerian conquest of Europe.

Yet "the puppet, called 'historical materialism,' is to win all the time." We call this puppet the dialectic, and it always wins because its object is the reconstruction of history as necessity: what happened had to happen, and the dialectic, the "historical materialist," knows this. We will see later on what benefits historical materialism is to gain from theology in this situation.

But this image, like that of the angel, has been read as the ironic acknowledgement of the end of history, if not, in a far more plausible and literal reading, the end of Marxism. We will see why this is a misreading in the pages that follow; perhaps it will be enough for the moment to remind ourselves that, whatever the fate of the political chess game, theology retains that belief in the Messiah of which "history" seems to have disabused the Left.

2

But theology, like historical materialism, is a whole code or language field, a constellation in its own right, and we have been at pains, in the preceding pages, to show that Benjamin's work is rich with any number of these, which coexist and whose face values cannot be easily reconciled: so many names which demand their own independent commentaries. The *Denkbild*, for example, the "thought-picture," supplies the missing name for a genre he practiced with virtuosity his whole life, the one we have called the prose piece, the art paragraph, the discursive episode, in order to avoid terms like "fragment" which suggest the very opposite of the closure with which he stylishly endowed them. It is, however, relatively ungeneralizable: no one sets out to write *Denkbilder*— at best, you might risk a "Benjaminian *Denkbild*" as a kind of homage or pastiche. Its usefulness lies not merely in underscoring the episodism of Benjamin's thought, but in the intent to invent a generic name for this unit of writing: what is, on the contrary, more likely to mislead and to short-circuit further theoretical development is the visual emphasis suggested by the word *Bild* or "picture." That a culture in which visuality has come to play so dominant a role (owing to the very technological

advances that interested Benjamin) should find its most facile theoretical solutions in the term "image" is inevitable; but we should be prepared
to ask ourselves whether the term stands for a genuine idea and is not
simply a way of papering over a difficult mediation between the sensory
and the conceptual. The dilemma was already present in the antinomies
of the theory of photography, with their paradoxical struggle between
past and present and their compromise in this or that notion of the trace
(an idea only less problematic in its more limited quotient of visuality).
Image-based theories of mass culture no doubt find it convenient not to
have to indulge in complex philosophical discussions of temporality
every time they confront their most characteristic exhibits. But
Benjamin, whose whole lifework turned centrally on history, was
obliged, implicitly or explicitly, to deal with time. Visuality worried him
very little; when it did, the concept of allegory was there to absorb it.
Meanwhile, the language of the image encouraged that evasion of philosophical abstraction in which he was, no doubt, a precursor of modern
theory as such.

It is in the coinage of one of his favorite slogans, the "dialectical
image," that these issues come to a head and are most misleading. His
definition of it as a "*Dialektik am Stillstand*" is characteristic. Omitting
the essential feature of his idea—namely the similitude between at least
two moments of history—it has, via a mistranslation, led his readers to
grasp it as yet another synonym for "the end of history" (Niethammer,
for example, has no problem ranging Benjamin among his specimens of
"*posthistoire*," as we shall see).[1] The English word "standstill," conveying
a breakdown or unwanted immobilization, then suggests that it is the
dialectic itself that has fatally broken down; and the two images we have
just discussed—the angel's paralysis and the warrior's secret recourse to
theology—only confirm this impression. But *Stillstand* is something
closer to freeze-frame photography than to a car wreck, and Benjamin's
characteristic presentation of "epic theater" gives us a more reliable
version of the process, which corresponds to what, in an older theatrical
practice, was called a tableau, a sudden arrest of the movement on stage:

> Imagine a family scene: the wife is just about to grab a bronze sculp-
> ture and throw it at her daughter; the father is opening a window to

1   Lutz Niethammer, *Posthistoire*, London: Verso, 1994.

call for help. At this moment a stranger enters. The process is interrupted. What appears in its place is the situation on which the stranger's eyes now fall: agitated faces, open window, disordered furniture.
(II, 779; II, 698)

The frozen moment does not bring the action to an end; rather, it allows
us to analyze it into multiple outcomes, multiple choices, on the basis of
a fundamental situation, a shared dilemma, which the arrest of movement reveals and produces, beyond all distraction, like an X-ray. The
technique then uses visuality itself against the very illusions inherent in
it, the false appearances aroused by movement and encouraged by our
pleasure in visual consumption.

The misconceptions perpetuated by the expression "dialectical image"
are then only confirmed by Benjamin's own complex and idiosyncratic
conception of contemporary temporality, which motivate characteristic
expressions like the following:

Marx says that revolutions are the locomotive of world history. But
perhaps it is quite otherwise. Perhaps revolutions are an attempt by
the passengers on this train—namely, the human race—to activate
the emergency brake. (IV, 402; I, 1232)

Nowhere, indeed, is Benjamin's profound anti-continuism so passion-
ately expressed as in his definition of the vocation of revolution "to
interrupt the course of the world" (IV, 170; II, 664). No doubt the Soviet
revolution did that; but he himself was also careful, as we shall see, to
distinguish the two senses of revolution—as a sudden violent interruption, on the one hand, and as a new kind of long-term social experiment
or construction, on the other.

I must feel that it is more prudent, in dealing with slogans like "the
dialectical image," to observe Benjamin's own recommendations for its
use: "what distinguishes images from the 'essences' of phenomenology
is their historical index. The historical index of the images not only says
that they belong to a particular time; it says, above all, that they attain to
legibility only at a particular time." As we have already noted, this phrase
has to do with "access," and we have to understand that the "particular
time" in question is our own present, the moment in which we find
ourselves able to read this moment of the past and to grasp its "now of

recognizability." Likewise, even more significant is a radiological figure: "history decays into images, not into stories" (AN 3, 1, 462; V, 577).

It will clarify this whole question, I believe, to assert that what Benjamin is trying to convey with his formula—which is designed to emphasize the empirical rather than the purely abstract, but also to reduce the narrative element in the process—is what today we would call the synchronic: a nonchronological "constellation" of concrete factors and interrelated phenomena. The synchronic, although often opposed to the diachronic or chronological, aims, above all, to minimize the temporal dimension of its material but not its historical "index": it is not to be confused with this or that notion of the present (and the Benjaminian expression "Now-time" or *Jetztzeit* is equally, I believe, meant to distinguish between actuality and some other form of "presence"); instead, it is meant to transform what look like causal dimensions of the phenomenon into structural ones which, as we know, he called "similitudes." What often looks like causality in Benjamin—for example, the simultaneity of a certain kind of gesture, striking a Swedish match as well as casting dice in a gambling bet (IV, 328; I, 630)—is not meant to evoke some new historical force causally at work in these various areas ("a development . . . taking place in many areas") but rather a structural similitude (to underscore a word and an idea of particular significance in his thinking). The contemporary conception of synchronicity is designed to displace and exclude as much as possible the unwanted temporality of "progress" or of Bergsonian "homogeneous" time, without removing historicity altogether from the process, as the alternate vocabulary of an "essence" or of the "eternal" would tend to do.

This first constituent feature of the "dialectical image," as I believe it is meant to be understood, can perhaps most dramatically be observed in a well-known dispute between Benjamin and Adorno on the detail of the former's Baudelaire exegesis, and in particular the inclusion of material on the wine tax of the period in a discussion of the poet's wine poems. The dispute involves issues of greater theoretical import than matters of historiography. In fact, what is at stake here, under the cover of an insignificant detail, is the base-and-superstructure distinction itself and the disagreement on the role it should play in cultural analysis. Adorno feels that the base should be invoked only in the most general way, as "capitalist production" (and, although he does not say so, by way of the mediation of the commodity form, of commodification, also *in general*), whereas it is clear that for Benjamin, and in light of the mass of data contained in the *Arcades* convolutes, the details themselves are fully as superstructural as they are economic.

The issue is the significance of the customs barriers around the city of Paris in Baudelaire's day and the way in which, as in some US state borders, alcohol is cheaper beyond the tariff boundaries and attracts a specific sociality. For Benjamin, what is at stake here is not only Baudelaire's poetic texts—the various kinds of intoxication—but intoxication itself: it is the very promise of culture and its consumptions (*promesse de bonheur*, the Frankfurt School liked to say, following Stendhal) which is the object of the debate. Adorno would like to see the wine tax as the allegory of capitalism as a whole, and he would like to replace this positivistic detail or fact altogether with the totality of which it is a characteristic mechanism. But Benjamin wants the ontological richness of the fact itself, thereby generating an opposition between subject and object, the spirit (intoxication, including that of the poetic language itself) versus the body or matter, the real liquid produced and sold and taxed. The dialectical image would then be precisely this *Stillstand* at the heart of all such dualisms, including those of Marxism itself, in which the base stands irreconciled with the superstructure, yet both are grasped together in a single image (which is a contradiction).

But there is more than this: Benjamin's reply appeals to classical philology for its defense of what Adorno takes to be a vulgar causality (IV, 101; B,790)—the practice (also of enormous importance to Gramsci, whose training lay in just such philology) of restoring the background of an entire world and way of life, with its implements and its laws, its concrete constituents:

> The appearance of self-contained facticity that emanates from philological study and casts its spell on the scholar is dispelled according to the degree to which the object is constructed in historical perspective. The lines of perspective in this construction, receding to the vanishing point, converge in our own historical experience. In this way, the object is constituted as a monad. In the monad, the textual detail which was frozen in a mythical rigidity comes alive. It therefore seems to me to be a misunderstanding of the situation to find in the text, as you do, a "direct connection between '*L'Âme du vin*' and the wine tax." Rather, the link has been legitimately established in the philological

context—much as one would have to do when interpreting an ancient
classical writer. This gives the poem the specific gravity it takes on
through a genuine reading—something which has not generally been
applied in Baudelaire up to now. It is only when this specific gravity is
registered in the poem that the work can be impacted—not to say
shattered—by interpretation. In the case of the poem in question, this
would link it not to tax questions but to the meaning that Baudelaire
attached to intoxication. (IV, 108; B, 784–95)

The crucial word here, however, is not the evocation of philology as
such, but, rather, that of the monad. For it is surely the monadic unity,
the complex interrelationships of what remains a kind of organic
whole—with outer limits, perhaps, rather than with boundaries—that
occupies the conceptual space in Benjamin of what today is dubbed the
synchronic—or, in another sense, figured under the image of the
Deleuzian rhizome. The history of the customs barriers on alcohol
would be fully as much a rhizomatic strand growing out of the monad as
any contemporaneous medical theories on intoxication or any journalistic accounts of social disorder around the outer fringes of Paris, where,
indeed, Baudelaire's rag pickers and other inhabitants of his urban
mythology also gather and find their family relationship.

   The wine tax is therefore not to be understood in terms of causality
nor even of a schema in which the superstructure mechanically "reflects"
the base; rather, the relationship between the economic measure and the
poetic elaboration is ideogrammatic and functions according to the
logic of Benjaminian similitude.

   It is in this sense that Benjamin's use of the term "origin" is also not
meant to be read in causal or chronological terms, but rather along the
lines of what the phenomenologists preferred to call "essence," a concept
whose possible ahistorical or Platonic overtones we have seen Benjamin
reject. It seems worthwhile to cite another version of his thoughts on the
matter and which he characterized, from notes he made in 1931, as

   my attempt to explain a theory of history in which the concept of
   development is entirely supplanted by the concept of origins.
   Understood in this way, history cannot be sought in the riverbed of a
   process of development. Instead, as I have remarked elsewhere, the
   image of a riverbed is replaced by that of a whirlpool. In such a

whirlpool earlier and later events—the prehistory and posthistory of an event, or, better, of a status, swirl around it. The actual objects of such a view of history are not specific events but specific unchanging statuses of a conceptual or sensual kind—for example, the Russian agrarian system, the city of Barcelona, population shifts in the Mark of Brandenburg, barrel vaulting, and so on. If this approach is determined by its firm rejection of the possibility of an evolutionary or universalist dimension in history, it is determined internally by a productive polarity. The twin poles of such a view are the historical and the political—or, to point up the distinction even more sharply, the historical and the event. These two factors occupy two completely different planes. We can never say, for example, that we experience history; nor can we maintain that a historical account brings the events so close to us that it has the same impact as a historical event (such an account would be worthless), or that we have experienced events that are destined to become history (since such a view is journalistic). (II, 502–3; VI, 443)

But this quote, like others we have cited, underscores another significant feature of the so-called "dialectical image," namely that it is always profoundly historical and thereby necessarily periodizing in Riegl's sense: it has to do with the past and the way in which every one of these dialectical images in question here is a picture or a snapshot of a particular past. In that sense, all of our cultural references have to do with the past, with the "archive," and thereby with this or that conception of a historical period. Baudelaire's Paris is, for us, just such a historical period, but so is Riegl's "late Rome" and Benjamin's "Baroque"; the Soviet city itself stands for a historical period (which Benjamin called a present, even if was not exactly his); and the fascism emerging from Weimar, however painfully actual it was, is not only for us a period, but already was one for viewers for whom the present was history. I venture to say then that for the kind of historicizing at work in Benjamin's thinking and imagination, there is no item of cultural, social or political analysis and investigation which does not come before him as expressive of a period of history: graphology is the reemergence of the archaic, Fuchs's collections of caricatures and pornography are indices of a Second-International mentality, Ranke's Christian-German patriotism that of a lost German liberalism of the Frankfurt 1848 convention, which it would have been desirable to resurrect at a perilous moment in the chaotic Weimar Republic. (I use the word resurrect advisedly, as you will see shortly.)

In short, to reiterate another term to which Benjamin attached importance in this context, the dialectical image is a monad, and a historical one at that. It involves what I will call "periodization without transition," in which each of these monads floats free of the others, like the constellations, and yet demands a relationship to the present without which we cannot gain access to it, to use another charged and profoundly Benjaminian term. The Weimar present, in other words—a monad which serves as Benjamin's own historical reality—contains enough "Expressionist" elements to enable us to gain access to that hitherto bizarre and incomprehensible image which is the Baroque; but it lacks the elements which would give us full access to ancient tragedy. Benjamin's historicism, therefore—in which a moment of the past draws enough energy from the present to gain a new (and perhaps only momentary) lease on life, like the ghosts who drink the blood Odysseus offers them in his underworld sacrifice—depends very much on the conditions of possibility offered by our own present: paradoxically, however, those conditions are not merely greater knowledge and preparatory material, they are at one with our own crises. We must need that past in order to revive it, as a famous passage in the theses on history reminds us.

> Articulating the past historically does not mean recognizing it "the way it really was" [Ranke's familiar formulation]. It means appropriating a memory as it flashes up in a moment of danger. Historical materialism wishes to hold fast that image of the past which unexpectedly appears to the historical subject in a moment of danger. (Thesis VI)

This account, however, which leads us to the second feature of the "dialectical image" we must consider in order to grasp it properly, requires yet another, perhaps more unexpected, return detour through theology: in other words, to the promptings of the wizened dwarf.

3

This is the place to emphasize Benjamin's implicit view that theology has its uses, not only because it develops collective categories unavailable in the purely empirical "bad infinities" of modern political science or in the still purely individualizing "values" of modern ethics or legality; but rather because theological categories give us access to historical and essentially narrative modes of thinking about mass realities.

It is a proposition I will illustrate with a non-Benjaminian historical example, namely a conception of fate and collective destiny unavailable to mythic antiquity and also seemingly lost in modern secularity. This is the spirit in which I claim that in the matter of historical necessity, Marxism (and the cluster of thinkers around it who have worried this issue like a bone) reproduces the old theological debate about predestination. The argument is quite different from the affirmation of a variety of non- or anti-Marxist writers that Marxism is a religion (or "just another" religion). Rather, it means that the theological debate about predestination (particularly, no doubt, in Calvinism, which one might argue, following Weber, constitutes the exasperated ultimate theoretical thrust of theology into emergent capitalism) turns on the same antinomy for the human mind as the later political debate on the same issue, and perhaps articulates its unthinkability in an even more useful way than the one conducted in a secular code. That issue is, of course, the future, raised in more ancient times by the soothsayers. The predestination debate posited the necessity of individual and collective history, all their details foreseen in advance by God, if not indeed stipulated by Him: a doctrine framed in terms of the individual, which will then be projected onto collective destiny as such without much modification. The drawback, for religious theorists and planners, is that it seems to withdraw all possibility of choice or free will in the matter: if you have been chosen from all eternity to be either one of the damned or one of the elect, there would seem to be very little you can do about it, and the attribution of freedom would seem to be an illusion. Luther then drew the conclusion that good works are insufficient for salvation and that the resultant agony was good for you. A remarkable novel by James Hogg, *Private Memoirs and Confessions of a Justified Sinner* (1822), dramatized this antinomy in the person of a figure who logically concluded that if he was one of the elect, he could do anything he wanted without losing that status (conferred from all eternity), while in the opposite case, as in Pascal's wager, it would not matter anyway. This novel is one of the rare works in any literature to have been able to give representation to contradiction as such virtually without figural mediation.

Calvin's "solution" was a masterpiece of casuistry: he reasoned that if one were chosen, destined from all eternity to be one of the elect, one's person, one's individuality and subjectivity, would somehow radiate this initial status and that the individual choices and behavior of the elect would then inevitably stand as the "outward and visible signs of inner election". This unsatisfactory but preeminently practical cutting of the Gordian knot of contradiction is a far clearer and more dramatic expression of the unthinkability of the problem of the future than the various ancient myths about destiny and its "forking paths" or the political and secular terms in which the dilemma was argued in modern times, where the "inevitability of the revolution" is balanced against the impotence of individual choice or will, with the result that the two ineffectual ideologies of voluntarism and fatalism confront each other over and over again in history with nothing but carnage and sacrifice as an equally inevitable outcome. The useless heroism of small groups of young Russian anarchist believers at the end of the nineteenth century here confronts the abject surrender of the German Social Democrats to the mindless slaughter of World War I and trench warfare.

My point in making this comparison between a theological and a political debate from two very different moments of history is not to give a dramatic example of what the so-called dialectical image really looks like, although it surely does that. It is, rather, designed to show that although what I have called the theological code cannot solve a "problem" which is closer to a Kantian antinomy than a Hegelian contradiction—nothing can do that—it reveals the structure of the antinomy more clearly in many ways than the more practical secular reformulation of the same false problem in concrete historical situations.

This is, I think, what Benjamin felt to be the conceptual advantage of the theological code—admittedly a figural rather than an abstract form of representation—over the secular and political (social-scientific and historical) ones. This is, incidentally, also why it seems to me misleading to reformulate the distinction in the biographical terms of a mystical younger Benjamin, later on "converted" to a political set of convictions.

These are alternate codes or language systems which are available for the different readings of the situation: they are not "beliefs."

The theological code, however, has one particular conceptual space in which it proves to be the privileged instrument in what is, in any case, an impossible situation: and that is the realm of the future. Its conceptual instruments—reconciliation, redemption, fulfillment, hope, prophecy, revelation, the very idea of theology itself—are moral or conceptual ideas which mark and denounce their own insufficiency at the same time that they keep their content alive. Secular prognoses ultimately unmask themselves as superstitions in disguise, as the regressive, the entrails consulted by soothsayers as well as by politicians claiming to decide when the time is ripe. "The Jews were prohibited from inquiring into the future," Benjamin reminds us (IV, 397; I, 704). He might have added that Lenin's *April Theses* were not a prognostication, either, but rather an act. "Politics," said Turgot prophetically, "is obliged to foresee the present." Prophecy, in other words, must deny its own existence in order to preserve its status as prophecy: a disavowal that has paradoxical consequences for the past as well.

For it does not seem quite so paradoxical to sustain these two contradictory positions simultaneously: that the past cannot be altered, and that every generation changes it. Benjamin's well-known observation that not even the past is safe if fascism wins does not seem so terribly distant in spirit from T. S. Eliot's transhistorical reading-room roundtable, in which each new work modifies tradition and the cultural past ever so slightly.

Where Benjamin's theology seems to exceed a left politics with which it is otherwise easily reconcilable lies in the suggestion of a doctrine of redemption which holds for human history in general, that "nightmare of history" (Joyce), which Hegel uncharacteristically also characterized as one immense charnel house. The redemption of the dead—the very phrase comes close to that breathtaking orthodox belief called apocatastasis, in which, after the trumpet of the Last Judgment, all of the dead of human history, sinners as well as saved without exception, will rise from the grave all equally redeemed, in some final and definitive bodily resurrection. Benjamin seems to have indulged this fantasy openly enough for it to merit a response from that wise orthodox Marxist who was Max Horkheimer, in the tolerant spirit of an adult correcting a naïve and enthusiastic adolescent: "Past injustice has occurred and is completed.

The slain are really slain . . . If one takes the lack of closure entirely seriously, one must believe in the Last Judgment . . . Perhaps with regard to
incompleteness, there is a difference between the positive and the negative, so that only the injustice, the horror, the sufferings of the past are
irreparable. The justice practiced, the joys, the works, have a different
relation to time, for their positive character is largely negated by the
transience of things" (quoted in A, 471, N8, 1; V, 589). It is the exact
opposite and an absolute negation of Benjamin's sporadic position.

Still, Horkheimer's insistence on the notion of completeness is suggestive: "The determination of incompleteness is idealistic if completeness
is not comprised within it," where completeness means the irrevocable.
Benjamin's response, which substitutes remembrance (*Eingedenken*) for
"scientific history," for the history of the irrevocable and the facts, for
death and absolute transience, seems on the face of it feeble enough and
a form of negative theology: "In remembrance we have an experience
that forbids us to conceive of history as fundamentally atheological,
little as it may be granted us to try to write it with immediately theological concepts" (A, N8, 1, 471; V, 589).

If, however, we understand "completeness" to be a secular synonym
for the theological idea of fulfillment, then this seemingly fanciful
exchange takes on real political content and significance. For fulfillment
is a central component of the theological doctrine of allegory; it derives
from the conviction that the New Testament "fulfills" the Old and that
the events of the latter—by no means unreal or merely symbolic, but as
definitive as suffering and death itself—are nonetheless incomplete in
themselves. They demand completion by events in the future; their
redemption is not a personal one, not a bodily resurrection, but a reenactment that brings them to realization and fulfillment.

This is, then, the ultimate meaning of Benjamin's enigmatic "dialectical image." We insisted on its dual nature, as a superimposition of the
present on the past; now it becomes clearer that this duality is a form of
allegorical figuration and that the moment of the past, the historical
monad, is, in its very failure, an incompleteness and a prefiguration of a
realization to come. This is, then, the political meaning of Benjamin's
often-quoted evocation of a past that "flits up" in a moment of danger:

To Robespierre, ancient Rome as a past charged with now-time
[*Jetztzeit*], a past which he blasted out of the continuum of history.

[This] is the tiger's leap into the past . . . The same leap in the open air of history is the dialectical leap Marx understood as revolution. (Thesis VI)

Robespierre and the Jacobin revolutionaries had, then, a dialectical image of the Roman republic, just as we have a dialectical image of them: they are present to us in a noncontemplative, "operative" way, not as models (aesthetic or otherwise), but as tasks to be completed; this is, to anticipate, the "theological" dimension of Benjamin's view of history. (I have tried as much as possible to avoid rewriting Benjamin as the anticipation of contemporary theoretical formulations; here, however, the closest approximation of the Benjaminian "dialectical image" might well be Deleuze's cinematographic "time-image," the Bergsonian way in which several presents of time overlap and seem to coincide, all the while constantly shifting their structural priorities over one another: this effect is, for Deleuze or Bergson, the result of an interruption in sensorimotor action, which might well then correspond to Benjamin's exclusion of linear or homogeneous time.)

In that sense, this is a moment to which we "have access"; indeed, this is a historical period which has for us become an Event, unlike other moments of the historical record, which we know as information but which do not live for us in the same fashion (or for which, as for ancient tragedy, we do not have equivalents at all—which remain for us a closed book). What makes such access possible? It should be stressed again that this view of a punctual, discontinuous yet living, vital and urgent relationship to a specific moment of the past is awakened under the category of similitude. Blanqui's insurrectional politics have little to do with those of Lenin (indeed, they are condemned by a Marxian view of revolution), yet Blanqui is the stand-in for Lenin in the time of Baudelaire; we cannot do without his implacable political will. It lives on in later eras, and very much in that new Dark Age of the Stalin–Hitler pact and the triumph of Nazi Germany over Europe. That unfulfilled will is a figure demanding completion in the future (if not the present).

Historicity is a peculiarly complex conceptual problem, but unlike its equivalent in photography, it is not blocked by the reification of the past in an image, it does not thereby become an antinomy. Still, the role of our own present in this unique resurrection of the past must not be grasped as a simple dualism: it is in reality a more complex, three-term structure, in which it is the overlap or similitude between two moments of the past which awakens our recognition in the present. Robespierre's electrifying relationship to the Roman republic not only transforms each of these moments into a monad, but it permits us to construct the present as a monad as well, allowing us to recognize our own moment in time, our own situation ("the moment of danger") as an equally "dialectical image" which makes a third together with these other two. As has been pointed out, the "now of recognizability" does not refer to our present but is in fact the "historical index" of that dual moment of the past, in which revolution itself emerges as a monad. It is worth quoting this dense note in its entirety:

> What distinguishes images from the "essences" of phenomenology is their historical index. (Heidegger seeks in vain to rescue history for phenomenology abstractly through "historicity.") These images are to be thought of entirely apart from the categories of the "human sciences," from so-called habitus, from style, and the like. For the historical index of the images not only says that they belong to a particular time; it says, above all, that they attain to legibility only at a particular time. And, indeed, this acceding "to legibility" constitutes a specific critical point in the movement at their interior. Every present day is determined by the images that are synchronic with it: each "now" is the now of a particular recognizability. In it, truth is charged to the bursting point with time. (This point of explosion, and nothing else, is the death of the *intentio*, which thus coincides with the birth of authentic historical time, the time of truth.) It is not that what is past casts its light on what is present, or what is present its light on what is past; rather, the image is that wherein what has been comes together in a flash with the now to form a constellation. In other words: the image is dialectics at a standstill. For while the relation of the present to the past is purely temporal, the relation of what-has-been to the now is dialectical: not temporal in nature but figural [*bildlich*]. Only dialectical images are genuinely historical—that is, not archaic— images. The image that is read—which is to say, the image in the now of its recognizability—bears to the highest degree the imprint of the perilous critical moment on which all reading is founded. (A, 462; N3, 1; V, 577–8)

Nor should we imagine that this "allegorical fulfillment" is a mere repetition in the Nietzschean sense of the eternal return or of Blanqui's cyclical pessimism. It cannot be a repetition inasmuch as the first figure itself was necessarily incomplete. All the revolutions in history, in other words, have been failures; each of them seemed to posit an "infinite task" and to demand completion by some future fulfillment. Just as the Commune's failure was not absolute but found its fulfillment in its Soviet reenactment, so little can one pronounce the latter to have been a failure either: Benjamin's "redemption" of the past calls not for resignation but for action and activism, for reenactment and "completion" on a higher plane. The pessimism hereby invoked is not that of Schopenhauer but rather of Sorel, an active and an energizing pessimism.

> The pessimist regards social conditions as forming a system bound together by an iron law which cannot be evaded, as something in the form of one block, and which can only disappear through a catastrophe which involves the whole. If this theory is admitted, it then becomes absurd to attribute the evils from which society suffers to a few wicked men; the pessimist is not subject to the bloodthirsty follies of the optimist driven mad by the unforeseen obstacles that his projects meet; he does not dream of bringing about the happiness of future generations by slaughtering existing egoists.[2]

4

I will argue that the burden of Benjamin's theses on history (IV, 389–411; I, 691–704, 1223–66) is the effort to separate historiography from history, that is, to get us to distinguish what we can know about history, what we can represent or imagine—our historical "picture" or worldview—from History itself, the real direction in which the wind of history is blowing in these "final two seconds" at the close of world history's "twenty-four-hour" day. There is a philosophy of history implied here, certainly, but the theses on history are above all concerned with the limits of our historical knowledge and imagination, with the shape of our own historicity.

---

2 Georges Sorel, *Reflections on Violence*, Cambridge: Cambridge University Press, 1999, 11.

The first thesis (the one marked II) interrogates our access to the future, a peculiarly impoverished one (we do not envy it) insofar as we are existential creatures. After that, it is recommended that we grasp history as the sum total of all human lives and all the instants of those lives, and that we distinguish that impossible totality from the ideological pictures of history abundantly supplied us by the tradition and the category of continuity. The "real" past, if that is the right way to put it, is exceedingly elusive and only available as glimpses (Thesis IV), which include recommendations as to how to keep a grip on these precious glimpses. At their heart is the reminder that although Utopia must remain a "regulative idea," it is not helpful for us (the Messiah is first and foremost the enemy of Anti-Christ; he is a figure of struggle and warfare and not a peaceful ruler).

Warning signals sound as we seek to identify the best way to grasp this real history, melancholy being one of the signs; it betrays our repression of the anonymous labor of the forgotten in our "cultural traditions." Indeed, tradition must itself be denounced, the only continuity in real history (Thesis VIII) is not cultural, it is that of catastrophe.

This is the point at which the "angel" appears, and its vision of history as catastrophe is also denounced. At this point, as well, the polemic direction of the theses shifts somewhat, and we are placed before a new contradiction: if everything is tainted by complicity, then is not the attempt to remain politically pure like a withdrawal into a monastery? (The other image, that of the whorehouse, will follow shortly on this one.)

The practical answer represents a narrowing of Benjamin's polemical sights and a return to his denunciation of the social-democratic belief in progress and the ideological vision of "historicism" that underpins it. (There is a return to Marx's critique of the Gotha program; not the domination of nature is to be asserted, which itself places labor in general in the position of exploitation; but rather creative—and cooperative—production.) "Progress," however, illustrates the dangers of a propagandistic use of the future (better to rely on past antagonisms—a later note will radically separate the embattled thinking required for revolution from the mentality required for socialist construction in order to remove class concepts from the Utopian thinking of a world without classes).

Here, the distinction between history and historiography becomes refined, for it is being shown that the vision of history that informs historiography has very real effects on history itself. Benjamin therefore directs his inquiry in a new way, which comes at our notions of history from that of temporality as such (homogeneous or empty, chronological time, the time of "universal history" of continuities versus the flash of the monad, the glimpse of the *Jetztzeit*).

At this point, something different is being made explicit: it is that triple time as which we defined the famous "dialectical image." This new monadic view of history (this shift from traditional historiography to something more radical and more effective, to a conception which will include what we called redemption or fulfillment) includes other times by foreshortening, by "time lapse": no transitions, but simultaneity. The traditional view of revolutions was a punctual, orgasmic one ("drained by the 'whore called once upon a time'"); this one will complete the past in a different way, in a kind of eternal simultaneity rather than either a linear or cyclical return. (We have already commented on the ambiguity of Benjamin's use of "standstill" and the misunderstandings it causes.) This time is double: it completes "the constellation into which [the historian's] own era has entered, along with a very specific earlier one," he adds in an afterthought (IV, 397; I, 703). The theses end with what has become a familiar clock of cosmological history, in which the entire last "two seconds" have become the human monad as such.

The theses on history, indeed, leave a number of such afterthoughts behind them, of which the usual additions, A and B, are only the more familiar pieces, and which are rich and suggestive and demand attention as well. These return to the question of "universal history"—that is, the "bad" history of the homogeneous or chronological kind (now the prototype of the historiography Benjamin has been denouncing in these theses). It turns out to be not so negative as we might have imagined. There is an odd and thereby perhaps revealing fluctuation in Benjamin's thought about "universal history." It is to be condemned as academic and bourgeois, relying on chronology and causality rather than on the logic of the monadic. And it is indeed in the latter that Benjamin seeks his own theory of history and of historiography alike (the *Arcades* project will be a monad, just as the Baroque was; the "dialectical image" is the conjunction of two monads, at the very least our own and a moment of the past). This bad universal history seeks to lump all the nameless dead together in a single narrative, whose protagonists are the victors.

Mallarmé suddenly springs to mind as an argument in support of
this repudiation of universal history, for he underscores its many
languages, which means that no single language can subsume the totality of the human population, living and dead. And then there are the
many peoples: Benjamin here seems to doubt the very unity of any
single one of those ethnic and linguistic groups ("the notion that the
history of humanity is composed of peoples is a mere refuge of intellectual laziness"). It makes sense even if you argue it by way of the
dialects, but even more if you remember that "race" (a form of people)
is as artificially constructed a unity as nation (the "national languages"
themselves were forcefully unified by compulsory education, military
service, legal requirement, markets and other deliberate political
processes and operations).

Meanwhile, it is also the very fact of historical narration itself which
is rejected ("history as something which can be narrated," he says scorn-
fully). Narration, it is implied, is a construct you make out of bits of
history or, as in bad universal history, that you try to impose on it for
ideological and political reasons.

But then Benjamin has one of those turns of thought which characterize the freshness of his thinking in the immediate and the unpreju-
diced, the undogmatic and unforewarned—the unexpected interrogation of those circumstances under which universal history might
nonetheless be possible and allowable, or at least imaginable. Now we
set out on the opposite path, working back from this state of alienation
to some non-alienated combination of circumstances. If "a universal
history *without* a constructional principle is reactionary," what might
one look like that was "not inevitably reactionary"? "The constructional
principle of universal history allows it to be represented in partial histories. It is, in other words," he adds, "a monadological principle" (IV, 404;
I, 1234). The logic of the monad, in other words, refracts the totality into
its parts, into all its elements, of whatever dimensions. The monadic
story, if it can be called that, comes in all shapes and forms; its smallest
element, its most insignificant human component, projects a story or at
least a figure, which is assumed and captured in its most dramatic
adventures.

The process is recapitulated (and the very principle itself illustrated)
in another feature of this constellation, a rather surprising one, which is
simply identified as "prose": "The idea of prose coincides with the

messianic idea of universal history," he abruptly concludes. These after-thoughts or preliminary notes contain references to Benjamin's other works, which have been suppressed from the final version of the theses: here, for example, we find a clue in the essay on Leskov of a few years earlier, "The Storyteller," albeit in a parenthesis: "great prose is the creative matrix of the various metric forms" (III, 154; II, 453). This would seem to be something of a reversal of the Viconian notion that the first language of humans was poetic.

But it can be perhaps be more adequately elucidated by reference to that even earlier essay, "On Language as Such," in which the various concrete languages of the world are, as it were, the projections of some primal language "as such" ("*imparfaites en cela que plusieurs*," adds Mallarmé). So, it seems fair to conclude that all the smaller partial histories are the projection of this primal one, just as the various meters and rhythms, the varied syntax, of the actually existing languages, are the emanations of prose as such (where our very formulation of this idea begins to approach Plotinus or at least Plotinian dimensions).

That this is the primal language and the primal universal history of what we have called the Benjaminian cosmos can surely not be doubted. That it is also the form taken by Benjaminian "redemption" is, then, the deductive tiger's leap, which, without leaving history, would place us at the heart of Benjamin's theological conceptuality and its most deeply political logic. This Benjaminian universal history is apocatastasis, as well as the Last Judgment ("every moment is a moment of judgment concerning certain moments that preceded it").

5

Still, Niethammer's eponymous book is scarcely the only interpretation to have concluded that the theses merited Benjamin a position among the thinkers of *posthistoire*, of this or that "end of history." And surely the storm which immobilizes the angel's wings, dooming it to eternal paralysis and retroactive contemplation of the garbage-heap of history forever—whether that storm be identified with the triumphant Nazi conquest of Europe or simply with a globalized neoliberalism—is likely to be considered by those who live in it an irreversible state of historical climate change. Nor do the enigmatic pronouncements on hope hold out much promise, or, likewise, the sparse evocations of the Messiah, which mainly seem to assure us of his inevitable unpredictability. Great prophecy seems to have been omitted, and Benjamin never formulates the idea of strong messianism as such.

The future is, to be sure, a very peculiar philosophical object: it has no being as such, but, on the other hand, a more-than-psychological exist-ence. It is scarcely to be thought or experienced as a thing-in-itself, outside of temporality as a whole; but there are multiple forms of tempo-rality, even of a limited kind, which are available to grasp a past-present-future as a continuum, and, meanwhile, the very name we give the future seems to endow it with an existence in its own right.

Theology reserves a uniquely specific virtue for the domain of the future: it is called hope, and hope is very much a Benjaminian preoc-cupation from the beginnings of his career to its premature end. Yet we will see that our access to the very idea of hope is class-conditioned, and it will be useful at this point to register Benjamin's most significant pronouncements on the subject of social class. Everything he wrote was steeped in his awareness of himself as a bourgeois intellectual and of the inevitable limitations this class status imposes: "the intellectual who espouses the proletarian cause will never himself become a proletarian." It is a conviction he develops in the important review of Kracauer's white-collar analysis in *Die Angestellten*:

> This left-radical wing may posture as much as it likes—it will never succeed in eliminating the fact that the proletarianization of the intel-lectual hardly ever turns him into a proletarian. Why? Because from childhood on, the middle class gave him a means of production in the form of an education—a privilege that establishes his solidarity with it and, perhaps even more, its solidarity with him. This solidarity may become blurred superficially, or even undermined, but it almost always remains powerful enough to exclude the intellectual from the constant state of alert, the sense of living your life at the front, which is characteristic of the true proletarian. (II, 309; III, 224–5)

This conviction explains why it was important for Benjamin to account for his own class politics in terms of his intellectual work and to advo-cate revolution as a solution to the professional and economic dilemmas writers faced in the West (he was keenly interested not only in proletarian participation in the public sphere, but also in institutions like the Soviet Writers' Union, all the while remaining conscious of the problems he himself, as a non-party left intellectual, would have faced in the Soviet Union). A certain conception of the class situation of the cultural intellectual under socialism clearly marked his own personal sense of futurity.

But another remark about the revolutionary future even more dramatically distinguishes the temporality of the revolution as an event from that of the revolution as a situation: "The existence of the classless society cannot be thought at the same time that the struggle for it is thought" (IV, 407; I, 1245). The psychology of the revolutionaries is necessarily radically distinct from that required by the "construction of socialism"; he had already implied as much in a critique of the social democratic insistence on the redemption of "future generations . . . This indoctrination made the working class forget its hatred and its spirit of sacrifice, for both are nourished by the image of enslaved ancestors rather than by the ideal of liberated grandchildren" (Thesis XII).

Yet his distinction between the thinking of classlessness and that of "the struggle for it" continues:

> The concept of the present . . . is necessarily defined by these two temporal orders. Without some sort of assay [*Prüfung*] of the classless society, there is only a historical accumulation of the past. To this extent, every concept of the present participates in the concept of Judgment Day.

It is a qualification which suggest that Klee's *Angelus Novus* has forgotten Judgment Day in its captivation with the slag-heap of an unredeemed past.

At any rate, that our very access to hope varies with our class position is suggested by one of Benjamin's most paradoxical sentences, the one which concludes, with an unrelated and incomprehensible flourish, his essay on *Wahlverwandtschaften*: "Only for the sake of the hopeless have we been given hope" (I, 356; I, 201). The pronouncement evidently has a deeper relationship to a remark by Kafka which fascinated Benjamin and which (now widely quoted) was related by his friend Max Brod. It is Kafka's response to a question Brod poses about the world's hopelessness, and whether there is any hope to be found "outside this manifestation of the world we know":

> He smiled. "Oh, plenty of hope, an infinite amount of hope—but not for us."
>
> (II, 798; II, 414)

So there can exist separate spheres: in one of which hope exists, and of which another is deprived. There is certainly a logic in the idea that, where hope is unnecessary, it need not or cannot exist; or, better still, it has a reason for existing only where it is absent and desperately needed. The place where it is needed, the place of the hopeless, is the place of the poor and the destitute: hope is the sign of a future for those who are hopeless (and this category exceeds the class category of a proletariat which is already potentially organizable and capable of social action).

Those who are not hopeless, however—ourselves, a class with privileges, a bourgeoisie (in the more general and loose sense), those who are, in the words of the *Threepenny Opera*, "in the light"—we do not have hope because we do not need it. This implies an ambiguous, twofold meaning about the future which goes with our class position: we do not have a future, either because we are so intensely caught up in our own present that we need none, or because our system itself has no future and we are existentially bound up in it. Whence the twofold cultural expressions of the present day: a dystopian imagination culminating in apocalypse or a fixation on the present of time so all-encompassing as to make futurity unnecessary and unimaginable. In any case, it is the longevity of the mode of production and its institutions—family, empire, business, buildings, landscapes—which provide the structure of our personal and existential fantasies and libidinal investments. Benjamin liked to quote Paul Valéry on the constitutive relationship between the idea of eternity and the temporality of handicraft production (III, 150; II, 449): in the same way, duration and its possibility is reflected back to us by the relative permanency of our object-world.

This is to say that hope "for us"—for that Western bourgeoisie for which Benjamin wrote and in which we still live—is an external experience; a reality to be glimpsed from the outside and at a distance. We cannot doubt its existence, but it does us no good to attempt to "believe" in it, something authenticated by Benjamin's citation of Lotze's curious remark about "the general lack of envy which every present day feels towards its future."

But then that thesis continues in an unexpected way, transforming this seemingly unfeeling relationship to the future into what we necessarily take as a theologically positive state, namely redemption (*Erlösung*). The pronouncement reads as follows:

> *Es schwingt, mit anderen Worten, in der Vorstellung des Glücks*
> *unveräusserlich die der Erlösung mit.* (I, 389; I, 693)

> The idea of happiness is indissolubly bound up with the idea of
> redemption.

"Indissolubly bound up," reads the standard English translation of "*unveräusserlich*," which one might wish had been rendered, with the proper legal terminology, "inalienable." In other words, however conscious or unconscious you may be about the legality of the matter, "redemption" will always be as it were "legally" connected with the experience of *Glück* (a word that, in German, means luck as much as happiness, shades of the old providence debate!). Here, then, theology comes back in full force and seeps into the very existential or phenomenological experience of personal happiness or fulfillment. Like it or not, our personal happiness is inseparable from the theological concept of redemption; and with this identification, Benjamin sketches what is probably his only ethics—namely the allegorical association of a well-nigh biological conception of individual happiness with a historical imperative. Unsurprisingly, the combination at once launches a foray into the past and its relationship with both present and redemption (now somehow identified and conjoined by way of happiness). This even more mysterious relationship is expressed in equally enigmatic terms:

> *Die Vergangenheit führt einen heimlichen Index mit, durch den sie*
> *auf die Erlösung verwiesen wird.*

> The past carries with it a secret index by which it is referred to
> redemption.

As far as the translation is concerned (and I am perfectly willing to agree, in Benjamin's own spirit of things, that it is untranslatable), one wishes for a stronger English equivalent for "referred." Yes, the past is, in that sense, destined for redemption as you might politely refer someone to their proper seat in the congregation: they are not yet seated, but a place is held for them and it is shown to them. Still, one does not want to place the responsibility for taking that place on the past itself. Perhaps further elucidation of "redemption" will clarify all this.

The real problem is the term "index," the same in both languages: does it simply mean marked? Not even marked out, but carrying a mark, like a scar or a tattoo, or, on the other hand, a ticket? To be sure, the "index" is secret and so in that sense we may never know what it looks like, only that, like a pointing finger, it "indicates." Both of these words belong in a Benjamin-style study, they are examples of his elegant evasion of the unspeakable or inexpressible, names for what has no name, words for the as yet unclassifiable (particularly inasmuch as classification governs the general or universal, while all of these things—the past!—are particular or specific, singular, and thereby only worthy of a name as such and not a "word").

"There is a secret agreement . . . Then our coming was expected . . . We have been endowed with a weak messianic power." And, finally and conclusively: "The historical materialist knows this!" No, not quite: *er weiss darum*—he knows something about it. Perhaps we will learn more about what he knows in the following theses.

6

Messiah, revolution, redemption, hope: so many radically heterogeneous concepts and language complexes which for Benjamin are strictly synonymous, but which cannot be uttered in the same breath. To grasp his reference to the Messiah, for example, one can evoke a variety of conceptual translation fields with which to identify this figure, the linguistic one being perhaps the most obscure in its combination of syntax and plenitude. The theological framework is precisely what remains to be translated for a secular and even postmodern reader; the psychological, existential, psychoanalytic frames are, alternately, the most facile, and Benjamin himself knew that they tended to include the phenomenological, which does not thereby escape subjectivity. A theory of history? That is obvious enough, but it presupposes that we know what it would be a theory of; and in any case, the category belongs with Heidegger's "world pictures" as a woefully modern term, not even a thought, but very much an ideologeme—in short, what Deleuze would have called a bad concept.

This is the sense, for example, in which the attribution to Benjamin of a narrative about modernity and the impoverishment of contemporary experience would be an ideological construction; and the same would have to be said for his supposed celebration of modern technological invention and new media. Benjamin certainly held both views simultaneously, in a coexistence which was neither a contradiction nor a synthesis. They are, on the contrary, simultaneous features of a historical situation—a current situation, or "Now-time" both monadic and differential—which it requires a new kind of time consciousness to think.

Biography, for example, would very much be an essential component of such a linguistic situation: the Stalin–Hitler pact, Benjamin's internment as an enemy alien, his physical debilitation, the characteristic (and now fatal) procrastination about flight and future destination—a linguistic procrastination, in which his chief concern was to prolong and preserve his productive and, as it were, artisanal relationship with the German language. A situation is not to be grasped ethically, nor in the affective terms—optimistic, pessimistic—which characterize ideological worldviews. I believe that it is only as a unique and idiosyncratic construction of a new kind of temporality that we can best encompass what look like incommensurabilities.

To affirm, for example, that the messianic in Benjamin simply means revolution is not false, but misleadingly conceals the gaps between these propositions, which it is more productive to approach literally. His own carefully chosen expression, "the weakly messianic," thereby becomes a more effective clue, and it leads us to interrogate what might in that case have been, for him, "strong prophecy." We also know that he practiced a monadic historicism, one which breaks with continuities and homogeneous time (or progress) and which incorporates our present and a Now-time into its multiple moments of the past, from which we are to draw the strength for our own future, or for our multiple futures.

The essential warning, the methodological hint, is to be sure furnished by what seems (now famously) to have been an afterthought to the original theses:

> We know that the Jews were prohibited from Inquiring into the future . . . This does not imply, however, that for the Jews the future became homogeneous, empty time. For every second was the strait gate in time through which Messiah might enter. (IV, 397; I, 704)

Or this alternate formulation:

> Spleen as a bulwark against pessimism. Baudelaire is no pessimist. This is because, with Baudelaire, a taboo is placed on the future. (IV, 162; I, 657)

We conclude that the soothsayers, elsewhere more explicitly condemned, were at best endowed with just that "weak messianic power" we here seek to elucidate. Even if their predictions turned out to be correct (on the order, perhaps, of the malignant oracles of antiquity—"when Croesus crosses the river Halys, a mighty kingdom will fall"—they remain on the level of doxa or sheer opinion, in comparison with the genuine knowledge, the philosophical episteme or apodictic conviction, that great prophecy once had, and that is forbidden us.

So it is that we cannot but construct a mental picture of a radically different future by using elements of our own present—the dilemma of Utopian thinking, surely one current form of the messianic. At best, perhaps, such thinking develops its power and brazenly displays its own limits in cyclical history. We remember Benjamin's fascination with Blanqui's final text, "L'Éternité par les astres," which he discovered in his own last years, and in which an eternal return discovers the aged revolutionary writing these same words again and again, along with all the failed insurrections that preceded them. What Nietzsche greeted with manic enthusiasm, and Dostoyevsky's devil characterized as "the most awful boredom," may be taken as the strong form of the pessimism we have already celebrated. Class struggle is, no doubt, just such an eternal return, as Lukács observed, in a Moscow anxiously awaiting the Nazi troops, when he calmly evoked the inevitable reemergence of class contradictions in Hitler's postwar cabinet. Nor does Kubrick's comic

Cold War apocalypse lack a certain sublimity, either: "We'll meet again, don't know where, don't know when . . ."

It is therefore wrong to conclude that the angel's wings, held open like an umbrella broken in a storm, signify the "end of history." The image, rather, expresses the experience of defeat, asking an unanswerable question about the way in which we are to receive the messianic emotion, namely hope as such. It has no place in a temporal system from which the future has been excised, and its philosophical expression is perhaps best conveyed by those late pages in which Althusser (another Blanqui, perhaps) tries to think the unthinkable—namely, the aleatory. Of all these formulations, however, the most faithfully Benjaminian, perhaps, remains Kafka's affirmation that hope exists (although "not for us"). This is not a happy ending, but it is not the end of history either.

Index

education, 41–2; as means of production, 240

Eiland, Howard, *Walter Benjamin: A Critical Life*, 105*n*5

Eingang, 14

einverleibt (experience), 49; and storytelling, 168

Eisenstein, Sergei, 6, 23, 193; montage as art that thinks without opinions, 28; "montage of attractions", 6, 26, 36, 39, 120, 122

empathy, 15

empiricism, tender, 8

Engels, Friedrich, 157; *Communist Manifesto*, 150

epic theater, 56, 124, 213–4, 222

"Epilogue to the Berlin Food Exhibition" (Benjamin), 40–2

episodization, 19, 32, 35, 73, 124, 178

"Epistemo-Critical Prologue" (Benjamin), 4, 73–5, 148

Erfahrung, 175; and aura, 185; central concern of Benjamin's work, 164; as experience, 6, 108; vs. experience, 173; and new technology, 217; and photography, 184; and storytelling, 100, 166

Erlebnis, 175; and photography, 184; as shock, 6, 173; and storytelling, 100, 166

escape: from psychology, 36; from society, 43–4

essays, 37; Benjamin impatient with essay form, 198; Benjamin never wrote an essay, 39; Benjamin's most perfect essay, 164, 175, 187; on Berlin, 115; and city, 114; as performance, 40; as program-essays, 37; tripartite periodization of, 114. *See also names of individual essays*

estrangement effect (V-effect), 6, 77, 98, 127, 174

L'Éternité par les astres (Blanqui), 45, 246

ethics, 10; and fate, 82

event, 84, 167; figure for absence of, at heart of Baudelaire's work, 92

everyday life, 153

exile, 96, 103

experience, 40; "boredom is the dream bird that hatches the egg of experience," 128; collective response, 201; of cosmos, 46, 48–9; deterioration of, 171–2, 185; dissolution of, 108; of history, 227; of Internet and TV, 217; and judgment, 78; of novel, 163–4; phenomenology, 130–1; politicalization of, 188, 205; of storytelling, 166–8; and temporality, 169; of tragedy, 66

"Experience and Poverty" (Benjamin), 171, 187

experimentation, 214

explanation, 168

Expressionism, 15, 79–80; and Riegl, 111; and Surrealism, 144

expressionlessness, 33, 76

facial recognition, 192

fairy tale, 55–6, 62; as anti-myth, 216; and memory, 174; and novel, 169–70, 174. *See also* literature; storytelling

fall, 51–4, 140; of language, 76–7

"False Criticism" (Benjamin), 144

family: family photo, 180–1; hatred for, 121

fascism: and aesthetization, 85, 156, 175, 188, 216; and capitalism, 208; vs. communism, 15, 207; and consumerism, 156; emergence of, 227; and history, 231; and myth, 55, 175; not mentioned after WWII, 206–7; and regression, 181, 202; and secularization, 151

fate, 60; and ethics, 82; and speechlessness, 82

"Fate and Character" (Benjamin), 82

fetishism, 152; of cultural objects, 159; increase of, 160; of "the creative," 181

figuration: for describing Benjamin's thought, 5; problem of universals understood as, 7; and theology, 11

film: and alienation, 195; apparatus of, and penetration of reality, 199–200; and aura, 191, 195, 218; close-up, 191, 195; Disney, 178, 202; distinguished from traditional art forms, 199;

37–8; reader as translator, 77; "The Task of the Translator" (Benjamin), 38, 77; of theological framework, 244; and Ur-language, 51; of "The Work of Art in the Age of Its Technological Reproducibility," 177–8
Trauerspiel (tragic drama), 14–5; and tragedy, 59, 64–8
traveler's notes, 24
Truman Show (movie), 155
truth, 76
types, 81–2, 101
Typhoon (Conrad), 23
Tzara, Tristan, 182

unconscious, 151, 159; collective unconscious, 13; fetishism, 160; optical unconscious, 190, 200–2
uniqueness, 193
universal history, 237–8
universals, philosophical problem of, 7–8, 52
Ur-form, 8, 18–9, 30, 179
Ur-language, 51

V-effect (estrangement effect), 6, 77, 98, 127, 174
Valéry, Paul, 88, 100, 109, 242
Vertov, Dziga, 21
violence, 139–43; artistic violence, 143; divine violence, 142–3; and law, 142; mythic violence, 142–3; *Reflections on Violence* (Sorel), 140; state violence vs. revolutionary, 141–3; and terrorism, 140–1. *See also* destruction
Virilio, Paul, 21
visuality: critique of, 50; as symptom of modernity, 46
Voices of Silence (Malraux), 180, 193
vorbeihuschen, 32

wage work, 153; and abolition of, 104; and bourgeoisie, 172; and gambling, 93–4; and strike, 140
Wagner, Richard, 86

Die Wahlverwandtschaften (Goethe), 37, 100, 143, 170, 241
walking, 103–4, 106
Walter Benjamin: A Critical Life (Eiland and Jennings), 105n5
Walter Benjamin and the Antinomies of Tradition (McCole), 175–6
Weber, Max, 11
Wilde, Oscar, 119
women: and fetishism, 160–1; prostitution, 25–6, 85, 91, 105–6, 113, 129
"The Work of Art in the Age of Its Technological Reproducibility" (Benjamin), 150, 171, 175; and authenticity, 192–3; censorship of, 178, 195; and episodization, 178; and film, 21, 163, 177–8; and masses, 191; as neutralization of aesthetic theory, 196; and photography, 178–85; political diagnosis of, 205–7; on production, 218; review of reproductive technologies, 192; second version of, 38; subject of, 177–8; translation of, 177–8
world, linguistic organization of, 48
World War I, 145, 171, 187
World War II, 206, 221
writing: Benjamin never wrote a book, 9, 39; as materialism, 25–6; narrative, 128, 131, 161; observation of masses as, 114; problem of universals understood as, 7; prose, 238–9; readerly vs. writerly, 1, 28; vs. thinking, 2–3. *See also* criticism; essays; quotation

youth movements, 27, 31, 145–6, 168

Zeitschrift für Sozialforschung (journal), 37, 170, 178
Zohn, Harry, 37
Zola, Émile, 183